Brexit and its Aftermath

Brexit and its Aftermath

Edited by
Sophie Loussouarn

BLOOMSBURY ACADEMIC
LONDON • NEW YORK • OXFORD • NEW DELHI • SYDNEY

BLOOMSBURY ACADEMIC
Bloomsbury Publishing Plc
50 Bedford Square, London, WC1B 3DP, UK
1385 Broadway, New York, NY 10018, USA
29 Earlsfort Terrace, Dublin 2, Ireland

BLOOMSBURY, BLOOMSBURY ACADEMIC and the Diana logo are trademarks of
Bloomsbury Publishing Plc

First published in Great Britain 2022

Copyright © Sophie Loussouarn, 2022

Sophie Loussouarn has asserted her right under the Copyright, Designs and Patents Act,
1988, to be identified as Editor of this work.

Cover design by ianrossdesigner.com
Cover image © Sean Gladwell/Getty Images

All rights reserved. No part of this publication may be reproduced or transmitted in
any form or by any means, electronic or mechanical, including photocopying, recording,
or any information storage or retrieval system, without prior permission in writing
from the publishers.

Bloomsbury Publishing Plc does not have any control over, or responsibility for,
any third-party websites referred to or in this book. All internet addresses given in this
book were correct at the time of going to press. The author and publisher regret any
inconvenience caused if addresses have changed or sites have ceased to exist,
but can accept no responsibility for any such changes.

A catalogue record for this book is available from the British Library.

A catalog record for this book is available from the Library of Congress.

ISBN: HB: 978-0-7556-4079-9
PB: 978-0-7556-4078-2
ePDF: 978-0-7556-4081-2
eBook: 978-0-7556-4080-5

Typeset by Deanta Global Publishing Services, Chennai, India
Printed and bound in Great Britain

To find out more about our authors and books visit www.bloomsbury.com and
sign up for our newsletters.

Contents

Preface	vi
List of contributors	viii
Introduction *Vernon Bogdanor*	1

Part I Brexit, Political Parties, the British Constitution and the Union

1	Brexit and the British Constitution *Andrew Blick*	13
2	Brexit's impact on the party system *Alan Wager*	28
3	Brexit and Scotland: Unfinished business? *John Curtice*	42
4	On the borders of contention: Brexit's physical and psychological impact on Britain's border with Ireland *Paul Breen*	57
5	The impact of Brexit on the future of the UK's financial services *Stephen Jones*	76

Part II The UK and the World

6	The future of British trade policy *Minister Hands*	117
7	Brexit and the 'special relationship' *Lord Robin Renwick*	129
8	Choppy waters: The future of the Entente Cordiale after Brexit *Sophie Loussouarn*	152
9	Brexit and the German position *Jochen M. Richter*	178
10	The new relationship between the EU and the UK *Sophie Loussouarn*	194

Index	213

Preface

The referendum on British membership of the European Union (EU) on 23 June 2016 was a major turning point in British domestic policy and in foreign policy. It opened an era of uncertainty and disrupted Britain's foreign policy after forty-three years of partnership with the EU. It also created new challenges for both the United Kingdom (UK) and the EU. Britain's decision to leave the EU is itself the symptom of an identity crisis and leaves the UK facing tough decisions.

Brexit is a vast field. This collection of essays covers the main areas of interest, especially the ways in which Brexit has changed British politics and the UK's position in the world.

This book captures the most recent dynamics in Brexit since the Trade and Cooperation Agreement was signed on 24 December 2020. It focuses on Brexit's implications on the UK's party system, the British Constitution, financial services, trade, foreign policy and key bilateral relationships, such as the bilateral relations with France and Germany.

It is a comprehensive, recent and student-friendly overview of Brexit. It is divided into two parts to highlight the internal and external implications of Brexit. Outside the EU, the UK has the ability to strike new deals with other nations, yet the UK is now more dependent on its relationship with the United States, even though it is no longer a bridge between the EU and the United States, which valued Britain's membership of the EU. The alliance with NATO remains crucial. The AUKUS deal announced on 15 September 2021 is a major strategic shift which will also strengthen the Five Eyes and the defence cooperation between the UK, Australia and the United States. Britain's priority has been to secure trade deals in order to safeguard its commercial interests. It will trade with countries of the Commonwealth, but this will not make up for the damage done to the customs union and the single market.

The chapters cover much new ground. They are written by a number of top scholars from this area (Professor Vernon Bogdanor, Professor John Curtice,

Dr Andrew Blick, Dr Alan Wager and Dr Paul Breen) as well as by prominent practitioners and policymakers (Minister Hands). A chapter could have been added on the Commonwealth and Britain's imperial past, yet it should not be overstated, because the Commonwealth will not compensate for the membership of the EU. An attraction of Brexit was that it allowed Great Britain to have close bilateral and commercial relations with certain Commonwealth partners, notably Australia and New Zealand.

Recently there have been some spats on the implementation of the Trade and Cooperation Agreement. There is tension between the UK government and EU over the Northern Ireland Protocol. Cooperation between the UK and the EU is under severe strain. What will the new relationship between the UK and the EU be like? Should defence and security links with continental European countries be strengthened, given the enhanced terrorist threat and the withdrawal of the United States from Afghanistan?

The book is addressed not only to students in politics or international relations but to a wider audience who are concerned about the upheaval that Brexit represents for British politics, the financial services and Britain's place in the world.

Sophie Loussouarn

Contributors

Andrew Blick is Director of the Political Department of King's College London and Senior Advisor to the Constitutional Society.

Vernon Bogdanor, CBE, is Professor of Government at the Institute of Contemporary British History, King's College London. He was formerly for many years Professor of Government at Oxford University. In 2019 he was a visiting professor at Yale University. He is a fellow of the British Academy, an honorary fellow of the Institute for Advanced Legal Studies, a fellow of the Royal Historical Society and a fellow of the Academy of the Social Sciences.

His books include *Beyond Brexit: Towards a British Constitution*, published by Tauris in 2019, and *Britain and Europe in a Troubled World*, published by Yale University Press in 2020.

Paul Breen is Senior Lecturer and author from County Fermanagh in Ireland, now living and working in London for the University of Westminster. He lectures on various courses for the university's Centre for Education (CETI) and on other courses in the School of Liberal Arts and Sciences. His research interests are primarily in areas relating to language, culture and identity. He has an extensive body of work in the areas of academia, fiction and political commentary.

John Curtice is Professor at the University of Strathclyde and NatCen Social Research.

Greg Hands has been Member of Parliament for Hammersmith and Fulham from 2005 to 2010 and Member of Parliament for Chelsea and Fulham since 2010. He was made Minister of State for Trade Policy in 2016 when Theresa May became Prime Minister. Boris Johnson appointed him Minister of State for International Trade from February 2020 to September 2021. In the Cabinet reshuffle, Greg was appointed Minister of State for Business, Energy and Clean Growth in September 2021.

Stephen Jones was the CEO of UK Finance from its creation in July 2017 until June 2020. As such he was responsible for the merger of six legacy trade associations to create a single entity to represent the UK activities of banks, building societies, cards issuers, payments networks, invoice finance, asset-based lending and payment service providers with government, regulators, the media and other industry stakeholders. He also served as a board member of the European Banking Federation, the International Banking Federation and TheCityUK over this period.

Sophie Loussouarn is an alumna of the Ecole Normale Supérieure (Ulm) and Oxford (Wadham College). She graduated from the Institute of Political Science in Paris and is an expert on British politics and economics. She is Associate Professor in British History at the University of Amiens in France and is Visiting Professor at the University of Alicante in Spain. She wrote a book on the Blair years, *The Political Odyssey of Tony Blair* (Séguier, 2009), and *David Cameron, a Conservative of the Twenty-First Century* (Séguier, 2010). She is often interviewed about British politics and the British economy on French radio and television (CNews, LCI, BFM Business, Canal Plus, France 24, TV5 Monde, RFI).

Lord Renwick of Clifton helped to negotiate the Fontainebleau agreement on the correction of the British budgetary contribution to the EU and the Single European Act. He served in the British Embassy in Washington during the Falklands War, then as British ambassador to the United States under Presidents George H. W. Bush and Bill Clinton. Robin Renwick has published several books including *Fighting with Allies: America and Britain at Peace and War* (2017), *How to Steal a Country: State Capture in South Africa* (2018) and *Not Quite a Diplomat: A Memoir* (2019).

Jochen M. Richter was Director General for Translation, European Parliament. He now lectures at the University of Luxembourg.

Alan Wager is a research associate at the UK in a Changing Europe initiative at King's College London.

Introduction

Vernon Bogdanor

Brexit has been, is and will be a momentous process both for Britain and for the European Union (EU).

Britain left the EU on 31 January 2020 and the transition period ended on 31 December 2020. Brexit was provided for in two legal instruments. The first was the Withdrawal Agreement agreed after Boris Johnson's election victory in December 2019. This agreement included an Ireland/Northern Ireland Protocol, which has proved highly controversial in Northern Ireland and led to protests by members of the Unionist community, some of them violent. The second legal instrument provided for Britain's future relationship with the EU – a Trade and Cooperation Agreement agreed on Christmas Eve in 2020. The 1,246 page agreement was ratified by Westminster in just one day.

It may seem as if these documents constitute a final settlement of Britain's relations with the EU, but they do not. They comprise more the skeleton or outline of a settlement than something final. They are incomplete. Some matters are left for future negotiation – for example, the Trade and Cooperation Agreement says very little about neither financial services or professional qualifications nor, most important of all perhaps in the modern world, non-tariff barriers to trade. Where matters are left for further negotiation, this will be done through a joint Partnership Council established by the agreement and by other bodies. The agreement is also subject to review in five years and can be terminated by either party with twelve months' notice. This is in contrast to the Withdrawal Agreement which cannot be terminated – with the exception of the Ireland/Northern Ireland Protocol, which provides for its possible rejection by a majority in the Northern Ireland Assembly after four years, that is in 2024.

The Trade and Cooperation Agreement is a success in the sense that each side to the negotiation achieved what it sought. The EU preserved its internal market, while the United Kingdom (UK) regained its legal sovereignty and a degree of autonomy. Britain now controls her laws, her borders and her trading relationships. UK negotiators faced the problem of whether to give priority to access or autonomy. The greater the degree of access to the EU, the more Britain would have to follow EU rules and so the less autonomy she would enjoy and the less she would be taking back control – to use the slogan of the Brexiteers in the 2016 referendum. Conversely, the more Britain took back control, the less access there would be to EU markets. Theresa May's government gave greater weight to access, while Boris Johnson's government gave greater weight to autonomy. Some have argued that the Trade and Cooperation Agreement gives Britain the worst of both worlds, yielding both insufficient autonomy and insufficient access. Only time will tell. But the nature of the agreement is such that the current relationship is not set in stone. It is open to a future government of the Left to seek a less divergent relationship but greater access by, for example, rejoining the EU customs union or the single market. It is also open to a more Eurosceptic government to move Britain further away from the EU. What is clear is that Brexit is a process rather than an event – and a process that is not concluded by the Withdrawal Agreement and the Trade and Cooperation Agreement. Some have gone so far as to suggest that the Trade and Cooperation Agreement is merely a prelude to a perpetual re-negotiation!

The issue of Europe has caused difficulties for almost every British government since the war. It has indeed proved a poisoned chalice for British governments since Britain first sought, unsuccessfully, to enter the European Communities in 1961 under the premiership of Harold Macmillan. When, in 1949, the Foreign Secretary, Ernest Bevin, was asked whether Britain should join the Council of Europe, which he mistakenly thought would be a supranational body, he told his officials, 'I don't like it.' He explained why. 'If you open that Pandora's box, you never know what Trojan horses will fly out.'[1] The British government helped to ensure that the Council of Europe was a purely advisory body and to that, Bevin had no objection. But Bevin's remark was perhaps the most prescient one ever made about Britain's involvement with the movement towards European integration.

---

[1] Quoted in Roderick Barclay, *Ernest Bevin and the Foreign Office*, 1932–1969, Roderick Barclay, 1975, p. 67.

It can be argued indeed that Europe has destroyed six of the last seven Conservative prime ministers – Harold Macmillan, Edward Heath, Margaret Thatcher, John Major, David Cameron and Theresa May. The only exception – Sir Alec Douglas-Home – was prime minister for only one year and a year when Britain's relations with the Continent were in abeyance.

There are two interconnected reasons why Europe has been so uniquely divisive an issue for Britain. The first is that it raises very profound issues of sovereignty and national identity. Every country of course was required to sacrifice some of its national sovereignty when it joined the European Community/EU. That, perhaps, was a greater sacrifice for Britain than some of the other member states, since she had a longer continuous existence than almost all of the others, and her system of government had not been disturbed by any violent change since the seventeenth century. On the Continent, by contrast, many of the member states had been required to refashion their constitutions after 1945, and many of them had a much shorter national existence. Some indeed had not been formed until the end of the First World War; others such as Slovakia and Slovenia had not come into existence until after the fall of communism in 1989. Britain, moreover, was the only member state that had to sacrifice not only national sovereignty but also parliamentary sovereignty, a reflection of her long evolutionary history. She had lived since 1660 under a historic constitution, a regime without a codified constitution, a regime of parliamentary sovereignty which dictated that Parliament could enact any law that it liked and that it could not be bound by any higher authority. This principle was incompatible with membership of the EU.

The second reason why Europe was so disruptive was that it divided both parties internally. In the 1970s and 1980s, Europe divided the Labour Party. Indeed, Europe was a main cause of the breakaway from Labour in 1981 by leading figures of the party such as Roy Jenkins, David Owen and Shirley Williams, all of whom had been prominent figures in Labour governments. They broke away to form a new party, the Social Democratic Party, which allied itself with the Liberals and in 1988 merged with them to form the Liberal Democrats. Britain had been taken into the European Community, as the EU then was, in 1973 by the Conservatives, and at first it seemed as if a pro-European orientation had very wide support in the party. But, from the time of Britain's exit from the Exchange Rate Mechanism of the European Monetary System in 1992 and the Maastricht Treaty of that year, it has been the Conservatives, the party since Disraeli of British nationhood, that has suffered the most from divisions in Europe. The party developed a powerful Eurosceptic wing which now controls it. In the general election of 2019, Boris Johnson required all Conservative candidates to pledge themselves to support the Withdrawal Agreement that he had negotiated so that pro-European MPs were in effect purged. But from 1992 to 2019, the party had been riven by the European issue. That is not to say that the Labour Party had achieved unity on Europe, but its divisions, partly because the party has been in opposition since 2010, have been effectively masked.

The political divisions within the parties coincide in large part with a cultural division, between a cosmopolitan and liberal constituency centred on London and many of the larger cities – London was the only region of England to record a Remain vote in the Brexit referendum of 2016 – and the so-called left behind areas of provincial England in the Midlands and North, most of which voted Leave in 2016. In the Labour Party, the division might be characterized as one between those living in Hampstead and those living in Hartlepool; and, because Labour appeared too pro-European for many of the left behind – though it was regarded as insufficiently pro-European by many Londoners – the Conservatives made striking gains in the so-called red wall seats in the general election of 2019. Brexit seems to have accelerated a process that was already occurring and one that has been occurring in many democracies – the decline of traditional class politics and its replacement by a new politics of identity. It may have permanently realigned British politics.

But the effects of Brexit are to be seen not only in party politics and in electoral behaviour. Indeed, there is hardly any aspect of Britain's political or constitutional life which is unaffected. Uniquely in British history, the basic decision for Brexit was made not by the government nor by MPs but by the voters in a referendum, against the wishes of the majority in David Cameron's Conservative Cabinet, against the wishes of the majority of MPs and even of Conservative MPs, a majority of whom favoured Remain in 2016. For the first time in British history, a supposedly sovereign Parliament was overruled by the people. A supposedly sovereign Parliament was constrained, not in terms of law but in terms of practical politics, by a popular vote. So Brexit raises in a very acute form the proper role of direct democracy. For what decisions are referendums appropriate? Should more precise rules be laid down for referendums? Further, in 1998 it was explicitly acknowledged that the UK was a multinational state. For it was in that year that legislation providing for devolution to the non-English parts of the UK – Scotland, Wales and Northern Ireland – was enacted. Devolution was an acknowledgement that there were separate political wills in Scotland, Wales and Northern Ireland. In a multinational democracy, is an overall UK majority sufficient for major constitutional change, or should a majority in all four parts of the kingdom be required to validate it? A further question is whether a majority of 52 to 48 is sufficient for so major a change or should a special majority be required? This question is likely to be resurrected were there to be another Scottish independence referendum. Britain left the EU even though 48 per cent of those who voted wanted her to stay. Could a large minority comprising, for example, over 40 per cent of the voters be similarly extruded from the UK against its wishes? Should not clear rules be laid down before further referendums are held and should these rules not be codified? Should they perhaps be codified in a constitution? Might it not be time for Britain to follow almost every other democracy by drawing up rules, by enacting a constitution?

But of course the most immediate question facing post-Brexit Britain is whether the country can be held together at all. The 2016 Brexit referendum had provided stark evidence of the existence of separate wills in the four parts of the UK. The UK as a whole voted to leave the EU but Scotland and Northern Ireland voted to remain. The UK vote for Brexit was around 52 per cent to 48 per cent. England and Wales both voted for Brexit by small majorities of around 53 per cent to 47 per cent. Scotland, however, voted to remain by a much larger majority, around 62 per cent to 38 per cent, while Northern Ireland also voted to remain by a large majority, around 56 per cent to 44 per cent. The Brexit verdict, therefore, was determined by voters in England and Wales. Scotland and Northern Ireland were to be extruded from the EU against their wishes. For this reason, Brexit has posed severe strains on the cohesion and unity of the UK.

The outcome of the 2016 Brexit referendum gave encouragement both to Scottish and to Irish nationalists. In the 2014 referendum on Scottish independence which the Unionists won by 55 per cent to 45 per cent, one of the arguments that had been used by Unionists was that only by voting to reject independence could the Scots be assured of retaining their membership of the EU. But, having duly rejected independence, the Scots then found that they were in fact going to lose their membership of the EU against their wishes.

Therefore, so nationalists argued, the Scots had been induced to support the Union under false pretences. So the Scottish National Party (SNP) calls for a second referendum on independence to preserve Scottish membership of the EU. It is now a wholly pro-European party. In the past it faced the problem of a cross-cutting cleavage since in the independence referendum of 2014 it appears that around one-third of its supporters favoured leaving the EU. But, since the Brexit referendum of 2016, there appears to have been a realignment. Brexiteers have left the SNP for other parties but have been replaced by Remainers who have joined the SNP from other parties. Electoral support for the SNP now comes almost wholly from those who voted Remain in 2016.

The SNP which, together with the pro-independence Greens, won a majority in the Scottish Parliament in the Holyrood elections of 2021 seeks a further referendum on independence. If, as is possible, the government in London denies it, nationalists will claim that the Union with Scotland rests not on consent but on force. The implication is that the Union is a voluntary one. However, Article 1 of the Treaty of Union of 1707 provides that England and Scotland will be merged 'for ever after'. But what can 'for ever after' mean in a system whose guiding principle is the sovereignty of Parliament which means that Parliament can enact any law that it likes and is not bound by any higher authority? It probably means very little. The 1801 Union with Ireland used similar wording but was in large part abrogated when the twenty-six counties seceded in 1921, and the Cameron government would have abrogated it in relation to Scotland had the independence referendum of 2014 yielded a different result. Nevertheless, many modern democracies either restrict secession constitutionally or, as in the United States, forbid it altogether.

In Northern Ireland as in Scotland, the Brexit referendum seemed to offer encouragement to nationalists, since with the Irish Republic remaining an enthusiastic member of the EU, there was clearly a large majority on the island of Ireland for continued membership. And Northern Ireland is unique in the UK as being the only part of it that could rejoin the EU without needing to re-negotiate entry. For Northern Ireland would not be forming a new state on its own as, for example, Scotland or Catalonia would were they to secede from the UK or Spain. Instead it would be joining an existing member state – the Irish Republic – just as East Germany became automatically part of the EU when it joined with the West after the fall of communism. The Brexit referendum, therefore, seemed to tilt Northern Ireland towards the republic and increase the prospects of Irish unity.

The Brexit campaign in Northern Ireland was quite different from that in England. Whereas in England, the main issues were control of immigration and control of British legislation by the EU, such issues played almost no part in Northern Ireland. Instead, the referendum campaign was dominated by the community conflict, by the possible consequences of Brexit for the peace process and by the prospects of economic and constitutional cooperation with the Irish Republic. The referendum proved to be yet another battleground for the struggle between the two communities. The main nationalist party – Sinn Fein – favoured a Remain vote. The main unionist party – the Democratic Unionist Party – favoured a Leave vote. It appears that an overwhelming majority of self-defined nationalist voters (around 88 per cent) voted to remain, while a smaller majority of self-defined Unionist voters (66 per cent) voted to leave.[2] The referendum served to intensify the community division, and it had a polarizing effect.

After the referendum, one commentator went so far as to suggest that 'for the first time in my life, the prospect of a united Ireland is not only credible but inevitable'.[3] Those in Northern Ireland who identified as British could argue that the decision for Brexit was a sovereign decision of the British people. But those who identified as Irish could argue that, despite the majority in the island of Ireland for remaining in the EU, the province was being extruded from it against the wishes of a majority of its people. Yet it would be a mistake to believe that all of the 56 per cent who voted Remain were also supporters of Irish unity. It is in particular highly unlikely that the 34 per cent of self-designated Unionists who voted Remain were also voting to join with the Irish Republic.

Brexit, of course, re-establishes a border between the republic which remains inside the EU and Northern Ireland which is outside. This is the only land border between the UK and the EU. The EU and the Irish Republic both believed that to make the land border a customs border would exacerbate the community conflict and perhaps encourage terrorism since it would seem to

---

[2] John Doyle and Eileen Connolly, 'Brexit and the Northern Ireland Question', in Federico Fabbini, *The Law & Politics of Brexit*, Oxford University Press, 2017, p. 142.
[3] Siobhan Fenton, *Independent*, 27 March 2017.

block the aspiration of nationalists for Irish unity. The Ireland/Northern Ireland Protocol, therefore, which is part of the Withdrawal Agreement, provides for Northern Ireland to remain within the EU internal market for goods. So it imposes a regulatory border in the Irish Sea. Article 4 of the Protocol declares that Northern Ireland remains part of the customs territory of the UK, which means that it, together with the rest of the UK, leaves the EU customs union. But Article 5 declares, in seeming contradiction, that EU customs legislation will apply to Northern Ireland. This means that in practice, Northern Ireland will be required to abide by EU customs rules. Northern Ireland, therefore, is placed in a different regime in terms of trade in goods from the rest of the UK. It means that goods travelling from the British side of the Irish Sea to Northern Ireland must meet country of origin formalities to ensure that a percentage of the contents derive from Britain rather than from elsewhere outside the EU. Goods thought to be at risk of going into the Irish Republic need to be checked to ensure that they pay the correct tariff, even if the tariff is zero, so as to avoid Northern Ireland becoming the back door into the EU single market. That means customs declarations and other paperwork raising costs and prices in the province. Sending parcels from one part of the UK to another could become akin to an international transaction. Moreover, Northern Ireland is required to accept EU regulatory rules – according to Annex 2 of the protocol around 300 EU directives and regulations – but without a vote on what they are – regulation without representation.

Some have suggested that the protocol will give Northern Ireland, from the economic point of view, the best of both worlds, since it will have the commercial advantages of being in both the UK and the EU single markets. The economic effect may well be to push the Northern Ireland economy closer to that of the republic. But Unionists in Northern Ireland argue that the protocol breaches the 1800 Act of Union which provides for Northern Ireland to enjoy 'the same Privileges' and 'Encouragements' in trade as the rest of the UK. The protocol would seem to establish Northern Ireland in effect as a condominium jointly governed by Britain and the EU. This of course raises fundamental constitutional issues.

Objections to the protocol have caused massive protests, some violent, in Northern Ireland by Unionists who say that as British taxpayers they are being deprived of their position of equal citizenship without their consent. Parallel to the threat of Irish Republican Army (IRA) terrorism if there is a hard border on the island of Ireland is the threat of Unionist terrorism if there is a hard border between different parts of the UK. So in Northern Ireland as in Scotland, Brexit has resurrected the issue of sovereignty, an existential matter. In Northern Ireland, Brexit has replaced the conciliation of the Belfast or Good Friday Agreement with an either/or. Wherever the border is, whether in the Irish Sea or on the island of Ireland, it is likely to prove destabilizing.

In 2021, the UK commemorated the centenary of its current borders which date from 1921 when the Anglo-Irish treaty recognized Irish independence and twenty-six counties in Ireland seceded. In 1973, when Britain entered the European Community, its borders seemed immutable and the future of the UK within its existing borders seemed assured. By 2021, that future had become a question mark.

To refashion a new form of Union, a settlement which all four territories of the UK can accept, is the task which now faces a post-Brexit British government. It will require statesmanship of the highest order to bring it about.

But the effects of Brexit will also be seen in Britain's foreign relations – the vital issue of Britain's defence and security relationship with the EU. What contribution can post-Brexit Britain make to European defence and security? Britain, after all, is with France the only nuclear power in Europe, and Europe is the only one of the four major power blocs in the world – the others being the United States, China and Russia – which relies on an outside power, the United States, to defend itself over seventy-five years after the end of the Second World War. There is, in the EU, as well as a democratic deficit, a defence deficit. So Brexit raises important questions concerning Britain's defence and security relationship with the Continent, questions which future governments will need to answer.

Britain then has to confront the question – What is her post-Brexit role in the world to be? In 1962, the former American secretary of state Dean Acheson famously said that Britain had lost an empire but had not yet found a role. That comment created a furore in Britain perhaps because it touched a painful nerve. Today it might be said that Britain has lost the EU but has yet to find a role. Could that new role involve a closer relationship with the United States – even though, as Robin Renwick points out in his chapter, it would be unwise to use the term 'special relationship'? In a virtual Chatham House interview with former British foreign secretary Jeremy Hunt in April 2021, Henry Kissinger suggested that Britain could still remain a bridge between the EU and the

United States. Whether that proves to be a correct judgement only time will tell. An alternative alignment, which some have suggested, would be with the Commonwealth. But could the Commonwealth whose diverse member states have no wish or pretension to act together really provide a viable alternative to the EU? Some Brexiteers have spoken of a Global Britain freed from the EU. But few were able to put flesh on the bones. What does Global Britain really mean in concrete terms?

If Britain's relations with the EU will, as I believe, remain an issue in British politics, it is an issue that can be resolved only by an informed electorate. These chapters form an essential means by which the British electorate can become more informed. They provide a basis for understanding the questions raised by Brexit and how they might be answered. While the essays cannot of themselves provide the answers, they do provide the material on which the answers must be based. I hope that this book will be widely read.

Part I

Brexit, Political Parties, the British Constitution and the Union

1

Brexit and the British Constitution

Andrew Blick

Departure from the European Union (EU) is more than simply a matter of policy pursued within the context of a given system. It pertains to the system itself. Brexit rests on competing views of what the constitution of the United Kingdom (UK) is and should be; it has been connected with significant strains upon it; and it entails substantial and in some cases difficult-to-anticipate strains upon it. This chapter considers these various aspects. It groups the subject matter into three main themes: the sovereignty of Parliament; the relationship between direct and representative democracy; and the dynamic interaction between Brexit and a variety of associated tendencies and occurrences. It uses the term 'Brexit' to apply to a broad political episode, commencing around the time of the EU referendum in mid-2016 and continuing up to the time of writing (late 2020) and presumably beyond.[1]

Parliamentary sovereignty

Brexit as a project had a significant constitutional component. Objections from within the UK to participation in European integration had – long before the UK even joined – included the idea that to do so was undesirable from the perspective of the UK system. A core feature of such reservations involved the doctrine of parliamentary sovereignty.[2] According to this traditional principle,

---

[1] For discussion and contextualization of the term 'Brexit', see A. Blick, *Stretching the Constitution: The Brexit Shock in Historic Perspective*, Bloomsbury/Hart, 2019: 2.
[2] See V. Bogdanor, *Beyond Brexit: Towards a British Constitution*, I. B. Tauris, 2019: 51–86.

the Westminster legislature is the supreme source of legal authority within the UK. The passing of an Act of Parliament, it is held, can accomplish any outcome whatsoever. The only limitations upon Parliament are self-imposed – what people within the institution judge to be practically and politically possible, and morally appropriate. This principle sets the UK apart from most other countries. A common international norm is for the ultimate legal force within a given polity to vest in an entity often known as a 'written' or 'codified' constitution. This text purports to be an expression of the will of the people – or popular sovereignty. It sets out some of the most important principles and rules of the system, provides a basis for key institutions of governance and the relationship between them, and regulates their relationship with the people, for whose rights it might provide. Changes to these rules are likely to require adherence to some kind of heightened amendment procedure, such as supermajority votes in legislatures or approval via referendum. The contents of the 'written' or 'codified' constitution are often enforceable by the judiciary, perhaps in a Supreme or Constitutional Court. Any action or legal measure found to be in violation of the text can be struck down.[3]

The UK system allows for no such arrangements. Through an Act, the UK Parliament can, in theory, make or unmake any constitutional arrangement, however fundamental its importance, through regular legislative procedures using simple majority voting. Parliament was able, for instance, to incorporate the European Convention on Human Rights into UK law in 1998 (through the Human Rights Act). The following year it removed all but ninety-two hereditary peers from the House of Lords (through the House of Lords Act, which had the effect of reducing the size of the second chamber by more than 50 per cent, changing its party balance and meaning that it was predominantly composed of life appointees).[4] Furthermore, there is no specific single text against which the judiciary can assess the constitutionality of legislation and actions of public authorities or – if found to be non-compliant – strike them down. Advocates of the doctrine of parliamentary sovereignty support it on a number of grounds. They argue, for instance, that it provides for a degree of systemic flexibility that the amendment procedures of a 'written' constitution

---

[3] A. Blick, *Beyond Magna Carta: A Constitution for the United Kingdom*, Bloomsbury/Hart, 2015: 25–284.
[4] V. Bogdanor, *The New British Constitution*, Hart, 2009: 39–40.

would lack. It is – so the argument runs – able, when the need for changes arises, to respond swiftly and incrementally, avoiding the rigidity and delay that eventually ends in more abrupt and disruptive transformation when the pressure for alteration can no longer be resisted. A further component of the case in support of parliamentary sovereignty is that it entails ultimate responsibility resting with a representative institution, Parliament, the pre-eminent component of which, the House of Commons, is directly elected, rather than with the judiciary, members of which are not directly accountable to the people in this way. Exponents of the doctrine in this sense make a democratic case for it.[5]

European integration raised difficult questions about the viability of the principle of parliamentary sovereignty. It introduced a new source of law – the European institutions – into the UK system. If an Act of Parliament came into conflict with European law, then the latter prevailed. For the first time, a court could 'disapply' provisions of an Act of Parliament, if found to be non-compliant in this way. There was complex debate about whether parliamentary sovereignty had in fact been compromised. It was the case that the means by which European law formed part of the UK order was itself via an Act of Parliament, European Communities Act 1972, which Parliament could, if it chose, repeal – as it ultimately did through the European Union (Withdrawal) Act 2018. However, at the very least, the so-called doctrine of implied repeal was compromised. According to this traditionalist version of parliamentary sovereignty, if a later Act of Parliament conflicts with an earlier Act then it supersedes it, even if it does not expressly state that it is intended to do so. The European Communities Act, however, was protected from this kind of repeal and took priority over both earlier and later Acts of Parliament. Only by specifically stating that the 1972 Act was repealed was it possible for the European Union (Withdrawal) Act 2018 definitively to achieve this outcome.[6]

Even for those who reject the idea that parliamentary sovereignty must encompass implied repeal, EU membership represented a practical limitation on the power of the Westminster legislature. That European integration posed a threat of some kind to the status of the UK Parliament was, then, a central component of objections to participation in this project. A concern often raised

---

[5] A. Tomkins, *Our Republican Constitution*, Hart: 2005.
[6] Bogdanor, *The New British Constitution*: 27–9.

was that the UK might find itself incorporated into a European federation. Such opponents came from across the political spectrum, for instance, from the radical left of the Labour Party during the 1970s and 1980s. But from the 1990s onwards, the most significant source of Euroscepticism was the political right. Alongside their desire to uphold parliamentary sovereignty, they sought to bring to end any role for what they perceived as a foreign body, the Court of Justice of the European Union (or European Court of Justice, ECJ), in the determination of UK law. Such views linked to a zero-sum conception of 'national' sovereignty, according to which any formal pooling of powers in areas such as inward migration represented an unacceptable surrender of autonomy. The striking slogan employed by the Leave side in the referendum, 'take back control', was in part an allusion to such concerns.[7]

For those of a populist-right inclination, exit from the EU could be part of a broader constitutional programme. An underlying theme of this project was a shift of power towards the electorate and those who were answerable directly to it, and away from supposedly unaccountable officials. It could encompass measures including restrictions of the scope of judicial human rights review under the Human Rights Act 1998, in accordance with the European Convention on Human Rights.[8] In theory, a constitutional reconstruction such as that envisaged by some within the Brexit camp would become more possible precisely because the UK had left the EU. The limitations that membership brought with it – and had proved objectionable for some because of their implications for parliamentary sovereignty – had to some extent provided an equivalent to the 'written' constitution that the UK lacked. As Vernon Bogdanor has noted, it was particularly notable that the UK removed itself from the protections provided by the European Charter of Fundamental Rights and made no attempt to copy it across directly into UK law at the time of Brexit, as it did with other provisions that arose from EU membership.[9] The assertion of a purer form of parliamentary sovereignty might lead to a circumstance in which the UK constitution was – from the perspective of the UK Parliament – a more malleable entity. Yet, as discussed further, in the period since the UK first joined the European Communities in 1973, other

---

[7] Blick, *Stretching the Constitution*: 108–9.
[8] D. Carswell and D. Hannan, *The Plan: Twelve Months to Renew Britain*, Douglas Carswell and Daniel Hanna, 2008.
[9] Bogdanor, *Beyond Brexit*: 146–58.

points of political authority had appeared which might make the practical exercise of this power problematic.

Direct and representative democracy

Brexit was executed partly in the name of parliamentary sovereignty. Yet, ironically, it was achieved using a device – the referendum – that presented a practical challenge to the status of the Westminster legislature and was opposed at the time of this vote by majorities in both Houses of Parliament.[10] The use of referendums for the making of major decisions in the UK dates to 1973. In the intervening period, thirteen such votes have taken place, ten of which were held at sub-UK level and three of which across the whole country. Of the three, the first (in 1975) and third (in 2016) were held on the subject of whether the UK should continue to take part in continental integration. Generally, referendums have been held on subjects of a constitutional nature – such as the possibility of establishing devolved institutions in a given part of the UK; the electoral system used for the House of Commons; or whether a particular territory should secede from the UK. They are sometimes employed in an effort to resolve issues that create divisions across the usual political lines and over which the governing party is divided. In 1975, the Labour administration of Harold Wilson held a popular vote on European Communities membership, a subject over which his Cabinet could not agree. In 2016, the Conservative Cabinet of David Cameron was similarly split. He had first committed to it in 2013, and it seemed to be for him a means of party management rather more than a means of enabling the public to make a decision. Cameron appears to have anticipated winning, and his government made only limited preparations for the advent of a Leave result.[11]

In both the 1975 and 2016 cases, it proved necessary to suspend a key rule of the UK system of government, collective Cabinet responsibility. According to this principle, while senior ministers can debate matters frankly in private, once a decision is reached they must retain a united public front, whatever their

---

[10] A. Blick and B. Salter, 'Divided Culture and Constitutional Tensions: Brexit and the Collision of Direct and Representative Democracy', *Parliamentary Affairs*, 2020.
[11] See L. Atkinson, A. Blick and M. Qvortrup, *The Referendum in Britain: A History*, Oxford University Press, 2020.

private views may be. In the case of the European referendums of 1975 and 2016, though the government made a formal recommendation in favour of continuing membership, government ministers were allowed to campaign on either side. This suspension had further constitutional consequences, raising complex issues regarding the relationship between dissenting ministers and their civil servants, who were by implication faced with the divergence between the individual politicians to whom they were accountable and the government for which they worked.[12]

While it is possible to discern certain patterns in the usage of referendums in the UK, a firm and shared understanding of their precise role within the UK constitution is lacking. The Brexit experience highlighted some of the uncertainty and disruption that such popular votes had the potential to generate. Referendums are a form of direct democracy, involving the public in specific decisions, used within the wider context of a system of representative democracy, under which politicians are ultimately accountable to the public via elections and other means make policy choices as part of programmes they develop and implement on behalf of the people. A justification offered for the use of referendums is that they are a means of resolving contested issues to which the use of regular representative mechanisms is not suitable. Supporters of the device argue that it is a means of separating out a particular item from the business of representative politics, allowing them to continue to a large extent as normal. They can, it is held, involve the people more fully in the democratic system, in the process providing definitive and lasting answers to difficult questions.

The reality of the 2016 EU referendum was more complicated. For a variety of reasons, it seemed to generate more controversy than it resolved. On a turnout that exceeded any general election since 1992, Leave won by more than one million votes (17.4 to 16.1). Yet the result – measured in percentage terms – was close: 51.89 to 48.81. A large group of more than sixteen million people was therefore on the losing side. Of all those who could have voted, only about 37.4 per cent supported Leave. Moreover, the legitimacy of the referendum was arguably called into question because certain significant categories were denied the right to take part at all. Neither sixteen and seventeen-year-olds nor

---

[12] House of Commons Public Administration and Constitutional Affairs Committee, *Lessons Learned from the EU Referendum*, House of Commons, 2017: 49–52.

EU citizens were included in the franchise. While people in these groups are not permitted to participate in UK general elections, they were allowed to vote in the Scottish independence referendum of 2014. There were further difficulties with the idea of the referendum as being the channel through which a clear answer to a question might be transmitted. It revealed and magnified a range of sharp divisions within the UK. In Scotland, Northern Ireland and London, there were clear Remain majorities. Alongside these territorial divergences, the referendum was connected to social divergences. Remain voters were generally younger, from more privileged social grades, with more formal education and of a generally more liberal outlook across a range of issues.[13] Taken together, these voting patterns suggested that while a majority of those taking part in the referendum had, across the UK as a whole, supported Leave, it was harder to argue that a high level of territorial and societal consensus had been achieved. By contrast, in the 1975 referendum, around two-thirds had supported the winning outcome, with majorities in favour of continued membership in each of Wales, Scotland, Northern Ireland and England.

The legitimacy of the referendum was called into question in other ways. Prior to the campaign, for instance, Leave supporters raised concerns about whether the government, given its support for Remain, would use official resources such as the civil service in a way that gave its side an unfair advantage. On the opposing side, before and after the referendum, there were various complaints about misleading claims regarding the benefits of departure from the EU. In the months and years after June 2016, scrutiny of aspects of the Leave campaign intensified. Various suspicions, complaints and allegations developed regarding matters such as finance; inappropriate use of data and online campaigning techniques; and the possibility of foreign interference. Support grew for an overhaul of the legal framework for referendums as provided for by the Political Parties, Elections and Referendums Act 2000.[14]

Far from settling the issue, the referendum inaugurated a prolonged period of pronounced political disruption that continues at the time of writing nearly a year after the UK departure from the EU, only partially masked during 2020 by the pandemic. One source of disruption was the lack of clarity about

---

[13] Blick and Salter, *Divided Culture and Constitutional Tensions*.
[14] House of Commons Digital, Culture, Media and Sport Committee, *Disinformation and 'Fake News': Final Report*, House of Commons, 2019.

what, precisely, a Leave vote meant. It had no binding legal force. Indeed – as the first *Miller* case revealed – the government needed further authorization from the legislature in the form of an Act of Parliament before it could activate Article 50 of the Treaty on European Union, commencing the process of UK departure.[15] Brexit, moreover, might take many different forms. The Leave campaign had not made precise statements on matters such as whether the UK would seek to remain within the single market and the customs union. To leave one or both brings about a degree of disruption that (to speculate) all those who voted Leave might not have supported had they known it was in prospect. Yet to remain within one or both would entail a scale of continuity that might call into question what had been the purpose of exiting the EU at all. Even if it did deliver a legitimate verdict in favour of the general principle of leaving, then the referendum did not offer clear guidance as to the preferred form such exit should take.

A principal problem was that most MPs and peers – though generally they initially expressed a desire to implement the result – had not wanted a Leave outcome. Even in the governing Conservative Party, within which Eurosceptic forces had become increasingly powerful over recent decades, a majority of MPs had favoured Remain. As noted earlier, the Conservative government backed this side, while allowing ministers publicly to dissent during the campaign. Yet because the result was characterized by ambiguity and did not have legal force, it was these same politicians, in Parliament and in the government, who would play a crucial role in determining the response to the referendum. Immediately after the 23 June 2016 vote the Conservative prime minister David Cameron judged that having advocated Remain and lost the referendum he had instigated, his position was no longer sustainable. His immediate successor, Theresa May, had herself been on the Remain side and partly for this reason lacked the full confidence of Leave supporters, contributing to her ultimate downfall. Then, in 2019, a leading Leave campaigner, Boris Johnson, became premier. That two prime-ministerial careers ended directly as a consequence of the Brexit issue was strong evidence of the referendum having brought about considerable instability within the system, as were the two ahead-of-schedule general elections of 2017 and 2019. The existing party system also came

---

[15] For analysis of the first *Miller* case, see M. Elliott, A. Young and J. Williams (eds), *The Constitution after Miller*, Bloomsbury/Hart, 2018.

under pressure. During 2019, two new parties appeared. One – Change UK, supporting Remain – was composed of MPs who had left the Conservatives and Labour. The other was a firm advocate of a decisive departure. The latter of the two, the Brexit Party, achieved the highest vote share at the May 2019 European elections, in which the UK participated because of the delay in its initially anticipated withdrawal date. At this same poll, the Conservative Party suffered considerably (coming fifth), prompting it to shift decisively towards a harder stance with regard to Brexit and its selection of Boris Johnson as its leader (and consequently as Prime Minister).

In part, the issues at stake was one of tension between two types of democracy: the representative model, with decisions taken by people governing on behalf of the people, accountable to them by elections; and the direct variant, with voters making specific decisions through referendums. With hindsight, the use of referendums had often contained within it the potential to create such difficulties. For instance, had the 1975 European referendum produced a result in favour of leaving the European Communities or had voters in Scotland opted in favour of independence in 2014, significant disruption would have followed. In 1979, a majority of those who voted supported devolution for Scotland. But the total number supporting this outcome did not reach the required 40 per cent of all those registered to take part. The policy therefore was not implemented, leading to the fall of the Labour government of James Callaghan. But before 2016 no referendum produced a result so at odds with the outlook of such a substantial portion of senior politicians; nor it had required such a far-reaching overhaul of the existing system, on a basis that had not been clearly defined in advance and over which there were such sharp and finely balanced popular divisions.

In the years that followed the 2016 referendum the UK government presented itself as the primary vehicle for the implementation of the result. Parliament – the principal organ of representative democracy in the UK – which had ceded a degree of control through providing for the referendum, gradually became more assertive in its efforts to reinsert itself into the process. Tension therefore developed between executive and legislature. The two landmark *Miller* cases, resolved in early 2017 and autumn 2019 respectively in the UK Supreme Court, both involved this conflict. The first reinforced the position of Parliament as the font of legal authority for the UK government, with respect to the activation of Article 50 of the Treaty on European

Union. The second ruled unlawful an attempt by the executive to prorogue Parliament, an initiative that was seemingly conceived as a means to reduce the potential of the legislature to hamper the UK government in its chosen approach to Brexit. One manifestation of this ongoing clash between direct and representative democracy turned on further confusion about the nature of the obligation the 2016 referendum had produced. As already discussed, the precise form that departure might take was not clear in advance. Further uncertainties surrounded whether representative institutions, including Parliament, might be able to provide for a further referendum, to confirm or reject the result of the first, or whether they could choose not to bring about or allow Brexit to take place. Majorities in both Houses – though reluctant to reject the Leave result outright – were willing to attempt to prevent departure without some kind of holding arrangement being in place. In 2019, Parliament twice passed legislation intended to force the government to confirm to this objective. Another set of representative institutions – at devolved level – also attempted to achieve some kind of influence in shaping the UK response to the referendum result. Levers they utilized included mechanisms in place to manage intergovernmental relations in the UK and recourse to the convention that some UK legislation was subject to consent from the devolved legislatures.[16]

Contiguous issues

The constitutional turbulence associated with Brexit heightened because it interacted with various other tendencies and episodes. These tendencies and episoders are listed in the following paragraphs.

Trends in the party system, in particular tensions within the Conservatives and Labour

While some constitutional analysis might not engage with the role of parties, they are central to the working of any such system. A discussion of Brexit and the UK constitution leads us to a consideration of parties. Within the Conservatives, there were ongoing disputes over the European issue that the

---

[16] G. Anthony, *Devolution, Brexit and the Sewel Convention*, The Constitution Society, 2018.

referendum failed – initially at least – to resolve. A significant minority of MPs were of radically Eurosceptic inclination. In holding this outlook they were in tune with the bulk of party members and activists, and set against the majority of Conservative MPs (and Conservatives in the Lords). The Johnson ascendancy represented power seizure by a politician who had aligned himself with these firm opponents of the EU. It was followed by a purge of Conservative MPs who were unwilling fully to commit to the Johnson programme, especially his emphasis being willing to exit the EU with no deal if an agreement deemed suitable could not be reached. For much of the Brexit period, Labour was led by the radical left leader, Jeremy Corbyn. His period as Leader of the Opposition was marked by conflict with the bulk of his parliamentary party. A factor in this dispute – though not the whole explanation for it – was his ambivalence regarding the EU, of which he had historically been an outright opponent. While Corbyn lacked the confidence of his MPs, he had an immense power base among the mass membership of the Labour Party – though on the issue of Europe, as a group his followers were far more supportive of membership than him. The appearance of new parties in 2019 was connected to these tensions within the Conservatives and Labour.

Elections

The referendum that lay at the centre of Brexit was a supposed alternative to the election as a means of popular political engagement. But elections played an important part in the whole episode. May seems to have sought an early general election in 2017 at least in part because the increased Commons majority she hoped to secure would strengthen her hand with regard to the Brexit issue. That – contrary to such expectations – the Conservatives lost their overall majority was not only a political disaster from her perspective but would serve to heighten the constitutional tensions associated with the Brexit experience. In particular, it made possible a clash between executive and legislature on a scale that lacked clear precedent in UK history. Buffeted by both those who were supportive of and those who were reluctant regarding UK departure from the EU, the UK government suffered a unique series of defeats in the Commons. The attempted prorogation of Parliament took place in this context. As 2019 progressed and the atmosphere became increasingly tense, fundamental constitutional principles came into doubt. In passing laws intended to force negotiating positions upon the UK government, Parliament arguably intruded upon an area of activity – the conduct of diplomacy – traditionally reserved to the executive. Even the meaning of the concept of Commons confidence in the government – a fundamental component of the UK system – came into doubt, compounding confusion already caused by the Fixed-term Parliaments Act 2011. A general election result, intersecting with the Brexit issue, helped bring these tensions into being; a further general election contributed to their resolution. The 2019 poll delivered a substantial Conservative majority in the Commons. Brexit seems to have played a part in this victory and may have contributed to the gains the Conservatives made in areas that have previously been regarded as safe Labour territory, for instance in the North East of England.

'Populism'

Arguably, both the Johnson and Corbyn leaderships were manifestations of an international ascendancy of populism. Aspects of it included a tendency for its exponents to depict themselves as champions of the will of the people in the face of resistant and manipulative elites. The Eurosceptic platform might be seen in such a light. The desire to assert sovereignty and resist what is presented as improper foreign impositions upon a given state is a classic feature of populism. So is the advocacy of referendums as a tool for circumventing supposed vested interest groups and the blockages they allegedly create to frustrate the will of the people. Public criticism of the courts for their involvement in the controversy and for finding against the government in the two *Miller* cases had a populist dimension to it. At the 2019 general election, the Conservative Party set out in its manifesto a commitment to overhaul aspects of the constitution, including the operation of judicial review. In explaining this objective, it depicted the Brexit as having exposed a system out of touch with the public – again, a populist scenario.

Social divisions

As discussed previously, support for Remain or Leave was often linked to a related set of characteristics and attitudes that cut across more established divisions. This emergent cleavage, which the referendum and the issue of

Brexit helped stimulate, seems to have played a part in the general election result of 2019 and the changes in party allegiances that occurred in places such as the North East of England.

Online politics

The Brexit episode became a focus for increasing – and often concerned – interest in the political role of the internet, with clear constitutional implications. In earlier times, optimistic views of this technology were more prevalent. Advocates of digital democracy saw it as a means of attaining a range of perceived desirable outcomes. They included making it easier for people to organize politically, increased participation, wider access to information and the exposure of the public to a diverse spectrum of viewpoints. In more recent years, partly in response to the use of social media during the 2016 EU referendum, alongside other events such as the ascendancy (seemingly now curtailed at the time of writing) of Donald Trump, more negative views have gained in force. Discussion of the internet now involves serious consideration of the idea that it is a threat to key aspects of the constitution in a democratic system such as the ability to hold free and fair elections, free from improper manipulation from within or without a given state, engage in inclusive and open discussion, achieve basic social consensus around shared values and maintain agreement about the existence of factual information upon which contesting interpretations can then be placed. The internet is often depicted as a vehicle for division and extremism. Such apprehension has given rise to calls for new regulatory mechanisms, for ends including the operation of a consistent and fair form of what is termed 'content moderation' to online platforms. These proposals raise difficult questions about constitutional principles, such as the right to freedom of expression.[17]

Geography

Constitutions exist not only as abstract structures and sets of values but also as systems that apply to a given physical territory. Geography was central

---

[17] See A. Blick, *Electrified Democracy: The Internet and the United Kingdom Parliament in History*, Cambridge University Press, 2021, esp. chs 2 and 8.

to Brexit. It was a manifestation of the perpetual tension arising from the relationship of the UK as an archipelago state with the continent of which it is a part. Brexit generated further territorial issues of its own. The most immediate problems involved the island of Ireland. Here the UK had a land border with the EU. The island was the site of an historic conflict, with the republic in the south having broken away from the UK in the 1920s, while Northern Ireland remained within the Union. The status of Northern Ireland and its relationship with the republic is subject to a peace settlement encapsulated in the Belfast or Good Friday Agreement of 1998 (which itself had been approved by separate referendums in Northern Ireland and the republic). Keeping the border open was vital to the agreement and to the material prosperity of the whole island. Yet UK departure from the EU was difficult to reconcile with preserving this position. At the time of writing doubts exist about how these twin outcomes can be achieved, without in effect detaching Northern Ireland from full membership of the UK. In the period since the 2016 referendum, this dilemma has caused immense controversy, both internally to the UK and in its external relations. Various outcomes, including a united Ireland and a resurgence of conflict, became more plausible than they had once been.

As we have seen, Northern Ireland – like Scotland and London – had produced a Remain result in the 2016 vote. As discussed, this divergence within the UK could be seen as compromising the legitimacy of the Leave result. In Scotland, the idea of a Brexit that it did not vote for seemed to give renewed impetus to the independence cause. In the 2014 referendum on possible secession, an argument advanced by the pro-Union side was that leaving the UK was undesirable since it would entail Scotland needing to reapply for EU membership. Now, being part of the UK would require Scotland no longer to be part of the EU, rather than guarantee continuity of presence within it.

Territorial politics raised challenges in other ways. Historically, an important feature of the UK as it came into being as a single composite entity was that the different components that made it up – Wales, Scotland, Ireland/Northern Ireland and England – were all integrated into a single market with no internal barriers, whether brought about through tariffs or regulatory variations. This model of state formation was influential upon early advocates of European integration, whose efforts eventually led to the European single market and customs union (and single currency). In the period since the UK joined the European Communities in 1973, it introduced legislative devolution in three territories: Wales, Scotland and Northern Ireland (where it had operated previously from the early 1920s through to the early 1970s). The UK single market was maintained in the context of a devolved UK partly through making the devolved institutions fully subject to European law. In order for it to be preserved post Brexit, it would be necessary to retain some degree of regulatory conformity for the whole UK. In practice, achieving this objective meant returning powers previously exercised at the EU tier to UK-level (as opposed to devolved) institutions. While the supremacy of EU law might have been acceptable at devolved level, perceived dominance from London seems likely to be less so. It might transpire that membership of the EU had been an unnoticed means of preserving the UK intact as a state and that it will be difficult to substitute. If so, this outcome will be one more of a number of profound constitutional aspects of Brexit.[18]

Bibliography

Atkinson, L., Blick, A. and Qvortrup M. *The Referendum in Britain: A History*, Oxford University Press, 2020.

Blick, A. *Beyond Magna Carta: A Constitution for the United Kingdom*, Bloomsbury, 2015.

Blick, A. *Electrified Democracy: The Internet and the United Kingdom Parliament in History*, Cambridge University Press, 2021, esp. chs 2 and 8.

Blick, A. *Stretching the Constitution: The Brexit Shock in Historic Perspective*, Bloomsbury/Hart, 2019.

Bogdanor, V. *Beyond Brexit: Towards a British Constitution*, I. B. Tauris, 2019.

McConalogue, J. (ed.), *The British Constitution Resettled: Parliamentary Sovereignty before and after Brexit*, Palgrave Macmillan, 2019.

Elliott, M., Young, A. and Williams, J. (eds), *The Constitution after Miller*, Bloomsbury/Hart, 2018.

House of Commons Public Administration and Constitutional Affairs Committee, *Lessons Learned from the EU Referendum*, House of Commons, 2017.

Simms, B. *Britain's Europe: A Thousand Years of Conflict and Cooperation*, Penguin, 2017.

Sobolewska, M. and Ford R. *Brexitland: Identity, Diversity and the Reshaping of British Politics*, Cambridge University Press, 2020.

---

[18] A. Blick, *Brexit: Removing the Connective Tissue of the United Kingdom?*, Federal Trust, 2020.

2

Brexit's impact on the party system

Alan Wager

On the night of the referendum on 23 June 2016, the British prime minister David Cameron was thirteen months into a five-year Parliament that he promised would be his last as Prime Minister. Over the next four years, instead of the Conservative Party under David Cameron protecting their slim but manageable thirteen-seat majority in the House of Commons, British politics was subsumed by the process of managing Brexit. In truth, even before the result was announced, Cameron privately knew the aftermath of the referendum would be bloody and his position unsustainable.[1] Yet few could have foreseen the scale of political turmoil unleashed by the decision of the United Kingdom (UK) to leave the European Union (EU). The rupture in the UK party system that followed Brexit ended the premiership of more than one Prime Minister, led to more than one leadership contest in both the Conservative and Labour parties, two general elections, the formation of new parties in the Brexit Party and Change UK, and the brief revival of an older one in the Liberal Democrats. All of this was driven by the party system catching up and adapting to a cleavage in the electorate – Leave and Remain – that gave a name to a social division in the UK that had long existed but which became increasingly central in shaping the UK's politics.

This chapter first sets out the key events of the period from June 2016 to December 2020 and the degree to which they were shaped by Brexit, and in turn how Brexit was shaped by party politics. Then, it will focus thematically on the domestic politics of Brexit across three areas: changes in the electoral coalitions of the major parties resulting from Brexit, the changing composition

---

[1] Interview with Ameet Gill, David Cameron's chief of staff. UK in a Changing Europe Brexit Archives.

and behaviour of the Conservative and Labour parties in Parliament, and the extent to which the attitude to party members impacted on the outcome of the Brexit process. Prior to Brexit, we had no precedent for what leaving the EU can do to the politics of a departing member state. The experience of the UK suggests the effect on party politics is destabilizing, divisive and ultimately transformative.

British party politics and Brexit, June 2016–December 2020

The history of Brexit politics after the 2016 referendum is a tale of five acts. The first year following the referendum saw the brief hegemony of Theresa May, a period in which the path of Brexit was set. The second saw the 2017 general election and the rise of Labour under Jeremy Corbyn, a phenomenon that had more to do with Brexit than is often presupposed. The third act was a period of suspended animation, both parties attempting to straddle a Brexit division in the electorate that widened as the length of time from the referendum continued. With the end of Brexit negotiations came an explosion within the Conservative and then the Labour parties, and with it the UK entered into a period of multiparty politics. The final dénouement saw Boris Johnson – the arch protagonist of the UK's decision to leave the EU – deliver victory for the Conservative Party in what was widely seen as a 'Brexit election' (Figure 2.1).

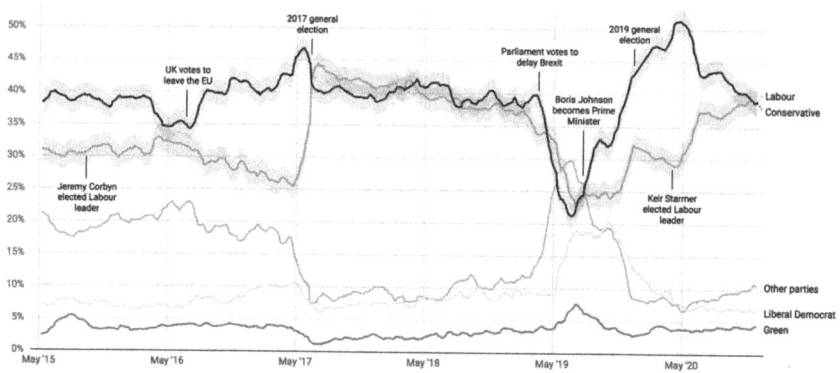

Figure 2.1 Aggregate opinion poll support for Britain's political parties, May 2015–December 2020. *Source*: *New Statesman* polling aggregation, 2015–20.

June 2016–17

David Cameron's director of communications described the EU referendum campaign as 'unleashing demons' (Oliver, 2016). Yet the Conservative Party establishment appeared to spend the immediate aftermath putting those demons back in their box. Within six hours of the result of the referendum being announced, David Cameron announced his resignation; within three weeks, Theresa May was anointed Conservative leader and Prime Minister, without a vote being put to Conservative members. The only serious candidate who had been an advocate for remaining in the EU – albeit while gaining the nickname 'Submarine May' during the campaign due to her deliberate inactivity – the new prime minister was the choice of 91 per cent of Conservative MPs who had campaigned for Remain (Jeffery et al., 2018: 276). Theresa May's rhetoric in public, and indeed the refrain of her advisers in private, was that 'Brexit means Brexit': in effect, the mandate of the referendum meant the path that her administration would follow on Brexit was self-explanatory.

Immediately following the referendum, May's candidacy had the support of only a quarter of Conservative members who had backed Leave (Sayers, 2016). Upon entering Downing Street, she was aware she was a leader of a party, and a country, who had voted to Leave. The appointment of three key Brexit advocates in Boris Johnson, David Davis and Liam Fox to run the three most Brexit-focused Cabinet positions – Foreign Secretary and heads of the new departments for exiting the EU and international trade respectively – was meant as a clear signal of her direction. Within the first few months, one clear belief guided Theresa May on Brexit: that leaving the EU meant ending freedom of movement. In a conference speech in September 2016 – to the chagrin and surprise of some of her Cabinet ministers, including her Chancellor – she signalled that the UK would leave the single market and trigger Article 50 by 31 March 2017. The path to what would come to be known as a 'hard' Brexit had been set. With it, the political positioning and appeal of the Conservative Party as the party of Brexit were beginning to entrench.

If the Conservative leadership contest advanced at pace and appeared to come to a quick resolution, the Labour Party's internecine warfare triggered by Brexit was long, drawn out and painful. Within four days, twenty-one members of the Shadow Cabinet resigned from the Labour front bench due to Jeremy Corbyn's ambivalence on Brexit and a perceived failure to campaign for Remain during the referendum. A confidence vote in which 81 per cent of Labour MPs voted against Jeremy Corbyn was followed by a leadership contest in which he won 62 per cent of the vote among Labour's grassroots members. The candidate Corbyn faced, the MP Owen Smith, supported a further referendum on any Brexit deal. Jeremy Corbyn, on the other hand, was clear that the Labour Party needed to respect the referendum result: he called for the immediate triggering of Article 50 the day after the referendum and in his 2016 conference speech set out his own Brexit agenda 'including the freedom to intervene in our own industries'. It was the first and clearest sign that if the Labour membership was forced to choose between their opposition to Brexit and support for their insurgent leader, for the Corbynite faithful there would always only be one winner.

By the turn of the year, six months after the referendum result, the polls showed Theresa May ascendant. In a speech at Lancaster House, the Prime Minister further fleshed out that Brexit would mean ruling out full membership of the EU's customs union as well as the single market. Theresa May's thoughts – supported by senior members of her Cabinet and her advisers – began, in the spring, to turn to a general election.[2] The rationale was that the Conservative Party, far from suffering from Cameron's resignation and Brexit, had instead gained additional support. This was driven in large part by May's apparent personal ratings in April 2017: when asked who would make the most capable Prime Minister, 61 per cent said Mrs May and 23 per cent said Jeremy Corbyn, the largest lead for a party leader since Ipsos Mori had begun asking that question since 1979 (Ipsos Mori, 2017). There was also some strategic discussion that a mandate and a majority that would last from 2017 through until 2022 would allow the UK and the EU the time and the space to negotiate and implement a deal within a single electoral cycle.

The Brexit election? The general election of 2017

In the end, despite Theresa May's framing, Brexit was conspicuous by its absence in the 2017 general election. Yet it was still top of the minds of many voters: the British Election Study, asking voters every day, found more than one

---

[2] Interviews with Fiona Hill and Joanna Penn, David Cameron's chief of staff. UK in a Changing Europe Brexit Archives.

in three people mentioned Brexit or the EU, compared to fewer than one in ten who mentioned the NHS and one in twenty who suggested the economy. The manifesto position of Labour – support for access to the single market – meant that Jeremy Corbyn's increasing popularity during the campaign drew in voters who supported Leave and Remain. Overall, 19 per cent of voters switched parties between the April/May survey and the election – unusually, Labour won 54 per cent of these voters who changed their mind during the campaign, compared to 19 per cent for the Conservatives (Mellon et al., 2018). Crucially, Labour was able to pick up the voters of those who prioritized both single market access and those who prioritized immigration control. Remainers flocked back to Labour as the best route to ameliorating Brexit, while Leavers were not convinced that overturning the 2016 referendum was a serious prospect. Theresa May's warning that she needed a majority, as Parliament was blocking the progress to leave the EU, was difficult to sustain given MPs had voted, by a majority of 384, to trigger Article 50. On Brexit, to use a phrase, Labour was able to have its cake and eat it.

One result of the 2017 general election campaign was that in England and Wales something akin to the two-party politics was able to reassert itself. Leavers deserted UKIP, which had lost (having lost) its raison d'être and its totemic leader Nigel Farage. Between the 2015 and 2017 general elections – the first fought with Farage as leader and the second without – its share of the national vote dropped from almost 13 per cent to just 1.8 per cent, and the number of seats in which UKIP polled at least 10 per cent of the vote crashed, from 450 to only 2 (Goodwin and Heath, 2017: 346). The Liberal Democrats were unable to cut through with an anti-Brexit position, not least given the social liberal voters that message would be dependent upon were not attracted to the party's leader Tim Farron. The result was a hung Parliament, with Theresa May reliant upon the Northern Irish DUP – the only party with seats in the House of Commons that had supported Leave position in June 2016 – to prop up a minority Conservative administration.

Party politics pushed to the Brexit extremes, June 2017–December 2018

One possible consequence of a hung Parliament – a cross-party approach to Brexit – was never seriously contemplated by the Prime Minister, as Theresa

May was kept in post by advocates of Brexit concerned about the prospects that further upheaval could see the result being reversed. Instead, UK politics entered a period in which the leadership of both the Conservative and Labour parties was put under pressure from their Eurosceptic and pro-referendum wings respectively. Following the referendum, the Leave and Remain campaigns came to provide labels for people's political identity that increasingly seemed to suit people better than traditional political labels. As a result, the British Election Study research found that in the summer of 2018, only one in sixteen British voters held no Brexit identity. This compared to one in five who did not identify at all with one of the parties.

At first, it seemed that the pressure within the Conservative Party would come from the small but persistent pro-Europeans in her parliamentary party – who undertook a series of rebellions to ensure that the Prime Minister would have to give the House of Commons the sign-off on any deal she made with the EU. However, it was Conservative Eurosceptics who the Prime Minister struggled to contain within her party. By the summer of 2018, a decision had to be made on Brexit by the Conservative Cabinet – and a decision was made, with the Cabinet signing off on the 'Chequers Deal', which would have kept the UK in the EU's regulatory orbit for goods. The senior Eurosceptics Boris Johnson and David Davis, who Theresa May had judged in 2016 needed to be in senior positions in her Cabinet to retain her Eurosceptic credentials, resigned. The subsequent Conservative Party conference – in which Johnson, addressing the fringes of a combustible conference, remonstrated that Theresa May should 'Chuck Chequers' – demonstrated that the Prime Minister appeared to have been proved right when she made that decision at the start of her leadership. A decisive section of her party could not be reconciled to the government's approach to Brexit. Boris Johnson was in tune with his audience: when Theresa May's deal finally did arrive, if given the choice just 29 per cent of Tory members would vote for May's deal compared with 64 per cent who would vote to leave without a deal. By January 2019, more Conservative voters (67 per cent) than Conservative members (51 per cent) thought Theresa May was doing a good job as Prime Minister (Menon and Wager, 2019).

It was not just Theresa May who may have come to wish she had insulated herself from her own party by forming a cross-party agreement on Brexit. Jeremy Corbyn's hope that Labour could go into the next election with a position of 'constructive ambiguity' on Brexit, much as it had in 2017, was difficult to square with a Parliamentary Labour Party increasingly attracted to a referendum. The 'People's Vote' campaign, launched in February 2018, made its primary task shifting Labour's position to support a referendum. They were helped by the fact that in the winter of 2018, 79 per cent of Labour members supported a referendum if May's deal was rejected in the Commons and over a third of Labour MPs openly backed a second referendum that was not party policy. Jeremy Corbyn's position that the UK should remain in a customs union with the EU – a position thought to be enough to signal Labour would once again be the party of 'soft' Brexit – was instead seen as a staging post in a gradual evolution on the long road to Labour becoming the party of Remain.

Multiparty politics: January–September 2018

The defeats that Theresa May endured on her Brexit deal once it returned to Parliament were historic. The first time a vote was scheduled, after five days of debate, the vote was cancelled. Once a vote on the deal was held, the Prime Minister lost by 230 votes, the largest defeat for a government in a vote in the House of Commons on the historical record. Almost 118 Conservative MPs, over a third of Conservative MPs and over two-thirds who did not hold a government job, voted against the deal. Six weeks later, with no meaningful concessions forthcoming, the government lost by a 149-vote margin – the second-largest recorded defeat for any government on a contested vote in the House of Commons in the post-war era. This was evidence that the House of Commons – a legislature designed to accommodate a cohesive governing party and an opposition – was struggling to cope with the splits created by Brexit (Russell, 2020: 9–10). This dysfunction within the party system was the root cause of the inability to find a solution to Brexit and the decision – ultimately a decision made on Theresa May's behalf by MPs – to seek an extension of the Article 50 process.

As these battles in Parliament played out, the two major parties began to come under external pressure. In January seven Labour MPs, and three Conservatives, left their parties to form the Independent Group – later Change UK – in part due to their opposition to Brexit and support for a further referendum. Meanwhile, on the other wing of the Brexit debate, Nigel Farage had viewed the chaos resulting from the failure of Theresa May to pass her Brexit deal as an opening – and eyeing the European Parliament elections that would be a legal consequence of an extension to Article 50 as a tactical opportunity. The Brexit Party was subsequently formed, their European election campaign launched in April and, within weeks, the party had 100,000 members and millions in donations. In May 2019, these European parliamentary elections provided the high-water mark for multiparty politics in the UK. The Brexit Party topped the polls with 31 per cent and twenty-nine seats; the Liberal Democrats finished second, with sixteen seats and 20 per cent. The creation of a new 'Remain' party had the paradoxical effect of triggering a revival of the Liberal Democrats – who had been in seemingly terminal decline since entering into a coalition with the Conservatives in 2010. Throughout the summer of 2019, the Liberal Democrats and the Brexit Party regularly traded first place in vote intention opinion polls. The Labour Party and the Liberal Democrats both received polling forecasts demonstrating that Labour could be abandoned en masse by voters who favoured a referendum.

The Conservative Party, meanwhile, began facing up to its Brexit Party problem. A survey by YouGov (2019) of Conservative Party members revealed 59 per cent of the party's members had voted for the Brexit Party in the European elections, and just 19 per cent had voted Conservative. The day after the vote, Theresa May announced her resignation. A Conservative leadership campaign, which had been barely concealed, began in public. From the start, the clear front runner was Boris Johnson – seen as the candidate most likely to reunite the party with those voters (and members) tempted by Nigel Farage. As a result, the contest was a Brexit arms race: all of the candidates bar one, Rory Stewart, said they would be willing to pursue a no-deal Brexit and, in a television debate, Dominic Raab suggested that Parliament could be prorogued to prevent the House of Commons from stopping a no-deal Brexit. But ultimately Boris Johnson was unstoppable: in the final ballot of Tory MPs Johnson received 160 votes to his nearest rival Jeremy Hunt's 77. In a run-off between Johnson and Hunt among party members, Johnson went on to win by two to one. It was the Conservative leadership contest dominated by Brexit that many had expected in 2016 and would be followed by an election where Brexit took centre stage – as many expected it might come in 2017.

Prime Minister Johnson and a Brexit election

Boris Johnson's mandate on Brexit from his party was clear. Yet the brutality with which the Parliamentary Conservative Party was transformed still took many MPs by surprise. In August, it was announced that Boris Johnson would seek to prorogue Parliament – making it much more difficult for MPs to stop a no-deal Brexit. In response, in the brief window before prorogation, MPs passed legislation making that would reduce the ability for the Prime Minister to push. The twenty-one Conservative MPs who opposed this decision were all previously Remainers and were largely party grandees – including nine former Cabinet ministers, the longest-serving Conservative MP Ken Clarke and Winston Churchill's grandson Nicholas Soames. While four of these twenty-one would go on to fight the subsequent election as Conservatives, this was a clear signal that the make-up of the Conservative Party in Parliament – on the issue of Brexit at least – was changing.

While some of these MPs ejected from the party would work with MPs across the House of Commons to limit the possibility of a no-deal Brexit, this cross-party working in 2019 was an innovation in British party politics that significantly empowered the legislature vis-à-vis the executive. However, there was a limit to their cooperation: not enough of these back-bench MPs were advocates of a stable referendum for a majority to be possible, and none would accept the idea of Jeremy Corbyn as the temporary head of an administration to make that happen. This was why when Boris Johnson returned with a revised Withdrawal Agreement, it looked likely that the pieces were falling into place for a Brexit deal to be passed. The Liberal Democrats – partly fuelled by their belief they could make significant gains in Conservative-held seats in the south of England that voted Remain – and the SNP moved towards supporting a general election.

In the election of December 2019, the Conservative Party's message that they would 'Get Brexit Done' was augmented by the Brexit Party's decision to stand down candidates in Conservative-held seats. The Remain campaign, on the other hand, was split between the Labour Party and smaller parties advocating a referendum. The division on Brexit, driven by a division on social values between more liberal and more socially authoritarian voters, was being decided by an election with one side broadly united and the other side divided. Yet, in truth, the fact that voters' preferences on Brexit had to be managed through a general election – in which their views on Brexit were refracted through a choice between a relatively unpopular Prime Minister in Boris and a historically unpopular alternative in Jeremy Corbyn – complicated the role of Brexit.

The Brexit effect on the UK party system

The events of the period from Brexit happening to the UK formally leaving the EU had a marked effect on the UK's two political parties. Drawing on questions that seek to measure the social and economic values (Wager et al., 2021), Figure 2.2 maps out where Conservative and Labour MPs, members and voters stand on social and economic questions in relation to each other. It demonstrates the organizational gaps between different strata of the UK's political parties and the extent to which intra-party differences have widened as a result of Brexit.

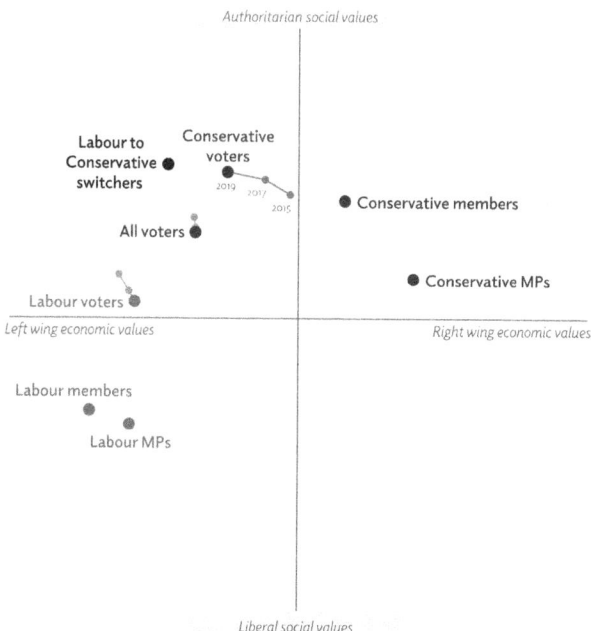

Figure 2.2 The social and economic values of Conservative and Labour MPs, members and voters, 2015–19. *Source*: ESRC Party Members Project survey, *YouGov*, fieldwork December 2019; UK in a Changing Europe MPs survey, *Ipsos Mori*, fieldwork January–February 2020; British Election Study Internet Panel, Wave 17, fieldwork November 2019, and Wave 19, fieldwork December 2019. Derived from 'Mind the Values Gap: The Social and Economic Values of MPs, Party Members and Votes'.

The UK's changing electoral coalitions

As Figure 2.2 demonstrates, the Conservative coalition became markedly more socially authoritarian between 2015 and 2019. The Labour Party's electoral coalition under Jeremy Corbyn became more socially liberal than it became economically left wing. The demographic and geographic trends that underpin these developments changed the nature of both parties. For the first time since the Labour Party was formed a century ago, the working class are now more likely to vote for the Conservatives than the middle class. While this is a process of realignment that has taken place elsewhere in Europe, it is certainly a process that has been accelerated by Brexit in the UK. This is a symptom of the fact that at least during the Brexit process, the economic cleavage of left and right became less important. Where voters sat on the liberal–authoritarian axis – a much more accurate determinate of whether or not a voter supported Brexit – in turn became a stronger indicator of which party a voter supported than it once did.

Much of the discussion has centred on Labour's loss of the 'red wall' in the 2019 general election and whether – if and when the 'Brexit effect' dissipates – these seats can be regained. In some constituencies, this looks unlikely. In Leigh, Labour's margin of victory over the Conservatives was 31 per cent in 2015. In Bolsover it was 27 per cent. In Redcar it was 25 per cent. All three constituencies, which voted solidly for Leave in 2016, are now Conservative held. However, this realignment also poses a geographical problem for the Conservatives: there are a number of Remain-leaning seats, predominantly but not exclusively in the south of England, where a high number of middle-class graduates live. Overall, these constituencies swung to Labour and the Liberal Democrats under Jeremy Corbyn's leadership. They form a defensive front, partly created by Brexit, which the Conservative Party will face pressure from a more moderate Labour Party in 2024.

Conservative and Labour party members

An important recent phenomenon that plays a role in explaining why the Brexit referendum took place, and how the politics of Brexit played out subsequently, was the increased relative power of party members. Within the Conservative Party, support for Leave was much higher than among members of Parliament, and Conservative advocates of a 'soft' Brexit or a second referendum began, in 2019, to face significant deselection challenges. The Labour membership was strongly in favour of remaining in the EU and became a significant weapon that advocates of a further referendum on EU membership used against the Corbyn leadership. By the summer of 2019, it was becoming increasingly difficult for the Labour membership to contain growing demands for a pro-referendum policy.

A desire to move on from the Brexit divisions that had riven the Labour Party united MPs and members, and in the first year in the job this was a clear priority of Keir Starmer – helped by the fact that changing the subject away from these social values questions to the economy has the effect, as Figure 2.2 shows, of uniting each part of the Labour Party organization. The form of Brexit pursued and achieved by Boris Johnson – prioritizing sovereignty and control over economic considerations – clearly retained the support of the vast majority of party members as well as MPs. The long-term question is whether this concordat between Conservative voters, members and MPs can be sustained as the economic recovery from Covid-19 poses a different set of questions to the unifying rallying call of 'Getting Brexit Done'.

The Parliamentary Conservative and Labour parties

It is perhaps unsurprising that the change in the nature of Conservative support in the country has been partially reflected in the House of Commons. Some 185 Conservative MPs (though not as many as David Cameron had expected) publicly supported remaining in the EU in the 2016 referendum, while 135 backed Leave. By December 2019, the Parliamentary Conservative Party had been transformed. Of the 365 Conservative MPs, 229 had publicly backed Leave and 129 had supported Remain (Bale and Minasyan, 2020).[3] The square sum of zero now advocated remaining in the EU, and all had signed up to a manifesto that included the possibility of a no-trade deal being agreed between the UK and the EU by the end of 2020. The Labour Party in the House of Commons has also accommodated itself to the fact of Brexit – most clearly seen in Keir Starmer's tactical decision as Labour leader to support the passage of the UK–EU trade agreement through the House of Commons with minimal dissent.

[3] The remainder did not have a public position.

Yet, as Figure 2.2 demonstrates, on the social values that underpin these Brexit attitudes, Labour MPs remain detached from voters and are indeed more socially liberal than party members. On the other hand, as Brexit has enabled the Conservative Party to expand its reach among economically left-wing and socially authoritarian voters, so the ideological distance between its libertarian MPs and its voters has widened. To take one example, when surveyed 5 per cent of Tory MPs think that there is 'one rule for the rich and one for the poor', compared to 84 per cent of those voters who voted for Labour in 2017 but were persuaded to support Boris Johnson in 2019.

All this raises the important question of the longevity of these changes and the long-term effect of Brexit on the UK party system. There is some early evidence that the importance of factors such as governing competence and the 'old' politics of the economy have reasserted themselves in the context of the Covid-19 pandemic (Green et al., 2020). If so, then some of the trends that drove the partial realignment of the UK political system could be reversed. However, the changed electoral map of the UK is likely to be long-term legacy of the aftermath of Brexit. It is likely to be felt for elections and for decades to come.

Bibliography

Bale, T. and Minasyan, H. (2020), 'Does Boris Johnson Have the Conservative Party's Permission to Extend Transition?', *UK in a Changing Europe*, 30 April. Available online: https://ukandeu.ac.uk/does-boris-johnson-have-the-conservative-partys-permission-to-extend-transition/.

Curtis, C. (2019), 'If Everyone Revealed How They Voted Last Week Labour Would Have to Kick Out Four in Ten Members', *YouGov*, May 30. Available online: https://yougov.co.uk/topics/politics/articles-reports/2019/05/30/if-everyone-revealed-how-they-voted-last-week-labo.

Green, J., Evans, G. and Snow, D. (2020), 'The Government Is Losing Support over Its Handling of Coronavirus, Especially among Its New 2019 Voters', Nuffield College Elections Unit, 9 December. Available online: https://www.politics.ox.ac.uk/news/latest-nuffield-elections-unit-british-election-survey-report-gives-government-stark-warning.html.

Goodwin, M. and Heath, A. (2017), 'The 2017 General Election, Brexit and the Return to Two-Party Politics: An Aggregate-Level Analysis of the Result', *Political Quarterly*, 88 (3): 345–58.

Ipsos Mori (2017), 'Political Monitor: April 2017', 25 April. Available online: https://www.ipsos.com/sites/default/files/2017-04/pm-april-2017-topline.pdf.

Jeffery, D., Heppell, T., Hayton, R. and Crines, A. (2018), 'The Conservative Party Leadership Election of 2016: An Analysis of the Voting Motivations of Conservative Parliamentarians', *Parliamentary Affairs*, 71 (2): 263–82.

Mellon, J., Evans, G., Fieldhouse, E., Green, J. and Prosser, C. (2018), 'Brexit or Corbyn? Campaign and Inter-Election Vote Switching in the 2017 UK General Election', *Parliamentary Affairs*, 71 (4): 719–37.

Menon, A. and Wager, A. (2019), 'Labour's Brexit Dilemma', In *Brexit and Public Opinion 2019: UK in a Changing Europe*, 2019, 31–4. https://ukandeu.ac.uk/wp-content/uploads/2019/01/Public-Opinion-2019-report.pdf,

Oliver, C. (2016), *Unleashing Demons*. London: Hodder & Stoughton.

Russell, M. (2020), 'Brexit and Parliament: The Anatomy of a Perfect Storm', *Parliamentary Affairs*, Early Access, 1–21.

Sayers, F. (2016), 'Theresa May Storms ahead of Boris among Tory Party Membership', *YouGov*, 29 June. Available online: https://yougov.co.uk/topics/politics/articles-reports/2016/06/29/theresa-may-storms-ahead-boris-among-tory-party-me.

Wager, A., Bale, T., Cowley, P., and Menon, A. (2021), *Political Studies*, Early Access, 1–25.

Brexit and Scotland

Unfinished business?

John Curtice

In contrast to the United Kingdom (UK) as a whole, Scotland voted decisively – by 62 per cent to 38 per cent – in the referendum on European Union (EU) membership held on 23 June 2016. That divergent outcome has triggered a sequence of events that has undermined support in Scotland for remaining part of the UK, the consequence of which is highly uncertain. There is at least the possibility that in leaving the EU, the UK government has put at risk the continued integrity of the British state whose sovereignty it was so keen to reclaim.

Introduction

Scotland has not always been a particularly Europhile part of the UK. In the 1975 referendum on the UK's membership of the then Common Market, 58 per cent voted in favour of staying in, well below the 67 per cent figure registered across the UK as a whole. However, in the 1990s, the Scottish National Party (SNP), whose raison d'être is to secure independence and which had campaigned against EU membership in 1975, developed a new vision of 'Independence in Europe'. By being an independent country within the EU, Scotland would, it was argued, be able to combine control over its own domestic affairs with continued access to a large domestic market and the benefit of its own place at the EU 'top table' (Dardanelli, 2005). The argument was a clear example of how globalization could potentially make it easier for a smaller country to pursue independence (Mau, 2005; Meadwell and Martin, 1996).

Thus, when a referendum on Scotland's constitutional status was held in 2014 (Curtice, 2021), continued membership of the EU was an integral feature of the portrait of independence that was presented to voters (Scottish Government, 2013). Indeed, whether an independent Scotland would necessarily automatically become a member of the EU became one of the central bones of contention during the referendum campaign. The UK asserted it would have to apply for membership afresh (HM Government, 2013), a view to which the then president of the European Commission, Manuel Barroso, appeared to lend support, while those campaigning for independence asserted the opposite. Yet, in the event, attitudes towards the EU seem to have played little role in determining whether people voted Yes or No to independence. According to the Scottish Social Attitudes survey, those who were sceptical about the EU (49 per cent) were somewhat more likely than those whose opinion could be characterized as Europhile (44 per cent) to have voted in the 2014 referendum in favour of independence (see note to Table 3.1). Despite the SNP's official stance on the issue, those who supported independence had always contained a group who doubted the wisdom of reclaiming sovereignty from London only then to share it with Brussels.

This was also the position in the 2016 EU referendum. According to the 2015 British Election Study Internet Panel, 62 per cent of those who had voted Yes to independence two years previously had voted to Remain in the EU, but so also did 60 per cent of those who had backed No. In short, prior to the vote in favour of Brexit there was little sign that the issue of Scotland's relationship with the EU made much difference to people's attitudes towards independence. So, although Scotland was now at risk of having its EU membership terminated against the wishes of a majority of its voters – seemingly the clearest possible illustration of the SNP's argument that as part of the UK, Scotland is always at risk of having its 'democratic wishes' overturned by the (allegedly) different outlook of voters in England – perhaps it was not surprising that the Brexit vote had little immediate impact on the overall level of support for independence. On average those polls that asked people how they would vote now in response to the question that appeared on the 2014 ballot paper, 'Should Scotland be an independent country?', found 46 per cent saying Yes in the second half of 2016 and 45 per cent in the first half of 2017. The latter figure was exactly in line with the 45 per cent that had been registered in the 2014 referendum.

Brexit begins to matter

Yet, in truth, underneath the surface Brexit was having an impact on who was and who was not supporting independence. Some of those who had voted No to independence in 2014 but had then backed Remain in the EU referendum in 2016 did swing in favour of independence. According to polling undertaken by YouGov in the autumn of 2016, only around three-quarters (74 per cent) of those who had voted No in 2014 but Remain in 2016 said they would vote No again, whereas over nine in ten (93 per cent) of those who had voted No and Leave would do so. However, the change of heart among this group was being counterbalanced by an equivalent, countervailing movement among those who had voted Yes in 2014. Among those Yes voters who had voted Remain in 2016, no less than 86 per cent were now saying they would back Yes again. However, this figure fell to just 65 per cent among those who had supported Leave. In short, now that it was apparently heading out of the EU, some of those who had backed independence in 2014 were converted to remaining in the UK.

As a result of these movements, attitudes towards the EU became intertwined with attitudes towards independence for the first time. This can be seen in Table 3.1, which uses data from the annual Scottish Social Attitudes survey to show how the level of support for independence evolved in the wake of Brexit. As we have already noted, prior to the Brexit referendum there was little sign that 'Eurosceptics' and 'Europhiles' had different views on Scotland's

Table 3.1 Support for Independence by Attitude towards the EU, 2013–19

% support independence	Eurosceptic	Europhile
2013	29	30
2014	35	31
2015	41	39
2016	44	53
2017	40	56
2019	43	62

Notes: Support for independence is the proportion choosing either independence within the EU or independence outside the EU in response to a choice of five possible options, including two varieties of devolution and one saying that there should not be a Scottish Parliament at all. Eurosceptics are those who in response to a five-option question said that either the UK should leave the EU or it should work to reduce its powers. Europhiles are those who were content with the EU's existing powers, wanted the EU to be more powerful and backed having a single European government.
The 2014 survey was conducted before the independence referendum, while the 2016 was conducted after the EU referendum.
Source: Curtice and Montagu (2020).

constitutional status. However, as soon as the referendum was over, support for independence began to be noticeably higher among Europhiles than Eurosceptics – as registered by the Scottish Social Attitudes survey conducted in the second half of 2016 – and the gap between them gradually widened further thereafter.

The 2017 election

In its manifesto for the 2016 Scottish Parliament election – held seven weeks before the EU referendum – the SNP did not commit itself to holding another ballot on independence. Rather, it merely asserted that the Scottish Parliament should have the right (which it currently does not have) to hold another referendum if either there was clear evidence that independence had become the majority view or 'there is a significant and material change in the circumstances that prevailed in 2014, such as Scotland being taken out of the EU against our will' (Scottish National Party, 2016). Thus, although the aggregate level of support for independence recorded by the polls had not increased, it was not surprising that after an attempt by the Scottish government to propose a relatively 'soft' Brexit had seemingly been rebuffed by the UK government (Scottish Government, 2016; May 2017), it sought and secured the authority of the Scottish Parliament to submit a request for the legal authority to hold another ballot. The request was greeted by the UK with the response that 'now is not the time' and a suggestion that any ballot should only occur after Brexit had been concluded.

Shortly thereafter, the then UK prime minister, Theresa May, called a UK general election in the hope that it would enable her to secure a larger parliamentary majority with which to pursue Brexit. That stratagem failed, but it did result in a political setback for the SNP. In the 2015 general election, held eight months after the 2014 independence referendum, the party had swept the board in Scotland winning 50 per cent of the vote and all but three of the country's fifty-nine Commons seats. It was therefore a disappointment when in the election in June 2017 support for the party fell to 37 per cent, leaving it with just thirty-five seats. The outcome was widely interpreted as a rebuff to the party's attempt to call a second referendum, an interpretation that the Scottish first minister, Nicola Sturgeon, seemed to share when a fortnight later she put her plans for another referendum on hold.

Yet, in truth, this interpretation of the SNP's electoral setback was wide of the mark. Just as support for independence was becoming intertwined with attitudes towards Brexit, so also were voters' party preferences (Curtice and Montagu, 2018; Fieldhouse et al., 2019). This is illustrated in Table 3.2, which shows the level of support for the three largest parties in Scotland broken down by how people had voted in the 2016 EU referendum. As we might anticipate, given the absence at the time of any link between attitudes towards the EU and support for independence, at the 2015 UK general election and the 2016 Scottish Parliament election, Remain voters and Leave supporters differed little in their propensity to vote for the SNP. However, at the 2017 UK election support for the SNP fell by as much as twenty points among Leave voters, while it barely fell at all among Remain supporters. Conversely, support for the Conservatives rose sharply (just as it did in the rest of the UK, Curtice and Simpson, 2018; Fieldhouse et al., 2019), while it no more than held steady among Remain supporters. Just as Brexit was reshaping the character of support for independence, so it was changing the pattern of party support too.

Thus, in the short term the pursuit of Brexit was disruptive of the nationalist movement in Scotland. It helped occasion a fall in support for the SNP while there was little sign of any increase in support for independence. It appeared that the constitutional question was on the back burner once more. Indeed, uncertainty about whether and how Brexit might be delivered meant that the idea of a second referendum was not revived as promised by Nicola Sturgeon the following year – instead that autumn the SNP lent its support to the call to hold a second EU referendum that might reverse the Brexit decision. That was no small move for a party that had long insisted that only one referendum would be needed to deliver independence and that there would be no need for a second ballot to approve whatever agreement was subsequently reached on the details of Scotland's exit from the UK.

Table 3.2 Election Vote 2015–19 by EU Referendum Vote 2016

	Remain voters			Leave voters		
	Conservative	Labour	SNP	Conservative	Labour	SNP
2015 (UK)	12	27	50	21	23	42
2016 (SP)	17	27	45	30	16	44
2017 (UK)	18	29	43	49	22	24
2019 (UK)	12	21	52	50	14	27

Source: 2015–19 British Election Study Internet Panel, waves 6, 8, 13 and 19.

Support for independence rises

In any event, there was still little sign of any rise in support for independence that might encourage the SNP to want to revive the issue. In the eighteen months after the June 2017 UK general election, support continued to average 45 per cent in the polls. However, the picture changed significantly in 2019 when, as Brexit came to dominate Britain's political agenda in the wake of a parliamentary stalemate over how the issue should be pursued (cross-reference), the polls began consistently to show higher levels of support for independence. On average a dozen polls conducted that year put support for independence at 49 per cent, only a little behind the 51 per cent who still wanted to be part of the UK. It was the first time that the polls had consistently recorded such a high level of support for independence.

There is little doubt that the trigger for this increase was opposition to the pursuit of Brexit. But polls over the last two years have not seen a persistent rise in Scottish support for independence. From 1 September to 22 November 2021, eight different polls found that support to remain in the UK was stronger in Scotland than support to leave. The latest Ipsos Mori poll between 22 and 29 November 2021 found that 52% of Scots would vote in favour of independence, 42% would not and 4% were unsure. This is apparent in Table 3.3, which charts the level of support for independence from the second half of 2018 through to the May 2021 Scottish Parliament election. As the first row of the table shows, although the overall level of support for independence still stood at 45 per cent,

Table 3.3 Vote Intentions in a Second Independence Referendum, 2018–21, by 2016 EU Referendum Vote

% vote Yes to independence	2016 EU referendum vote	
	Remain	Leave
June–December 2018	50	34
April–October 2019	56	32
November–December 2019	55	30
January–March 2020	56	31
June–December 2020	59	37
January–February 2021	56	34
March 2020	53	32
April 2021	54	31
Final election polls 2021	55	30

Source: Average of polls conducted by BMG, Ipsos MORI, Lord Ashcroft, JL Partners, Opinium, Panelbase, Savanta ComRes, Survation, YouGov. Not all companies published a poll in each period.

by the end of 2018 a half of those who voted Remain supported independence while only around a third of Leave voters were doing so. The process that had started two years earlier whereby some No voters who had voted to Remain in the EU were switching to Yes, while some who had backed Yes and Leave were now in the No camp, had by this stage resulted in a clear difference between Remain and Leave voters in their attitudes towards independence.

It was always likely that this process would eventually have an impact on the overall level of support for independence. After all, those who had voted No and Remain were twice as numerous as those who had backed Yes and Leave. Eventually in 2019 it did. The increase in the overall level of support for independence was accompanied by a widening of the gap between Remain and Leave voters in their level of support for independence. By the end of the year support for independence had increased by five points among Remain voters, whereas it had fallen back by four points among Leave supporters. In short, all of the increase in support for independence registered by the polls in 2019 was to be found among opponents of Brexit. Although it might have taken three years to emerge, there was now little doubt that the pursuit of Brexit was undermining support for Scotland's continued membership of the UK.

Not least of the reasons is that more people feel that Brexit will be deleterious for Scotland than believe leaving the UK would be (Curtice and Montagu, 2020). According to the 2019 Scottish Social Attitudes survey, 61 per cent of people in Scotland believe that Britain's economy will be worse off as a result of leaving the EU, while just 18 per cent believe it will be worse off. In contrast, while 33 per cent feel that Scotland's economy would be worse as a result of independence, rather more (43 per cent) believe it will be better. Moreover, among those who believe that Brexit will worsen Britain's economy, as many as 51 per cent feel that Scotland's economy will be better as a result of independence, whereas only 33 per cent of those who believe that Brexit will not do harm to the economy feel that independence will be beneficial for Scotland's economy.

Much the same contrast is apparent in perceptions of the impact of independence and Brexit on the international status of Scotland and the UK. A half of people in Scotland (50 per cent) believe that Britain will have less influence in the world as a result of Brexit, while just 15 per cent take the opposite view. In contrast, 54 per cent feel that independence would give Scotland a stronger voice in the world, while just 24 per cent believe it will be worse off. Meanwhile, as many as 63 per cent of those who believe that

Brexit will weaken Britain's influence in the world say that independence would strengthen Scotland's voice, whereas only 46 per cent of those who reckon Brexit will not reduce Britain's influence feel that independence would strengthen Scotland's voice. Brexit has provided a point of comparison that for some voters at least has now made independence look rather more attractive.

The fate of Brexit itself was finally determined by the outcome of the 2019 general election; the Conservatives won an overall majority of eighty, which enabled the government to secure parliamentary approval for its withdrawal treaty and ensure that the UK left the EU at the end of January 2020. The SNP played a crucial role in triggering that election. Under the terms of the Fixed Terms Parliament Act 2011 the Prime Minister could no longer call an election at a time of their own choosing, but rather needed to persuade two-thirds of MPs to vote in favour of a ballot. However, at the end of October 2019 it emerged that the SNP and the Liberal Democrats were willing to back legislation that would only need a simple majority to trigger an election. One motive was a concern that if the Brexit stalemate persisted, the government would eventually simply leave the EU without a withdrawal treaty. However, it was also suggested that, given the SNP's current standing in the polls, an early election held out the prospect of reversing some of the losses the party suffered in 2017. Indeed, the party won 45 per cent of the vote and forty-eight seats. However, as the bottom row of Table 3.3 shows, this progress rested primarily on the party securing a record share of the vote among Remain voters rather than reversing the heavy losses it had suffered two years earlier among Leave supporters. Meanwhile, the Conservatives became even more dependent on the support of Leave voters. Brexit continued to leave its heavy imprint on the pattern of party support.

Brexit and devolution

The implementation of Brexit gave rise to some important questions about the existing devolution settlement. Many of the areas of policy that hitherto lay within the competence of the EU were ones, such as agriculture and the environment, that domestically lay within the ambit of the devolved institutions and therefore in Scotland the parliament in Edinburgh. Consequently, when the UK eventually left the single market, an event now timetabled for the end of December 2020, the powers currently exercised by the EU would transfer to the devolved institutions, thereby opening up the possibility of regulatory divergence between the four component parts of the UK. Such a prospect was an anathema to the UK government, and it proposed the introduction of 'common frameworks' that would avoid undesirable divergence, and some progress was made in agreeing these.

However, this approach was largely overtaken when in autumn 2020 the UK government introduced the Internal Market Act (Sargeant and Stojanovic, 2021). Inter alia, this set out the principle that goods that could legally be sold in one part of the UK should be capable of being marketed in any part. Any attempt by a devolved administration to introduce distinctive regulations could only have an effect on goods produced within their own country, and goods imported from anywhere else in the UK could not be banned from sale because they failed to meet those standards. The provision therefore significantly limited the effective scope of the devolved institutions' regulatory powers. Together with other provisions in the bill, including reserving to Westminster the provision of state aid to industry, this legislation was portrayed by the Scottish government as a 'power grab'. Although this disagreement appeared to have had a limited impact on the wider public, the legislation did little to improve the already strained relations between the Scottish and UK governments. In any event, the development underlined the potential impact of Brexit on the future governance of Scotland.

The pandemic

The rise in support for independence registered in 2019 did not simply come to a halt. Rather, within weeks of the UK's departure from the EU at the end of January 2020 support rose further, such that for the first time in Scottish polling history the polls began consistently to suggest that there was now majority support for independence. After support for Yes hovered around the 50 per cent mark in the first five months of 2020, a run of nineteen polls between June 2020 and January 2021 all put Yes ahead – on average by 54 per cent to 46 per cent.

This rise, however, cannot be ascribed to a reaction against the implementation of Brexit. As the entries for this period in Table 3.3 show, if anything support rose more among Leave voters than it did among their

Remain counterparts. What did happen within weeks of the UK's withdrawal from the EU was the onset of the coronavirus pandemic – a crisis for which all the health and public health measures were the responsibility in Scotland of the devolved administration, thereby representing the biggest public policy challenge faced by the Scottish government since the advent of devolution in Scotland in 1999. Indeed, thanks to the pandemic, the Scottish government had yet again to abandon any attempt at making progress on holding another independence referendum.

During the pandemic, voters reacted very differently to the style of leadership offered by the Scottish first minister, Nicola Sturgeon, and that provided by the UK prime minister, Boris Johnson. The former was widely thought to have handled the pandemic well, while the opposite was true of Boris Johnson. For example, in July 2020 Panelbase found that 74 per cent believed that Ms Sturgeon had done a good job of responding to the coronavirus outbreak, while just 23 per cent said the same of Mr Johnson. Similarly, in August YouGov reported that 79 per cent believed Ms Sturgeon was handling the pandemic well, but that only 18 per cent reckoned that Mr Johnson was doing so.

More importantly, for some voters these very different evaluations of the two leaders gave them reason to re-evaluate their views on the constitutional debate. In August 2020 YouGov found that as many as 43 per cent thought that Scotland would have handled the pandemic better as an independent country while only 16 per cent felt it would do so worse. In November Ipsos MORI reported that 39 per cent were of the former view and only 20 per cent the latter. Of course, most of those who felt that the pandemic would have been handled better were already supporters of independence – but among their number were between 15 per cent and 20 per cent of those who had voted No in 2014. It seems likely that this perception helps explain why support for independence rose in the second half of 2020 among Leave as well as Remain supporters.

However, by the spring of 2021 this mood seemed to have dissipated, and by the time of the Scottish Parliament election that took place in May, YouGov was reporting that there were now as many people who believed that an independent Scotland would have handled the pandemic worse as there were those who believed it would have been handled better. Meanwhile, by this time the polls in general were finding that support for independence had on average dropped back down to the 49 per cent level that had been registered immediately before the UK left the EU. At the same time, as the last row of Table 3.3 reveals, the level of support among both Remain (55 per cent) and Leave (30 per cent) voters had also returned to exactly the same level. The impact of the pandemic on support for independence may have proven temporary and contingent, but it appeared that the imprint left by Brexit was enduring.

The 2021 election

Thus, when the scheduled Scottish Parliament election was held in May 2021, it did so against a backdrop of a Scottish government that, because of Brexit, had been wanting for four years to hold another independence referendum and an electorate that, again thanks to Brexit, was expressing increased support for independence, such that the country was now more or less evenly divided on the issue. It was thus not surprising that the constitutional question became the central issue of the election.

In contrast to the position in 2016, the SNP were explicit and unconditional about their wish to hold another independence referendum. 'We are seeking your permission at this election for an independence referendum to be held after Covid', the party wrote in its manifesto (Scottish National Party, 2021). This stance was backed by the Greens who had backed the call for a referendum in March 2017. The main parties on the other side of the argument, the Conservatives, Labour and the Liberal Democrats, argued with equal passion that a pandemic was not an appropriate time to be contemplating a referendum, an argument about timing that echoed the UK government's response to the original request for a second ballot made in March 2017.

The constitutional question proved to be a fault line in how people voted. Voters had two votes – one for their local constituency Member of the Scottish Parliament (MSP) and the other for a regional closed party list. The polls conducted immediately before polling day suggested on average that 88 per cent of those who were currently in favour of independence were voting for the SNP on the constituency ballot, while just 8 per cent of those who opposed independence were anticipating voting that way. A poll conducted by Savanta ComRes immediately after polling day reported that 87 per cent of independence supporters had backed the SNP, while just 8 per cent of opponents had done so. The division on the list vote was no less marked.

This degree of polarization was unprecedented. Never before had so high a proportion of those in favour of independence backed the SNP while never before had so few of those opposed to independence done so. For example, according to the Scottish Social Attitudes survey, at the 2016 Scottish Parliament election only 81 per cent of those who at that stage would have voted Yes to independence supported the SNP, while as many as 22 per cent of those who would vote No still backed the nationalist party. Hitherto, the SNP had often been heavily dependent on securing the electoral support of those who were opposed to independence but who felt that the party was best able to run Scotland's devolved institutions (Curtice, 2019). However, in a post-Brexit environment in which Scotland's constitutional status had become a hotly contested issue, such behaviour had now almost entirely disappeared.

As a result, people's attitudes towards Brexit continued to be reflected in their party choice, just as they had been in the UK elections of 2017 and 2019 but had not at the previous Scottish Parliament election in 2016. According to the final pre-polling day polls, as many as 56 per cent of those who voted Remain in 2016 backed the SNP while only 29 per cent of Leave supporters did so. Conversely, support for the Conservatives stood at 41 per cent among Leave voters but just 14 per cent among Remain supporters. Only Labour continued to bridge the Brexit divide with 24 per cent support among Remain voters and 20 per cent among their Leave counterparts.

Meanwhile, the overall outcome of the election corroborated the claim of the polls that Scotland was now evenly divided on the constitutional question. On the constituency ballot, just over half (50.4 per cent) of the vote was cast for one of the three main parties backing Scotland's continued membership of the UK, while on the list vote just over half (50.1 per cent) supported parties that backed independence. Thanks, though, to the way in which the less than perfectly proportional electoral system operated, the election produced a Scottish Parliament in which a clear majority (72) of its 129 members are in favour of holding another ballot on the issue. As a result, there is now likely to be a constitutional clash between the UK government that delivered Brexit and wishes to avoid another ballot and a Scottish government that because of Brexit wants to revisit Scotland's constitutional status.

Scotland's new choice

Indeed, Brexit has not only created an impetus for revisiting the question of Scotland's constitutional status but also reshaped the choice with which voters would be faced in another referendum. Given that both the current Scottish government and a majority of the public favour rejoining the EU, no longer would the choice simply be in or out of the UK. It would now also be about whether or not Scotland should be part of the EU even though the rest of the UK is outside.

Such a prospect potentially raises important questions that have as yet been little debated (Hepburn et al., 2021; Hughes, 2020). In particular, it would mean that the border between Scotland and England would become a EU single market border. Even if the British and Irish Common Travel Area were to remain in place and thus the new border would not hinder the free movement of persons, it would become a regulatory and customs border. As the experience of Northern Ireland, which has remained in the single market after Brexit, has indicated (Spisak, 2021), this could prove a significant non-tariff barrier to the movement of goods, as well as have significant implications for the delivery of services. Meanwhile, there is relatively little enthusiasm in Scotland for the prospect of joining the Euro.

At the same time, the prospect of a Scottish application to re-enter the EU would raise potentially sensitive issues for the EU itself. On the one hand, facilitating Scottish membership would represent an opportunity to reverse some of the impact of Brexit. On the other hand, such an application might prove less palatable for those member states, such as Spain, whose own integrity is potentially threatened by nationalist movements. It remains to be seen how voters in Scotland will react if and when these issues receive more attention in the public debate than they have done so far.

Conclusion

The Brexit process has resulted in fresh moves to revisit Scotland's constitutional status and has both increased and changed the character of public support for independence. It also changed the choice that Scotland now faces. Remaining part of the UK would mean that the country would still have unconstrained access to its largest trading partner and be part of a system that generates substantial fiscal transfers from which the country is currently profiting, but would also mean being part of a relatively small internal market. Becoming an independent country in the EU, in contrast, would restore the country's free access to a much larger single market, but one that currently only represents its second-largest trading partner, and place the country in an institution that has only recently begun tentatively to put its toe in the waters of fiscal transfers. However, what remains to be seen is whether or not voters in Scotland will eventually be asked to make that choice.

Acknowledgement

This chapter was written while the author was funded by UKRI-ESRC as a fellow of 'The UK in a Changing Europe' initiative.

Bibliography

Curtice, J. (2019), 'The Electorate and Elections', in Hassan, G. (ed.), *The Story of the Scottish Parliament: The First Two Decades Explained*, Edinburgh: Edinburgh University Press.

Curtice, J. (2021), 'The Scottish Independence Referendum of 2014', in Smith, J. (ed.), *The Palgrave Handbook of European Referendums*, Cham: Palgrave Macmillan.

Curtice, J. and Montagu, I. (2018), 'Scotland: Has Brexit Has Created a New Divide in the Nationalist Movement?', in Phillips, D., Curtice, J., Phillips, M. and Perry, J. (eds), *British Social Attitudes: The 35th Report*. London: NatCen Social Research. Available at https://www.bsa.natcen.ac.uk/media/39220/ bsa_35 _scotland.pdf.

Curtice, J. and Montagu, I. (2020), *Is Brexit Fuelling Support for Independence?*, London: NatCen Social Research. Available at https://whatscotlandthinks.org/wp -content/uploads/2020/11/SSA-2019-Scotland-paper-v5.pdf.

Curtice, J. and Simpson, I. (2018), 'The 2017 Election: New Divides in British Politics', in Phillips, D., Curtice, J., Phillips, M., and Rahim, N. (eds), *British Social Attitudes: The 35th Report*, London: NatCen Social Research. Available at https:// www.bsa.natcen.ac.uk/latest-report/british-social-attitudes-35/voting.aspx.

Dardanelli, P. (2005), *Between Two Unions: Europeanisation and Scottish Devolution*, Manchester: Manchester University Press.

Fieldhouse, E., Green, J., Evans, G., Mellon, J., Prosser, C., Schmitt, H. and van der Eijk, C. (2019), *Electoral Shocks: The Volatile Voters in a Turbulent World*, Oxford: Oxford University Press.

Hepburn, E., Keating, M. and McEwen, N. (eds) (2021), *Scotland's New Choice: Independence after Brexit*, Edinburgh: Centre on Constitutional Change. Available at https://www.centreonconstitutionalchange.ac.uk/sites/default/files/2021-03/Scotlands-New-Choice.pdf.

Hughes, K. (ed.) (2020), *An Independent Scotland in the EU: Issues for Accession*, Edinburgh: Scottish Centre on European Relations.

HM Government (2013), *Scotland Analysis: Devolution and the Implications of Scottish Independence*, Cm 8554, Norwich: The Stationery Office.

Mau, T. (2005), 'Globalisation, Regional Integration and the Evolution of the Independence Rhetoric of the PQ and the SNP', *British Journal of Canadian Studies*, 18 (2): 313–39.

May, T. (2017), 'The Government's Negotiating Objectives for Leaving the EU'. Speech given at Lancaster House, 17 January. Available at https://www.gov.uk/government/speeches/the-governments-negotiating-objectives-for-exiting-the-eu-pm-speech.

Meadwell, H. and Martin, P. (1996), 'Economic Integration and the Politics of Independence', *Nations and Nationalism*, 2 (10): 67–87.

Sargeant, J. and Stojanovic, A. (2021), *The United Kingdom Internal Market Act 2020*, London: Institute for Government. Available at https://www.instituteforgovernment.org.uk/sites/default/files/publications/internal-market-act.pdf.

Scottish Government (2013), *Scotland's Future*, Edinburgh: Scottish Government.

Scottish Government (2016), *Scotland's Place in Europe*, Edinburgh: Scottish Government.

Scottish National Party (2016), *Re-Elect: SNP Manifesto 2016*, Edinburgh: Scottish National Party.

Scottish National Party (2021), *Scotland's Future: SNP Manifesto 2021*, Edinburgh: Scottish National Party.

Spisak, A. (2021), *After Brexit: Northern Ireland and the Future of the Protocol*, London: Tony Blair Institute for Global Change. Available at https://institute.global/sites/default/files/articles/After-Brexit-Northern-Ireland-and-the-Future-of-the-Protocol.pdf.

4

On the borders of contention

Brexit's physical and psychological impact on Britain's border with Ireland

Dr Paul Breen

Introduction and contextualization

Ireland has historically been a blind spot in British politics and again assumed such a role in Britain's 2016 EU referendum (Lonergan, 2019). Northern Ireland's realities pass 'under the radar of Britain's press' with their role portrayed as that of 'reluctant piggy in the middle between two warring Irish religious tribes' (Greenslade, 2019). This myth of military neutrality and benevolence is a recurring motif, deeply entrenched across all segments of British society, where many people pride themselves upon their Dunkirk spirit of standing alone in defence of freedom. Such mythology gives rise to the exceptionalism which fuelled Brexit (O'Toole, 2016; O'Brennan, 2019) and fevered a desire for 'taking back control' (Walsh, 2019, p. 142). For several decades, anti-European sentiment saturated right wing media to a point where expertise became distrusted and disinformation accepted as indisputable fact.

Despite ideological foundations where emotion trumped reason, a slim majority supported Britain's exit from the EU in June 2016, giving little consideration to the 'far-reaching consequences for the political geography of the island of Ireland' (Walsh, 2019, p. 137). In trying to close the front door to mainland Europe, the Irish border's back door had been largely ignored (McCall, 2018, p. 10). Tragically, for much of its history, the Northern Irish state enjoyed a 'quasi-quarantined status' in the British psyche (Gormley-Heenan & Aughey, 2017, p. 7). Through the twentieth century, a habitus evolved of criticizing far-flung places such as South Africa while ignoring the apartheid conditions that existed on their own doorstep. Even today, those who might justifiably chastise the treatment of such minorities as China's Uyghurs fail to see parallels with Britain's own internment practices, less than half a century ago. The British public have made an art form out of averting their gaze from Ireland.

In 2016, this place of 'dreary steeples' (Churchill, 1922) would again rise up from the margins of British politics when the deluge of a fanciful referendum victory had subsided. The Irish border would prove a sticking point in negotiations that the British side often framed in a language that risked a return to 'zero-sum territorialism' (Walsh, 2019, p. 149). This both contradicted and threatened the entire architecture of the Good Friday Agreement of 1998 (Todd, 2017, p. 7), which was born out of 'a lengthy and often precarious peace process' (Brown & Macginty, 2003, p. 85). Although more of a bandage than a permanent solution (Little, 2003; Vaughan-Williams, 2006; Breen, 2018) largely built upon 'rocky foundations' (Byers, 2019), this agreement facilitated a reconfiguration of the border in the public imagination from 'barrier to bridge' (McCall, 2018, p. 11). It shifted from 'a bounded container space within the UK to a relational space' dependent on relations within a broader shared British, Irish and European context (Walsh, 2019, p. 137).

Before the 'contentious' result of the European Union (EU) referendum (Gormley-Heenan et al., 2017), the border had become functional rather than physical. This facilitated symmetry between 'hard governance structures and the growth of soft spaces' (Rafferty & Blair, 2019, p. 182) that allowed 'a multitude of cross-border initiatives' to develop 'within the public, private and community sectors on the island of Ireland' (Walsh, 2019, p. 148). Of equal importance, it softened the entrenchment of borders 'in the mind' (Gormley-Heenan & Aughey, 2017). The free movement of goods and people ironically created a situation where the border's physical existence came to be almost as forgotten in the Irish psyche as in the British. Then, the foundations of this everyday ease quaked with the 'existential shock to British and EU politics' (O'Brennan, 2019, p. 157) that arose from a vote to leave the EU.

According to Colum Eastwood, leader of Northern Ireland's Social Democratic and Labour Party, the 'tremendous destabilising effect' of this on the psyche of Irish nationalists cannot be 'overstated' (Gormley-Heenan & Aughey, 2017, p. 14). Significantly too, this destabilization is not limited to the nationalist perspective. Driscoll (2019, p. 242) points out that Britain's exit threatens 'the EU citizenship of British nationals in Northern Ireland' and jeopardizes their equality with nationalists in this regard. That may be further threatened by the risk of a hard border leading to the hardening of nationalists' aspirations for a united Ireland.

Throughout the post-referendum literature on Brexit and Ireland, there is a recurring sense of a great damage having been done. After all the hard-fought progress of the past few decades, it seems absurd that Northern Ireland is turning towards shadows of the 1980s when Irish author Colm Tóibín set out from Derry to walk the length and breadth of the border. Then, this line of demarcation mapped in military infrastructure had given rise to a gangrene 'of death, destruction and bitterness prevalent in a land economically deprived and politically divided' (Tóibín & O'Shea, 1987). Although Brexit was finally enacted in January 2020, even in late 2021, there remain issues around the Northern Ireland Protocol (2019). This is a measure designed to ensure smooth flow of goods and people at the border within the island of Ireland (Tóibín & O'Shea, 1987). Essentially, it differentiates between Northern Ireland and the rest of the United Kingdom (UK) in terms of rules to such an extent that the region truly now does seem a place apart. Effectively, it is a sea border in everything but name.

This protocol was implemented to avoid what McCall (2018, p. 11) refers to as a 'reintroduction of customs, agri-food inspection and immigration checkpoints on cross-border arterial routes'. Such a scenario could have caused 'the closure of hundreds of secondary cross-border roads' and the 'establishment of a border security regime', giving rise to further spectres showing why Brexit's damage should not be measured in economic terms alone (McCall, 2018). This would have included the possibility of risking what Tánaiste Simon Coveney refers to as 'our hard-won peace' (O'Brennan, 2018, p. 168). Since the decades before and after Sean O'Casey's seminal 1923 play, *The Shadow of a Gunman* has never been far from the surface of Irish politics and today, though peripheral, it remains very timely (Hoey, 2018). Worryingly too, street protests have emerged as a form of response among working class, urban Protestant communities to the Northern Ireland Protocol's de facto sea border, which challenges their idea of the UK as a unitary state.

Identity and affiliation are again at the heart of the greatest schism that Brexit has caused on the Irish border since the original partition. Through 'common UK and Irish EU membership' that border had been 'transformed from a sharp dividing line between states into a meeting point between friendly neighbours and partners in the European Union' (Hayward, 2018; O'Brennan, 2019, p. 162.) Now, once again old binaries of identity have returned to Northern Ireland's frame of political reference (Gormley-Heenan & Aughey, 2017, p. 12). From that, a question arises of whether or not there can ever be a shared acceptance of regulatory frameworks along the Irish border. On the one hand, things have to continue working at an all-island level to maintain the 'soft spaces of cooperation' created by the 1998 agreement (Walsh, 2019, p. 149). Conversely, unless Unionists are content with these arrangements, that all-island dimension is likely to be met with opposition. On all sides, though, there seems to be a demand for solutions to these lingering issues.

Research study and methodology

Anything written about Northern Ireland can be contentious and ethics must be the scaffolding around which studies are based, especially after such cases as that of the Boston College tapes (Sampson, 2016). These were part of what was named 'the Belfast Project', in which oral histories of the Northern Irish conflict were recorded for archiving in the Burns Library at Boston College, Massachusetts (Boston Word Press, 2019). Unexpectedly, in March 2011, the British government issued a 'sealed subpoena for all materials relating to two interviews in the archive' (Sampson, 2016), effectively trying to sever the seal of academic confidentiality. Although these tapes ended up being 'inadmissible' (Sampson, 2016), the unprecedented demand for access sent reverberations through politics and academia.

Northern Ireland then is a place apart, misaligned socially and politically not just from practices in its broader milieu (Fenton, 2018; Walsh, 2019) but also to the extent of sensitivity around political discussion. As such, great care had to be taken in managing this research study. I have opted for a small-scale qualitative study, within which the voices of participants have been collected through verbal or written interviews and then synthesized for the purposes of discussion. The goal is to shape the narrative around participants' voices, allowing readers to thread their own interpretation into the tapestry of views presented. Since Northern Irish identities are becoming increasingly fluid and less binary (Breen, 2018), participants are labelled numerically by chronology of response rather than possible political affiliation. Furthermore, due to the sensitivities of Northern Ireland, minimal information is given about each participant with just enough to provide a basic sense of who they are as people.

To capture a snapshot of these people's perceptions of Brexit's impact on the Irish border, I opted for an approach similar to that of the International Centre for Local and Regional Development's (ICLRD) survey conducted in 2017 detailed in Rafferty and Blair (2019, p. 185). Twenty-four participants took part in that study, from across fields that included public administration, civil society, the private sector and the academic community (Rafferty & Blair, 2019). Others have conducted similar studies, as in Morgan-Jones et al. (2020) who carried out 'a co-joint survey experiment to assess preferences about post-Brexit border arrangements' (p. 1).

Many such studies lament the absence of a 'border voice' in the literature but at the same time present one that seems alien in many ways based on empirical experience of those of us from this actual region. Growing up a mere 13 miles from the border, I find myself in a position to directly access and listen to the voices of people 'on the ground'. Through this access, my approach to selection was to choose a specific sample, offering them the opportunity to participate in a study that participants recurringly referred to as being 'deep' but 'straightforward'.

One hundred people from a range of backgrounds and locations were invited to respond, with the main proviso being that they had lived in, worked in or been born on the island of Ireland. Additionally, the latter category included one or two people of Irish parentage who live in England but identify as Irish. The reason for their inclusion is that this demographic is one that has largely been historically ignored but which feels just as Irish as those born on the actual island. Such a sentiment has resonance with the sociocultural notion of 'borders in the mind' (Beckett, 1966; Gormley-Heenan & Aughey, 2017). Having chosen a specific group of respondents, the next stage involved contact through email or social media, outlining the nature of the research and inviting responses. Around two-thirds agreed to participate. Though only thirty would eventually submit on time and three answers were quite short, the final study still had a similar participation level to ICLRD's (2017) study. Most of those who answered opted for written responses though some requested phone calls or physical interviews, with the latter made more difficult by the

Covid-19 pandemic at the time of researching. That and the general uncertainty of Brexit's finished form possibly caused the 30 per cent response rate out of the original hundred invitations that I sent out.

Participants were asked to answer two questions: (1) What do you see as Brexit's main *physical impacts* on the island of Ireland? (2) What do you see as Brexit's main *psychological impacts* on the island of Ireland?

Blurred boundaries at the outset

Having gathered the responses and started out on my analysis, one striking characteristic emerged at the outset. Female respondents appeared more likely to challenge the distinction made within the research questions of separating physical and psychological impacts. Indeed one female respondent (R20) from the greater Belfast area suggested that even *'the term island of Ireland can cause a heated debate in certain quarters'*. She points out that *'yes, it is an island but for the purposes of Brexit it is not'*. From this perspective, Ireland is composed of *'two attached but separate countries as seen in mainland Europe but without any Schengen Agreement which does operate in mainland Europe'*. A unique gravity, though, occurs from the fact that *'there is a (possibly) unique set of playing pieces'* in the reality that *'we also have many persons in the country who do not see the separate jurisdictions'*.

Within the literature, many have sought imaginative solutions to the potential physical impasse of Brexit along the Irish border (Todd, 2017; McCall, 2018; Driscoll, 2019; Rafferty & Blair, 2019; Walsh, 2019). The British government itself (2019, pp. 292–3) also made a no-border promise (Pinos & Sacramento, 2020, p. 12). However, the border means different things to each of the two main communities in Northern Ireland, namely those who identify as Irish and those who identify as British. Gormley-Heenan and Aughey (2017, p. 9) define this as being the product of a society that has 'no ideological mortar – common national identity – holding things together'. That at least is the generic perception of things. However, responses from participants R9, R18 and R20 challenge this view in presenting notions of a shared identity as a solution. R20 depicts Northern Ireland in the form of a pie chart of four distinct identities, namely '*Northern Irish first and British second*', '*Northern Irish first and Irish second*', straightforward '*British*' and straightforward '*Irish*', allowing for '*a foot in each pie*'. R25, a retired politician from Dublin, appears to support this idea of Northern Ireland as a place apart with Brexit '*inevitably*' moving '*Irish people away from the UK and UK people*' which '*will tie us into Europe and the EU further*'.

R9 and R18 take the perspective that trauma serves as the ideological mortar of these multiple Northern Irish identities. The former (R9) suggests that '*Psychologically, I have not recovered from the troubles*' but '*The Good Friday Agreement made me proud to be Northern Irish and to achieve something like this was the best moment for me in our shared history*'. As such she does not want '<u>us</u>[1] *to become a divided community again*'. Similarly, R18 states that '*in a world where tolerance and respect for all is under the spotlight, it would be heart breaking for Ireland to retreat back in any way to the shadows of the past*'. However, throughout the responses, there is a very real fear that such shadows are looming in Brexit's 'existential shock' (O'Brennan, 2019, p. 157).

The shadows of gun people in Irish history

Though Brexit may have offered dissident republicans 'an unexpected shot in the arm' (Hoey, 2018, p. 82) they appear to lack any ideological vision that might sustain a return to violence. With a world view largely framed in an early twentieth-century sense of national sovereignty (Hoey, 2018, p. 76), their perspectives ironically echo those of noted Brexiteers such as Boris Johnson and Nigel Farage (Manley, 2016; Hoey, 2018). Sadly, though, the release of bombs and bullets into the equation is not dependent upon the strength of underlying philosophical paradigms. Concerningly, some respondents see a potential for a return of not just dissident activity but other more neglected forms such as '*domestic violence*' (R6) that grows out of the associated poverty and disorder. R26 echoed this with references to an increase in '*suicide*' and '*depression*', particularly south of the border, where the economy is weaker. Nobody, though, at the time of this research, predicted any form of violent loyalist reaction. At most, that was expected to be discontentment rather than direct action.

---

[1] My emphasis for the purposes of accentuating the idea of a shared identity.

R10, though, refers to how *'violence begets violence'* while R1 who grew up close to the border speaks of needing to avoid physical infrastructure that could instigate *'the slippery slope towards conflict'*. Quite interestingly, the interviewee with the greatest skin in the game of past conflict does not believe that a return to violence is likely. This former political prisoner who is now a community worker (R16) suggests that there will be *'no reactivation of trouble'*, but *'resentment'* against a sense of *'capitalism and neo-colonialism'* might have *'other outcomes'*. He also makes the point that *'psychological factors'* can lead to *'physical expression'* and that borders *'create division within people's minds'*.

Obviously, for ethical reasons, I could not force discussion towards the type of struggles which might ensue, but R16's prediction of this seemed more rooted in protests on either side of the border than eradication of the dividing line. Again as with R6 and R26, there was a powerful sense that *'the main physical effects will be felt by the more vulnerable citizens'*. Ironically, though, as a consequence of that aforementioned Northern Ireland Protocol, much of the protest and dissent has taken place on the opposite side of Northern Ireland, east not west. This is largely because those of a British identity, within the state, are concentrated in areas closer to the larger towns around Belfast than to the Irish border. This feeds into a cultural climate, where *'symbols of Britishness dominate the public sphere and those representing Irishness are only tolerated in areas where Catholics are in a majority'* (McKay, 2021).

Despite this, a growing sense of the all-Ireland dimension has developed within discussions about Brexit and the Irish border. The issue of Irish unification was another that recurred. In an earlier study on 'attitudes and aspirations of contemporary Northern Irish Catholics' (Breen, 2018) there seemed no immediate appetite for unity. However, participants from all backgrounds now believe this is a real possibility (e.g. R2, R4, R8, R12, R23, R28). At the very least it will become more of a discussion point on both islands (R11) and possibly increase demand for a border poll (R7, R15). The latter scenario, pushed most strongly by Sinn Fein (Pinos & Sacramento, 2020, p. 13), could create issues for an Irish government that needs to balance the satisfaction of nationalists with overtures towards Unionists. This might come about through *'a process of open dialogue, greater cooperation and cross border projects'* (R11).

The latter remark about greater cooperation is striking from the perspective that it seems to challenge much of the literature on soft spaces and functional geographies. Within the responses, another dividing line has taken shape in the functional geographies of the 'new' Northern Ireland that has emerged since the Good Friday Agreement. This is seen in the different responses from people according to their distance from the border and the fact that people to the east of Ireland, north or south, seem less concerned with mental and emotional factors as in responses from Dubliners R17 and R25 compared to R14 from Donegal. The closer people live or have lived to the actual physical border, the more attuned they are to its psychological impact.

Perhaps that is best exemplified by taking responses from two Ulster Protestant males, who both lived through the conflict of the 1960s to 1990s. The respondent living closest to the border (R2) suggests that among Unionists, '*Brexit is forcing their community to reconsider their relationship with the UK and Brexit is just one reason why a United Ireland is on the agenda*.' However, a respondent from the opposite side of Northern Ireland (R21) argues that the Brexit situation might bring '*definitive closure of a united Ireland with us no longer being a part of the European political system and very much an integral part of the United Kingdom*'. R28 also speculates that reinforcing borders was a motive of the DUP's support for Brexit for reasons of '*psychological impact*' rather than physical. This, though, is seen as something that could '*backfire*' in the long run (R28). Such a prediction has come true with the advent of the Northern Ireland Protocol (2019), which has opened up a source of contention around identity issues not widely anticipated beforehand.

This lack of anticipation was perhaps because of respondents focusing on positives, for the main part. Throughout the responses there is a recurring sense of solutions needing to be found. These range from an acceptance of the need for the Republic of Ireland to avoid imposing the '*hard borders*' that Britain does not want (R21) and the imperative on all sides to '*avoid barriers imposed by those playing a political game*' (R18). Avoidance of such barriers would help disperse the flickers of dissidence back into the shadows since historically, border checkpoints (Manley, 2016 in Hoey, 2018, p. 82) have been a gaslight to moths. Even those on the southern side of the border believe that '*most Irish people would take exception to the construction of any physical barriers which would hinder free movement of people and goods on the island*' (R14).

However, the avoidance of some type of border inspection regime seems impossible in regulatory terms (R2, R16, R20, R22). Several respondents showed great acumen in predicting that this would eventually come in the form of a sea border (R2, R4, R20, R27, R28). For those of an Irish identity, such a scenario helps to placate the fears of border communities as well as facilitating the continuation of soft spaces operating in the shadows of hard governance (Rafferty & Blair, 2019, p. 182). At the same time, through the implementation of de facto sea border arrangements, those espousing a British identity have been antagonized. Some Unionists see the present regulatory arrangements as challenging the territorial integrity of the UK. As a consequence, much of the focus has shifted from those dissidents discussed by Hoey (2018) to loyalist protestors whose aspirations are less straightforward to articulate. This is because so much of their angst seems to be directed not simply at the sea border but at the equalization of identities within Northern Ireland.

The opening up of a territorial Pandora's box

Although much of the focus among respondents was on the threat of trouble emanating from the Irish Republican side, some commentators had foreseen issues on the British side as well. Pinos and Sacramento (2020, pp. 3–4) spoke of a 'potential destabilisation' that would open up a 'territorial Pandora's box'. Citing the examples of Scotland and Gibraltar, they predicted a transformative impact on British identity. R11, a male born in Northern Ireland but living in Scotland, raises the spectre of Scottish independence, asking if this would *'mean England becoming even more inward looking and hasten the end of the Union'*. Here, the impact is conceptualized in not just Irish but also British terms where Brexit is seen as an 'act of national self-harm' (O'Toole, 2018, p. 3). That, according to the same respondent, has been caused by the *'fact that the Irish border has yet again been brought up as part of a political game with the EU by Johnson/Cummings'* (R11). The idea of *'playing a political game'* appears too in the responses from R18 and from R6 who puts the fact of this down to *'the selfishness of the British government'*.

R14, a male from an Irish border county now working in England, echoes O'Toole (2018) in talking about how *'the British (or the English) famed for their pragmatism seemed to have committed an act of self-harm'*. He further suggests that within Ireland *'there was also an element of schadenfreude'* and interestingly *'a boost to Irish national self-esteem with the realisation that in terms of negotiations, Ireland was in a position of relative strength due to the support of EU partners'.* That sense of '*schadenfreude*' was again mentioned by R27 who also comes from the southern side of the border. Recurringly, then, there is a sense of change in the Irish nationalist mindset with R27 suggesting that '*there has been a marked improvement in recent years of people beginning to "trust" the British again and that feeling has now disappeared*'.

R19, a second-generation Irishman with bases in both Britain and Ireland, also speaks of how '*Brexit could have a positive effect on the confidence of the Irish as a nation*'. He gives the example of how '*even after independence the Irish still lived very much in the shadow of the UK, but the Brexit negotiations have shown that the Irish don't have to dance to the UK's tune because they are part of a much larger trading bloc*'. Pinos and Sacramento (2020, p. 16) go further than this in suggesting that Brexit has 'been pivotal in advancing the Irish republican cause at the EU level'. At the same time, this could be seen as a 'tribune' republicanism (Mitchell et al., 2009), where the goal is not so much to achieve Irish unity but to preserve the idea of that as a legitimate aspiration. It also allows for 'the constructive ambiguity', which has 'long characterised the EU model of governance' (O'Brennan, 2019, p. 158) and shaped the rhetoric of the Irish constitutional aspiration to unity by consent (Pinos & Sacramento, 2020, p. 14). For today's nationalists this is a crucial principle, and there cannot be '*definitive closure*' (R21) on the idea of a united Ireland. Altering this idea could open up a more dangerous Pandora's box.

Much of this comes down to a combination of English 'mythology' (O'Brennan, 2019, p. 159) and the fact of Ireland being a historical blind spot in the British psyche (Greenslade, 2019). Fittingly, then, drawing on Pinos and Sacramento's 'territorial Pandora's box' (2020, pp. 3–4), one version of the myth tells how a man named Epimetheus opened the box. Relaying that story which originates in *The Adages of Erasmus* (1508), Epimetheus becomes wise after the act (Barker, 2001, p. 34). Thus, the name has come to mean 'late-wise' (Barker, 2001) or afterthought. Herein, from the responses of participants, it is apparent that the Irish border situation has been an afterthought and one that even in the aftermath of Brexit being implemented, the British are still not wise to the interests of. Sentiments of this nature come across in multiple responses with references to '*uncertainty*' (R1), (R2), (R5), (R14), (R15); (R24); '*caveats and unknowns*' (R3); '*so much flux*' (R8); '*fallout that could potentially occur for Ireland*' (R10); and finally '*worry of the unknown*' and '*the fact that the British negotiating team cannot be trusted*' (R12).

Perhaps it is the matter of trust that could open the greatest Pandora's box of all not just in a sense of bad faith as regards territorial politics but in terms of long-term planning (R15) and economic uncertainty (R5). '*Brexit has the potential to severely damage the Irish economy, North and South, and to completely erode what little trust and affection exists between our two islands*' (R6). R9 suggests '*we have again been shafted on both sides by the British government and mistrust begins*', which is echoed by R13 writing from a hospitality industry perspective, suggesting that '*Northern Ireland will get the short straw as always*'. This is because '*the hotel industry in NI*' has been burdened with different VAT rules to the republic and '*just couldn't compete with the rates they were giving*', during which time '*England couldn't or wouldn't give us a break*' (R13).

This, though, is long engrained in the Irish sensibility. R10 makes reference to literary figures such as '*GB Shaw and Somerville and Ross*' in stating that '*there can be no other country in the world that should have a better understanding of the nature/character of the Englishman than its neighbour*'. As such, she suggests that '*looking to the future, Ireland will need to capitalise on this genetic knowledge and experience to bridge the physical and psychological separations*' (R10). But that according to R1 is '*trickier than envisaged*' because it is hard to separate the physical and psychological from something that is '*so political*'. As in much of the literature, there is ultimately a sense that Brexit's impact will be either hardened or softened by everyday physical interactions at the border. Presently, at the time of writing, that impact has been softened by the Northern Ireland Protocol (2019) but with loyalist antagonism and perceptions of bad faith on the part of the British government, there is a lingering sense of this always being subject to change.

Getting Brexit done and getting on with life along the border

'Getting Brexit done' served as the catchphrase of Boris Johnson's campaign in his British general election landslide victory of 2019. However, the months that followed this were characterized by uncertainty. R22 draws upon language common to the Covid-19 pandemic of 2020 by pointing out '*there have been multiple waves of preparation in this prolonged journey and many have braced for a hard Brexit only to find the deadlines have shifted at the last minute'*. That added to a sense of there being a *'game'* the British negotiators were seen to be playing (R11, R18) *'in a project driven by internal Tory party politics'* (R14) and the UK putting *'its own narrow interests before all else'* (R27). The British Conservatives wanted to get Brexit done but were not quite sure what would come after (R1, R16, R27, R29). They also failed to realize how quickly the situation could *'implode'* (R22).

Within responses to this study, a large part of the discussion was on economic aspects of implosion rather than in terms of political discontent. R22 went on to warn that there could be *'significant implications for NI-UK trade pretty quickly'* in such areas as *'supply chain'* management. R26, a Northern Irish businessman who grew up along the border, echoes this by suggesting that there will be *'price increases, supply chain issues, reduced choice for produce and materials and a lot more paperwork'*. R12, R13 and R16 also pointed out the immediacy of possible challenges for various sectors from tourism to waterways if solutions were not found. R1 makes a further salient point that although *'Ireland "only" sends something like 11% of its exports to the UK, the fact that most of this is accounted for by the food and small business sectors mean that the impact will be felt more keenly in non-urban areas'*.

In a society where significant urban–rural disparity already exists, the impact of this could have dangerous implications. R27 highlights the fact that if trade dries up between the UK and Ireland, existing ferry routes could face economic collapse, causing job losses for workers in the ports. R25, though, argues that *'from a trade point of view, trade is like water and will find the easiest and quickest way'*. To support this, he gives the example of how *'significant delays with trade through the UK on the way to the continent'* could lead to *'trade redirection over time'* with direct routes being established between Rosslare and France. This gives an impression of Ireland being ahead of Britain in planning terms or at least in the articulation of those plans to the public. Possibly, much of Britain's problems have originated in the fact that they have not equipped their society with a practical understanding of Brexit. That certainly appears to have been the case for Northern Ireland's Unionists.

Even in early 2020, changes were happening under the radar rather than being a source of discussion in the public domain. Though no great supporter of the British government's handling of Brexit affairs, in the summer of

2020, R16 spoke of how '*some physical work has already started at places such as Larne and Warrenpoint*'. Unionists, though, appear not to have been mentally prepared for the psychological impact of such physical changes. Irish nationalist respondents such as R3 were far more confident that '*Britain will not repudiate the Withdrawal Agreement and the physical changes will be control posts at Warrenpoint, Belfast, Larne and Foyle and for freight at George Best and Aldergrove*'. Similarly, R15 had predicted acceptance of the '*Dublin government*' approach of '*allowing NI businesses to export around the world using EU free trade agreements*'. Some other suggestions, despite being creative, did not or have not yet materialized. These included the idea of '*lorry and goods checks away from the border in so-called "lorry parks" or inland sites*' (R7), an Irish equivalence of Calais with tailbacks of machinery rather than migrants. Possibly, in light of the protocol issues, this could be seen as a compromise on both sides but again it is kicking the can down the road rather than solving the problem, which has been characteristic of British governance in Ireland.

Throughout the responses, a common refrain is that any kind of physical border would be '*detrimental to the unity, goodwill and prosperity which has been an organic offshoot of the Good Friday Peace Agreement*' (R10). As such, R1 echoes Hoey (2018) in saying that '*Ireland will go to great lengths to avoid the erection of anything physical as this would simply inevitably lead us on the slippery slope towards conflict*'. This ties in very much with the idea of the psychological being inseparable from the physical (R9, R16, R18) and the great dangers of '*those smaller wins*' on an everyday level being '*undone with one act of politics*' (R18). R16 also echoes those such as Byers (2019) in pointing out that the full work of the Good Friday Agreement is '*not yet done*' with so much that remains to be completed around the promises of gradual societal transformation.

The problem, though, has arisen from the fact that by addressing the physical concerns of those who identify as Irish, a new set of psychological issues have emerged on the other side. Regulatory aspects are having more of an impact of the psyche of those who identify as British. This is not universal, though, reflecting the divisions and even schisms that exist within Northern Irish Protestantism. Though from an Ulster Protestant background, R2 holds the view of a '*so-called Border down the Irish Sea*' being '*probably the lesser of two evils*', even though it still creates '*difficulties for some NI businesses in terms of delay and red tape*'. R21 who is from a similar sociocultural background to

R2 but living on the opposite side of Northern Ireland disagrees with a sea border. He suggests that '*the UK has said that they are not interested in hard borders or physical checks at the border between Ireland and Northern Ireland*' and that '*all goods checks can be done at the source or at its destination*' (R21). This, though, is not something the EU is prepared to accept.

Conclusion and recommendations on the basis of this study

McCall (2018, p. 11) outlines how the road network along the Irish border is so dense that 'the direct route from Cavan Town (in Ireland) to Dungannon (in Northern Ireland) through the Drummully Salient crosses the border no less than 5 times'. This serves as a good example of how the demarcation is often seen in the public imagination, but this study has shown that there are other variables at play here. Since the 'borders in the mind' (Gormley-Heenan & Aughey, 2017) are more to the fore of Northern Ireland's identity politics, there is a need to take physicality out of 'bordering' (McCall, 2018, p. 2). That, though, has been a challenge which only the 1998 Good Friday Agreement has surmounted, being more successful in transcending a fixed sense of national boundaries than even the EU itself (Walsh, 2019). Although imperfect in certain respects (Breen, 2018), this agreement is one which cannot be unpicked or that could bring the shadows of gunmen back into play, exploiting the chaos of what might variously be described as the opening of a Pandora's box or the unbinding of deep, unhealed wounds. Even in the midst of a pandemic, Britain moved towards Brexit as if in a game of blind man's bluff without set rules. Worst of all, they failed to equip their population with a sense of what Brexit would entail. Thus, many Unionists who voted for Brexit have been completely blind-sided by the problems that have emerged. Sadly, though, there are no easy solutions to regulatory frameworks readily acceptable to all parties.

Northern Ireland's stalemate is now providing firm evidence for those who argued that the UK's suicidal chess game was always an English nationalist fantasy grounded in no tangible sense of reality. There are no winners in such a situation, though. Sadly, after five years of obfuscation, nobody has offered a solution to the Irish border question unanimously acceptable to all sides. Driscoll (2019) proposed four possible solutions, three of which would seem to be acceptable to participants within this study. The first of these is the retention of the Common Travel Area arrangement between the UK and Ireland, which allows for free movement between the two states (Driscoll, 2019, pp. 231–4). The second entails the UK joining the Schengen visa area (pp. 234–6) and the third involves a proposal to 'maintain EU citizenship for all citizens of Northern Ireland' (pp. 236–9). Each might seem palatable to respondents herein, but her fourth suggestion to 'reverse Brexit' (pp. 239–41) would curry no favour with such participants as R17 and R22.

The problem with all of these suggestions, though, is that an agreement has already been negotiated which incorporates the Northern Ireland Protocol (2019). It seems that going back to the drawing board is not an option on the table right now, particularly from an EU and Irish government perspective. Potentially, the prospect and configuration of a united Ireland seems easier to implement than any other impending regulatory change. Though unpalatable to many Unionists, this may indeed be the end result of Britain's disastrous Brexit fantasy. With proper planning, it neither needed to be disastrous nor fantastical, but the whole project was based upon a notion of separation at odds with political and geographical reality. So long as Britain shares a land border with another EU member state, there can be no simple solution. At the same time, for the sake of societal harmony, the unionist side needs greater confidence in regulatory arrangements which their folly has contributed towards.

That most contentious of conundrums – the Irish question – has come to the fore once again. However, in looking to the recent past, we may find future solutions. The Good Friday Agreement has worked because its design has allowed for necessary ambiguity (Ruane & Todd, 2001, p. 923). The same now needs to happen for the post-Brexit landscape of the Irish border in both physical and psychological terms. Even though built on shaky foundations as suggested in Byers (2019), the Good Friday Agreement must remain 'sacrosanct' (O'Brennan, 2019, p. 168) as 'a backbone to our hard-won peace' (O'Brennan, 2019). Even though psychological borders remain in places, there can be no retracing of footsteps akin to Colm Tóibín's when he walked a more physical border. The breath of peace has softened pathways across what was once a cratered divide. Whether Irish or British, people on the island of Ireland have learned to live together in an imperfect but workable union of national identities. Now, in our uncertain future, so much of that seems at risk.

There are no easy solutions to this issue, and it remains very much a work in progress, apparently susceptible to change at any moment. Despite being among the loudest advocates of change, Northern Ireland's Unionists might have the most to lose out of all this. Whatever happens next, Brexit has been a disaster for this receding demographic who perhaps thought a hard border would slow demands for a united Ireland. Instead, it has accelerated such demands. That, though, is a whole other chapter in the story of a future shaped by a major mistake in 2016, assuming that Brexit could be done and nothing would change. The fact that five years after the referendum, Britain is stumbling around, seeking to redefine arrangements already agreed to, suggests that everything about this venture has been ill-considered. Unfortunately, as has happened often in Anglo-Irish history, England's actions might have greater consequence in Ireland than anywhere else. Drunk on a distorted sense of nationalism, they have allowed a genie of Irish discontent to escape the bottle. The end result may well be the break-up of the UK itself.

Bibliography

Barker, W. W. (2001). *The Adages of Erasmus*. University of Toronto Press: Canada.

Beckett, J. C. (1966). *The Making of Modern Ireland – 1603 to 1923*. Faber and Faber: London.

Boston College Subpoena WordPress. (2019). *The Belfast Project, Boston College, and a Sealed Subpoena*. Accessed 30 October 2020. https://bostoncollegesubpoena.wordpress.com/.

Breen, P. (2018). 'Healing Past Wounds with More Than an Elastic Bandage – A Small-Scale Evaluation of Attitudes and Aspirations of Contemporary Northern Irish Catholics'. *National Identities*, 21(2), 151–69.

Brown, K. & Macginty, R. (2003). 'Public Attitudes toward Partisan and Neutral Symbols in Post-agreement Northern Ireland'. *Identities: Global Studies in Culture and Power*, 10(1), 83–108.

Byers, S. (2019). '50 Years since the Troubles'. *Tribune*, Autumn 2019.

Churchill, W. (1922). 1922 *Speech on the Ireland Situation Made in the House of Commons*, 16 February 1922. Full text accessed 1 November 2020. http://www.ukpol.co.uk/winston-churchill-1922-speech-on-the-ireland-situation/.

Driscoll, E. E. (2019). 'Equal Treatment for the Identity: The Inequality of Irish and British Citizenship in Post-Brexit Northern Ireland'. *BU Int'l LJ*, 37, 211.

Eastwood, C. (2016). *Oral Evidence to House of Lords European Union Committee Brexit: UK-Irish Relations.* Accessed 3 November 2020. https://www.publications.parliament.uk/pa/ld201617/ldselect/ldeucom/76/7607.htm.

Fenton, S. (2018). *The Good Friday Agreement.* Biteback Publishing: London.

Gormley-Heenan, C. and Aughey, A. (2017). 'Northern Ireland and Brexit: Three Effects on "the border in the mind"'. *The British Journal of Politics and International Relations,* 19(3), 497–511.

Gormley-Heenan, C., Aughey, A. and Devine, P. (2017). 'Waking Up in a Different Country: Brexit and Northern Ireland'. *The British Journal of Politics and International Relations,* 19(3), 498–512.

Greenslade, R. (2019). 'The Belfast Blindspot: How Britain Still Doesn't Get Northern Ireland'. *New Statesman,* 23 October 2019.

Hayward, K. (2018). 'The Pivotal Position of the Irish Border in the UK's Withdrawal from the European Union'. *Space and Polity,* 22(2), 238–54.

Hoey, P. (2018). 'Dissident and Dissenting Republicanism: From the Good Friday/Belfast Agreement to Brexit'. *Capital & Class,* 43(1), 73–87.

Little, A. (2003). 'The Problems of Antagonism: Applying Liberal Political Theory to Conflict in Northern Ireland'. *British Journal of Politics and International Relations,* 5(3), 373–92.

Lonergan, A. (2019). 'Former Brexit Secretary David Davis Admits UK Government Should Have Put More Resources into Solving Irish Border "Blind Spot"'. *The Irish Post,* 17 January 2019.

Manley, J. (2016). 'EU Referendum Throws Up Odd Couplings'. *The Irish News,* 17 June 2016.

McCall, C. (2018). 'Brexit, Bordering and Bodies on the Island of Ireland'. *Ethnopolitics,* 17(3), 292–305.

McKay, S. (2021). 'The Irish Language Can Give Us All a Sense of Home – If We Save It from Sectarianism'. *Guardian Newspaper,* 10 August 2021. https://www.theguardian.com/commentisfree/2021/aug/10/irish-language-belfast-preschool-unionist.

Mitchell, P., Evans, G., and O'Leary, B. (2009). 'Extremist Outbidding in Ethnic Party Systems Is Not Inevitable: Tribune Parties in Northern Ireland'. *Political Studies,* 57(2), 397–421.

Morgan-Jones, E., Sudulich, L., Cochrane, F. and Loizides, N. (2020). 'Citizen Preferences about Border Arrangements in Divided Societies: Evidence from a Conjoint Experiment in Northern Ireland'. *Research & Politics,* 7(3), 2053168020929927.

O'Brennan, J. (2019). 'Requiem for a Shared Interdependent Past: Brexit and the Deterioration in UK-Irish Relations'. *Capital & Class,* 43(1), 157–71.

O'Casey, S. (1923). 'The Shadow of a Gunman'. In O'Casey, S. (1998). *Three Dublin Plays: The Shadow of a Gunman, Juno and the Paycock, & The Plough and the Stars*. Macmillan.

O'Toole, F. (2016). 'Brexit Is being Driven by English Nationalism: And It Will End in Self-Rule'. *The Observer*, 19 June. https://www.theguardian.com/commentisfree/2016/jun/18/ england-eu-referendum-brexit.

O'Toole, F. (2018). *Heroic Failure: Brexit and the Politics of Pain*. Head of Zeus Ltd: London.

Pinos, J. C. and Sacramento, J. (2020). 'The Sovereignty Paradox: Brexit's Territorial Consequences for Gibraltar, Scotland and Northern Ireland'. Danish Institute for International Studies working paper.

Rafferty, G. and Blair, N. (2019). 'Emergent Cross-Border Functional Geographies on the Island of Ireland: Pre- and Post-Brexit'. *Irish Geography*, 52(2), 175–91.

Ruane, J. and Todd, J. (2001). 'The Politics of Transition? Explaining Political Crises in the Implementation of the Belfast Good Friday Agreement'. *Political Studies*, 49(5), 923–40.

Sampson, F. (2016). 'Whatever You Say . . . ': The Case of the Boston College Tapes and How Confidentiality Agreements Cannot Put Relevant Data beyond the Reach of Criminal Investigation'. *Policing: A Journal of Policy and Practice*, 10(3), 222–31.

Todd, J. (2017). 'From Identity Politics to Identity Change: Exogenous Shocks, Constitutional Moments and the Impact of Brexit on the Island of Ireland'. *Irish Studies in International Affairs*, 28, 57–72.

Tóibín, C. and O'Shea, T. (1987). *Walking along the Border*. MacDonald, Queen Anne Press: London.

UK Government Department for Exiting the European Union. (2019). Agreement on the Withdrawal of the United Kingdom of Great Britain and Northern Ireland from the European Union. 19 October 2019. Accessed 3 September 2021. https://www.gov.uk/government/publications/new-withdrawal-agreement-and-political-declaration.

Vaughan-Williams, N. (2006). 'Towards a Problematisation of the Problematisations that Reduce Northern Ireland to a "Problem"'. *Critical Review of International Social and Political Philosophy*, 9(4), 513–26.

Walsh, C. (2019). 'Brexit Geographies: Spatial Imaginaries and Relational Territorialities on the Island of Ireland'. *Irish Geography*, 52(2), 137–52.

Yeats, W.B. (1921). *'Easter 1916'* in *Michael Robartes and the Dancer*. Cuala Press: Dublin.

The impact of Brexit on the future of the UK's financial services

Stephen Jones

The United Kingdom's (UK) financial services industry matters greatly to the UK not only in its contribution to the country's economy through employment provided and tax receipts generated but also because of the other services for which the industry acts as the dominant client and which it therefore helps to sustain. In aggregate the industry and related clusters are estimated to support 2.3 million jobs, two-thirds of which are outside London and the South East of England,[1] and to contribute £75.5 billion or some 10.5 per cent of total UK tax receipts.[2]

As well as highly regulated domestic banking, insurance and asset management sectors offering the full range of finance, savings, assurance, pensions and wealth management services to UK-based customers, the UK has developed a highly sophisticated financial centre serving the needs of global corporates, governments, investors and insurers. This financial centre has come to dominate wholesale financial markets across the European Union (EU), as well as other geographies, and has consistently vied with New York to be ranked the number one global financial marketplace for the last fifteen years.[3]

It is no surprise therefore that financial services – in particular UK-based financial services – have proven to be highly contentious in negotiations on the UK's exit from the EU. More surprising, however, is how little British

---

[1] TheCityUK, *Key Facts about UK-Based Financial and Related Professional Services*, April 2020.
[2] PwC and City of London, *The Total Tax Contribution of UK Financial Services in 2019*, 12th Edition, January 2020.
[3] Z/Yen, 'Long Finance and FS Club', *The Global Financial Centres Index 28*, September 2020.

government's energy and focus have been devoted over the four years of Brexit negotiations to securing the UK's position as Europe's leading financial centre. As British prime minister Boris Johnson understatedly put it in the immediate aftermath of a deal being announced at the eleventh hour on 24 December 2020, 'on financial services the deal perhaps does not go as far as we would like'.[4]

During the course of negotiations, the tone of the UK's public position ebbed and flowed as UK governments and negotiating teams changed following the Brexit referendum in 2016 but at no point was the passion and energy devoted by France to securing, for example, the interests of its fishing industry matched by the British government in its efforts on behalf of the UK economy's largest industry, the financial services.

Against this backdrop, the future of the UK as a global financial centre in post-Brexit world is difficult to predict, but a steady reduction of wholesale market activities currently undertaken by EU-based wholesale market counterparties in London and Edinburgh is almost inevitable. Whether and how much of their business is diverted to Frankfurt, Paris, Amsterdam, Luxembourg or Dublin remains to be seen.

The pace of continuing onshoring of financial services activities from the UK to the EU will depend on political and regulatory initiatives to continue to repatriate to the EU certain activity in pursuit of the EU's emerging doctrine of 'strategic autonomy' as applied to financial markets activity.

The British government and regulators have tools available to them to combat this inevitable loss of EU customer business. Whether they choose to do so is as yet unknown.

Even harder to call is whether Europe as a whole, including the UK, is deprioritized by North American and Asian actors who may choose to relocate activities to New York, Singapore, Hong Kong, Shanghai and Tokyo.

In this chapter we will explore the reasons for the relative pre-eminence of the UK's financial markets in the second half of the twentieth century, analyse the conduct and results of Brexit negotiations between the UK and the EU since 2016, and consider the factors that will determine what the medium-

---

[4] Harry Yorke, 'Exclusive Boris Johnson Interview: From Bruges to Brexit, This Is the End of Our 30-year Struggle', *The Telegraph*, 26 December 2020.

term consequences of Brexit could be for the UK-based financial and related services ecosystem.

What accounts for the growth of the UK's financial services industry?

The coffee house culture of the City of London in the seventeenth century resulted in a concentration of particular types of financial activity in individual establishments leading, for example, to the establishment of the London Stock Exchange in Jonathan's Coffee House in Change Alley and the Lloyd's of London insurance market taking its name from Edward Lloyd, a coffee house owner in Tower Street.[5]

Ever adaptable, the City of London financed wars, colonies and global trade on a massive relative scale as the concentration of relevant skills in a single location allowed innovation, risk sharing and rules to evolve quickly to meet the dynamic and ever-changing needs of a trading and industrial nation.

London's role as a leading financial centre accompanied the development of the UK at the centre of a colonial empire, financing and insuring the shipment of commodities from producer nations across the globe to the consumer nations of Europe. By the end of the nineteenth century, the Industrial Revolution had heralded the creation of a modern industrial British economy with its factory production, railways, steamships and telegraph communication systems, resulting in an enormous further increase in international trade flows and the financing and risk sharing required to facilitate this transformation.[6]

Fast-forward to 1947, the forces of globalization underpinning international economic activity began to reassert themselves following the interwar years and the Great Depression of the 1930s, which had seen the introduction of capital controls and the abandoning of free trade.

During the 1950s and 1960s, London benefited from preferential capital flows being permitted between the UK and sterling area countries such as Australia, New Zealand, Singapore, Malaya, South Africa and Hong Kong. But the real acceleration of wholesale markets' activity came from the emergence

---

[5] City of London, *City History*, 19 June 2020.
[6] Richard Roberts, *Schroders Merchants & Bankers* (London: The Macmillan Press, 1992), chapters 3–5.

of the Eurodollar market in London, where US dollar bank deposits, loans and bonds were taken, made and issued by banks on behalf of customers around the world. As the importance of sterling as a global currency diminished, the British authorities condoned the development of a market denominated in US dollars, showing a pragmatism and understanding of how facilitating global capital flows through London could earn valuable foreign exchange from the provision of these financing services.[7]

The development in the 1960s of the Eurobond market from London was greatly facilitated by the accumulation of these US dollar balances outside the United States. External investment by US multinational corporations expanding overseas, US balance of payments deficits and fear of US dollar accounts being frozen in the United States and Regulation Q, which had capped the rate of interest that could be earned on US dollar deposits placed with US banks, allowed foreign banks to attract US dollar balances by offering higher rates which could not be matched by their US peers. Holders of these offshore dollars became big investors in securities issued by non-US, often European, corporations and governments.[8]

In parallel, the United States was attempting, ultimately in vain, to prevent the Bretton Woods system of fixed exchange rates from collapsing by curbing the flow of US dollars from the United States. In 1963, it imposed an Interest Equalization Tax of 1 per cent on the cost of US dollar borrowing by all foreign entities in the United States, heavily curtailing the use of domestic US dollar bond markets by overseas issuers.

In that year, S. G. Warburg, the London-based merchant bank, launched the first Eurobond for the Italian issuer Autostrade, raising $15 million at a coupon of 5.5 per cent with a final fifteen-year maturity. An Italian borrower building infrastructure in Italy had accessed long-dated funding from the offshore US dollar market in London facilitated by the innovation of a leading merchant bank with German origins based there.[9]

In 1965, the US' Voluntary Restraint Programme imposed voluntary restriction on US corporations investing overseas and on US banks making

---

[7] Catherine Schenk, 'The City and Financial Services: Historical Perspectives on the Brexit Debate', *The Political Quarterly*, 14 February 2019, Volume 90 S2.
[8] Richard Benzie, 'The Development of the International Bond Market', *BIS Economic Papers* No 32, January 1992.
[9] ICMA, History of the Eurobond Market, *About ICMA/ History*, https://www.icmagroup.org.

loans to non-US borrowers for longer than one year. When these restrictions became mandatory in 1968, many US corporations were forced to use the emerging offshore Eurobond market in London to fund their overseas subsidiaries.

Meanwhile, the German authorities had been struggling to contain upward pressure on the valuation of the Deutschemark. As a result, German investors were allowed to buy foreign, that is London-issued, Deutschemark bonds since this outflow from Germany helped ease pressure on the currency, while a 1964 withholding tax created a strong disincentive for non-German investors to hold domestic Deutschemark bonds. As non-German securities houses became involved in the underwriting and distribution of these offshore Deutschemark securities in London, so the conventions surrounding the issuance of bonds in this currency in London increasingly resembled those prevailing in the US dollar Eurobond market.

Despite the abolition of the US Interest Equalization Tax in 1974 following the collapse of the Bretton Woods system in 1972 – resulting in floating exchange rates – the infrastructure which had come to underpin the US dollar Eurobond market in London, and strict SEC regulations applying to new bond issues in the domestic US Yankee bond market by non-US issuers, helped to ensure that the Eurobond market did not migrate back to New York.

With floating exchange rates requiring more active cross-currency balance sheet management by borrowers, the Eurobond market developed across multiple currencies. Issuance expanded eightfold between 1981 and 1986 as interest rates fell, the swap market expanded and the liberalization of financial markets, particularly in the UK and Japan, followed.[10]

The Bank of England's *Quarterly Bulletin* in November 1989[11] analysed the factors underlying London's position as 'a major centre for international eurocurrency business, Eurobond transactions, insurance, foreign exchange, fund management and corporate financial advice' as well as 'the location for a significant volume of international equity business'. Pointing to the 'relatively restrictive regulatory and fiscal conditions in other centres – though also owing something to the innovativeness of London firms', the bulletin highlighted

---

[10] Benzie, 'The Development of the International Bond Market'.
[11] *Bank of England Quarterly Bulletin*, London as an International Financial Centre, November 1989, 516–28.

the outsized share of international markets that had accrued to London (and Edinburgh in the case of fund management).

Factors to which this success was attributed in 1989 are relevant to not only that time but also today in the context of the UK's uncertain future as a global financial centre following its exit from the EU. As the Bank of England put it then:

> London has offered a pool of suitably trained labour; relatively free access to markets which have not been heavily regulated; . . . declining levels of corporate and personal taxation; a reasonable tax regime for financial instruments (e.g. ability to issue bearer bonds that pay interest gross); a supply of suitable premises; the absence, since 1979, of exchange controls; prudential and monetary regulations that have not historically tended significantly to raise the cost of funds, distort or prevent competition (compared, for example, with heavy reserve requirements elsewhere); the English language; and political stability. There has also been a degree of confidence among firms that regulations will not be altered without good reason and appropriate consultation.

UK policymakers and regulators in 2021 would do well to reflect on the extent to which these factors prevail today as market participants address the diseconomies caused by the UK's exit from the EU and are forced to make decisions about how to reorganize and where to relocate their business activities serving European customers and markets. The extent of change to the UK's position as a global financial centre that may result following Brexit will depend on many factors. The Bank of England's 1989 conclusions are relevant to all who today are considering the competitive position of the UK as a leading global financial centre:

> London has developed over a long period as a leading international financial centre and the financial sector plays a central role in the UK economy. London's success owes much to its history of openness, in contrast to other countries where for many years restrictions on entry or operations hindered the development of their financial sectors. Recent moves, and others afoot, to dismantle many of these restrictions combine with rapidly advancing technology to present an international environment in which competition between locations is intensifying. However, the wealth of experience available in London, the advantages of an established centre displaying the full range of financial and ancillary services and the determination to

improve systems where necessary suggest that London should be well placed to meet the competitive challenge. But neither the authorities nor firms operating there can afford to be complacent.

A wide range of financial services activity

London's position has been consistently assessed as one of the two leading global financial centres alongside New York since the Global Financial Centres Index (GFCI) began in 2007. The Top 5 include Shanghai, Tokyo and Hong Kong, with Zurich the only (non-EU) European centre to be ranked in the Top 10.[12]

The key factors driving this competitiveness ranking are led by the business and regulatory environment. Respondents note that the regulatory balance must strike the right mix of regulation to reduce corruption without stifling innovation and development, and ensure greater transparency. The availability of high-quality human capital is critical, so open immigration and flexible compensation rules, as well as good infrastructure and lifestyle, still attract the highest scores. The need for information technology (IT) skills has continued to grow as fintech and artificial intelligence become mainstream and as the need increases for world-class IT and connectivity infrastructure to facilitate machine-based trading and virtual working.

Since the deregulation of financial markets in the 1980s, commentators and market participants have widely attributed the attractiveness of London and the UK to language, time zone, Anglo-US business culture (with flat hierarchies and less bureaucracy), reputation and the rule of law, principles-based regulation, flexible employment laws and the large concentration of skilled workers available in a single geographic concentration. Favourable tax and immigration policies, as well as strong and predictable regulation, provided strong tailwinds to the UK's success as a global financial centre in the run-up to the 2008 global financial crisis (GFC).

Over the post-2008 GFC period, the corrective actions taken by UK regulators to improve financial strength and consumer protection have been among the toughest globally across banking, insurance and asset management. UK influence is also perceived to have driven some of the more onerous EU

---

[12] Z/Yen, Long Finance and FS Club, *The Global Financial Centres Index 28*, September 2020.

policy responses, for example, Solvency II capital standards in insurance and AIFMD rules in asset management. The UK's taxation of banks with continuing levies and corporation tax surcharges remains the longest enduring of major economies impacted by the GFC.[13]

Despite this forceful and inevitable response to the GFC given the relative size of the UK-based financial services sector to the overall UK economy, the other advantages of a concentrated centre of expertise and talent referenced in the GFCI surveys have tended to outweigh negative sentiment generated by UK gold-plating of global regulatory norms in the eyes of those financial businesses established or establishing in the UK. Many have predicted that where the UK goes in terms of conduct and prudential regulation, others will follow. The UK's tough tax policy, particularly towards banks, remains a source of friction with many of the largest global banking institutions heavily invested in the UK: for them future UK tax policy will be a critical factor in determining their ongoing commitment of capital and activities to the UK.

The relative size of the financial sector in the UK, and the concentration of EU financial activity undertaken there, is remarkable on the one hand and remains a source of concern to policymakers in the EU. In 2018, Olivier Guersent, then director general at DG-FISMA, the European Commission directorate with responsibility for financial services, told me that for Eurozone member states to have such a significant concentration of Euromarkets activity concentrated outside the Eurozone, even if in an EU member state, was already a source of discomfort for EU policymakers concerned about financial stability and systemic resilience. So such concern would inevitably be even greater once the UK left the EU.

The unilateral decision by London-based LCH to increase collateral haircuts required against southern European government bonds at the height of the so-called PIIGS southern European sovereign debt crisis in 2012 created enormous resentment in Brussels, Paris and Frankfurt and the relevant capitals, and highlighted the perceived risk to the financial stability of Eurozone member states of dependence on London, an offshore financial centre outside the Eurozone.[14]

---

[13] PwC for UK Finance, *Total Tax Contribution of the UK Banking Sector*, a publication prepared by PwC for UK Finance, Fifth Edition, October 2019.

[14] Angela Armakolla, Raphael Douady, Jean-Paul Laurent, Francesco Molteni, 'Repurchase Agreements and the European Sovereign Debt Crises: The Role of European Clearinghouses', *Working Paper*, 6 October 2017.

No wonder that in December 2020 Mairead McGuinness, the EU's financial services commissioner, warned in discussing the future relationship between the UK and the EU: 'Our interest is making sure that we are not captured by a system that we don't regulate, or controlled by it.'

In 2019, the UK was the largest net exporter of financial services in the world with an estimated surplus of $77 billion, with the EU member states the largest block accounting for over a third of the UK's financial services exports.[15]

As a centre for more than 250 foreign banks based in London, it was the world's largest centre for cross-border lending and borrowing with global market shares of 15 per cent and 18 per cent respectively in 2019.

The Bank for International Settlements estimated that 43 per cent of global foreign exchange volumes were traded in London in April 2019. By contrast, France accounted for 2 per cent and Germany 1 per cent.[16]

The Swiss Re Institute estimated the UK insurance market to be the largest in Europe in 2019 with $366 billion in premiums, accounting for a quarter of total premiums in advanced European economies over that period.[17]

In fund management, assets under management in the UK totalled $12.6 trillion, with a strong international orientation – more than 70 per cent of equities and more than 50 per cent of bonds under management were held in non-UK markets. The UK is the second global centre for hedge funds with $447 billion in assets under management underpinned by strong administration, prime brokerage and custody services sectors.[18] UK-based private equity funds invested $42.2 billion in 2019, the greatest amount in Europe.[19]

Derivatives markets underpin the management of financial market risks by governments, financial institutions and corporates. By far the largest of these derivative markets trades interest rates where the UK accounts for over half of all global over-the-counter activity.[20] Again, strong infrastructure and regulation underpin these markets, enabling counterparties to manage exposures to one another efficiently. The London-based clearing platform

---

[15] TheCityUK, *Key Facts about the UK as an International Financial Centre,* December 2020, 7–9.
[16] Bank for International Settlements, 'Triennial Central Bank Survey', Foreign Exchange Turnover in April 2019, 16 September 2019.
[17] Swiss Re Institute, *sigma No 4/2020*, World Insurance: Riding Out the 2020 Pandemic Storm, 10.
[18] Investment Association, 'Asset Management in the UK 2019 – 2020', *The Investment Association Annual Survey*, September 2020, 9, 19, 20, 104.
[19] TheCityUK, *Key Facts*, December 2020, 18.
[20] Bank for International Settlements, *OTC Interest Rate Derivatives Turnover 1995–2019,* 8 December 2019.

LCH, part of the London Stock Exchange Group, dominates the clearing of derivatives across Europe.

The ecosystem of infrastructure and advice supporting all these activities, as well as the competence of regulators and willingness of the British government to back-stop such enormous scale of financial markets activity relative to the overall size of the UK economy, helps explain why any dilution of the scale of UK financial centre is unlikely to happen quickly following the UK's exit from the EU.

The impact of Brexit negotiations on financial services

The British government and the financial services industry were both taken by surprise by the Leave vote. David Cameron resigned as Prime Minister on 24 June 2016 in the immediate aftermath of the UK's Brexit referendum vote to be replaced by Theresa May. Industry leaders, their trade associations and lobbyists in the UK worked frantically to seek to establish common ground and put forward to their government a unified position which could be used to underpin a negotiation strategy on behalf of each industry potentially impacted by the UK's exit from the EU.

Representatives of the financial services industry, though shocked by the referendum result, were at least confident in the assessment that the importance of UK-based financial services would result in so-called passporting – or something very close to it – being prioritized by the British government as a core part of its overall exit negotiations. The 'passport' is the mechanism that enabled UK-established financial institutions subject to UK regulation and supervision to service continental European customers directly from the UK, and continental European financial institutions to serve UK customers from their bases in the EU in the same way, as well as access the UK's wholesale financial centre without being required to have a physical presence in the UK.

For many international firms, passporting was the critical permission that underpinned their European corporate structures, enabling them to build headquarters and invest significantly in the UK from where they could conduct their continental European business activities. But the extent of passporting went beyond large global investment banks: some 5,500 UK financial firms were estimated to be relying on passports to do business in the rest of the

EU in September 2016, with some 8,000 EEA firms estimated to be reliant on passporting in the other direction to do business in the UK.[21]

There was also an assumption by many in the industry, particularly larger global investment banks with European activities headquartered in London, that the UK would strain to secure a comprehensive exit deal with the EU and that the EU would wish to secure its access to London's outsized financial centre as a matter of economic necessity. These assumptions and assessments were gradually all turned upside down.

'Project Fear', the playbook adopted by pro-EU politicians and other thought leaders before the 2016 referendum in the UK, had even cast the Monetary Policy Committee of the Bank of England in a role. In its measured language, the underlying message in May 2016 had been clear: 'A vote to leave the [EU] could materially alter the outlook for output and inflation ... [which] could lead to a materially lower path for growth and notably higher path for inflation.'[22]

As the pro-Brexit wing of the ruling British Conservative Party replaced the departing 'remainers' in government in the aftermath of the June 2016 referendum, TheCityUK, the umbrella lobby group representing financial and professional service businesses across the UK, commissioned consultant Oliver Wyman to assess the risks of a bad deal or no deal emerging from the UK's exit negotiations with the EU.[23] Oliver Wyman did not pull its punches, concluding that were the UK to move to a third-country status on exit without a trade deal, 40–50 per cent of financial services activity with EU clients would be lost, costing up to 35,000 jobs and £5 billion of tax revenues directly, with further related ecosystem losses accounting for up to 40,000 further job losses and a further £5 billion of tax revenues. It concluded:

> EU businesses have an interest in retaining access to the UK as an international financial centre, not only for the services provided directly but also as a conduit for global investment into the EU. The best outcome would

---

[21] Martin Arnold, '"Significant" Brexit Risk for 5,500 UK Groups Using EU Passporting', *Financial Times*, 20 September 2016.
[22] Bank of England, *Monetary Policy Summary and Minutes of the Monetary Policy Committee Ending on 11 May 2016*, 12 May 2016.
[23] Oliver Wyman, *The Impact of the UK's Exit from the EU on the UK-Based Financial Services Sector*, 5 October 2016.

recognise these dynamics and deliver mutually beneficial results for the EU and the rest of the world.

The industry's initial ask of the British government to seek to preserve as near as possible existing passporting rights fell on deaf ears. David Davis, then secretary of state at the UK's newly formed Department for Exiting the European Union (DExEU), told industry representatives in October 2016 that the industry did not need help from the government and was powerful enough on its own to adapt.

It was also clear by the end of 2016 that the broad financial services industry, despite its collective weight and relative economic importance, was struggling to establish a single vision of the best path forward. Though the voice of the largest investment banks operating cross-border models headquartered in London was loudly in favour of maintaining maximum integration with the EU in financial services, other voices were less keen on the continued perceived 'rule-taking' from Brussels that would be the necessary corollary of continued passporting access rights.

Domestic banks and building societies without European presence were keen to take advantage of the opportunities of leaving the EU to slim down a perceived 'one size fits all' rule book.

Voices in the asset management industry were not united about passporting – and accompanying EU rule-taking – representing the best path forward. The sector, dominated by centres in London and Edinburgh looking after 40 per cent of continental Europe's assets under management, was determinedly global in its assessment of future growth prospects, highlighting the continued need for competitiveness relative to the United States in order to compete in Asia and other fast developing markets, where the savings needs of the emerging middle class were seen as a key growth opportunity. In this context, EU regulations were often perceived as unnecessarily bureaucratic and costly, for example AIFMD, with continuing EU references to the industry as 'non-bank finance' or 'shadow banking' frustrating senior asset management leaders who felt that the industry was being shoe-horned into bank-shaped, rule-heavy boxes by an EU lobby acting for an inefficient and heavily protected domestic EU banking industry.

There were different voices in the insurance sector. One part of the industry was largely domestic in outlook – life insurance, motor, property and corporate players – reliant on UK savings, pension and welfare provision, and domestic capital and broking for which passporting and EU rule adherence served little purpose and added little benefit. On the other side stood international players and specialist marketplaces like Lloyd's of London, underwriting, broking and reinsuring global risks, accessing specialist pools of capital, attracting global insurance firms to base their European activities from London, for whom international connectivity and competitiveness were vital.

Not only did the wider financial services industry have a range of views of what should be asked for, but it was also clear that the British government itself had been surprised by the referendum vote and did not have a detailed prospectus of what it wanted from Brexit and how it should handle negotiations with the EU.

Boris Johnson, then foreign secretary, was ridiculed for suggesting in November 2016 to Italy's then economics minister, Carlo Calenda, that the UK should be granted access to the EU's single market 'because [Italy does not] want to lose prosecco exports'.[24] Officials in Brussels, Berlin and Frankfurt expressed frustration bordering on anger to me on several occasions in 2017 about UK ministers and some industry representatives who would be arriving to discuss financial services arrangements with an attitude that 'EU needs access to the British markets for financial services more than the United Kingdom needs access to EU markets'.

By January 2017, TheCityUK on behalf of the wider financial services industry had abandoned the idea of seeking to retain the financial passport in favour of proposing instead a 'bespoke deal' for the UK industry building on the existing EU concept of 'equivalence' embedded in some of the EU's financial regulation.

Equivalence allows entities established in third countries outside the EU that are judged by the EU to have equivalent regulatory standards to trade freely across borders based on the rules and regulations in their home markets. But the equivalence model was immediately viewed by its detractors to be flawed. It did not apply to large parts of financial services, for example commercial banking, deposit-taking and insurance broking. It relied on a unilateral EU technical assessment of sufficiently mirrored rules and regulations but could

---

[24] Rowena Mason, Peter Walker and Patrick Wintour, 'Boris Johnson Ridiculed by European Ministers after Prosecco Claim', *The Guardian*, 17 November 2016.

be withdrawn by EU authorities without challenge on thirty days' notice, offering insufficient commercial certainty for businesses that needed greater regulatory predictability to operate.

And UK regulators, ever vigilant to protect their rule-making sovereignty, were not convinced by EU equivalence. Mark Carney, then governor of the Bank of England, warned in early 2017 of the UK losing influence and control over its own markets, stating:

> Of course the rules that are there in the EU are influenced by international standards and by the presence of UK officials in their development. Once we're not there, we will get . . . increasingly rules with which we don't agree and which may cause risk to financial stability.

The existing EU equivalence model, as deployed by the EU in financial services with other third countries, was flawed in the eyes of impacted UK-based firms and their regulators. However, the EU was unwilling to engage at all on matters of substance regarding the future relationship until an Article 50 exit timetable had been set and issues regarding the free movement of people and Ireland had been agreed. This was a matter of EU tactical brilliance. By setting a rigid and sequential timetable for Brexit negotiations, the EU blunted any significant ability of the British government to engage on matters of technical substance until the Withdrawal Agreement addressing the EU's priority issues was eventually signed in October 2019.

Nevertheless, the UK's financial services industry lobby continued to develop its proposals for the desired regulatory model in the absence of real challenge from and debate with EU officials. In April 2017, the International Regulatory Steering Group (IRSG), a practitioner-led body of leading figures from the UK's financial and professional services industries chaired by former British government minister Mark Hoban, published its call for a bespoke mutual market access between the UK and the EU across financial and professional services.[25] Its proposed framework was based on 'mutual recognition' of each other's regulatory and supervisory regimes. It proposed criteria for access based on rules established by global standard setters, dialogue mechanisms to monitor regulatory evolution and supervision and,

---

[25] IRSG, *IRSG Report on Mutual Recognition – a Basis for Market Access after Brexit*, 11 April 2017.

in particular, management of possible future divergence of rules in advance. It also proposed a dispute resolution mechanism involving global experts and standard setters.

In public the IRSG report was met with silence by the EU. In private EU officials expressed incredulity at the assumption that the EU should wish to engage in compromising its existing autonomy in setting rules and regulations for the EU financial services industry.

In May 2017, some eleven months after the UK's exit referendum vote, the British government published its initial views on the future relationship between the UK and the EU. Less than a page was devoted to financial services, much of which was a factual summary. The British government called for the 'freest possible trade in financial services between the United Kingdom and EU Member States', referenced the interests of the UK and the EU 'to avoid market fragmentation and the possible disruption or withdrawal of services' and then proceeded to lecture the EU that its '[c]itizens, business and public sector bodies across the continent rely on the City [of London] to access the services that they need'.[26]

It was a remarkably poor prospectus. It lacked any detailed thinking about how the UK and EU authorities might work together to regulate and supervise respective financial institutions seeking to continue to serve customers cross-border. It also reverted to a narrative seen by many in the EU as insulting by asserting that continental Europe would remain dependent on the UK for the provision of essential financial services.

Meanwhile the EU study 'Implications of Brexit on EU Financial Services', presented to the European Parliament in June 2017, was more thorough in its analysis, mapping potential impacts of a range of Brexit final scenarios on EU financial services.[27] It highlighted strong interdependencies of the UK and EU economies in the amount of EU financial services activity undertaken in the UK, in particular the fact that 69 per cent of Euro-denominated derivatives activity was traded and cleared there with a resulting financial stability risk to the Eurozone from this offshore concentration of risks in clearing. It pointed to the increased costs of financial services that would inevitably result from

---

[26] UK Government Department for Exiting the European Union, *The United Kingdom's Exit from and New Partnership with the European Union White Paper*, 15 May 2017.
[27] EU Directorate General for Internal Policies, *Implications of Brexit on EU Financial Services; Study for the ECON Committee*, June 2017.

the need to relocate and duplicate certain UK-based activities into the EU27 as the benefits of the concentrated ecosystem efficiencies in the City of London fragmented. It addressed the urgent need to close the legal uncertainties following exit to ensure a sound underpinning for financial services in a post-Brexit world. Finally, it referenced the opportunity for the EU27 to establish a major financial centre on the European mainland by completing so-called European Capital Markets Union (CMU).

The EU's position was analytical and thorough, based on existing EU rules, frameworks and mechanisms, just as the UK's made assumptions about the EU's willingness to rely on an offshore centre and construct an entirely new regulatory framework to enable it to do so.

Mutual regulatory recognition, the big idea proposed by the UK's industry leaders in the IRSG paper of April 2017, was formally adopted by the British government as its position in March 2018 but then abandoned completely following the publication of the British government's follow-up White Paper of July 2018.[28] Some two years after the Brexit vote, this document sought to articulate the British government's vision for the future relationship between the UK and the EU based at its core on a free trade area for goods with the UK largely applying the EU's rule book. Though services accounted for around 80 per cent of the UK's economy, the White Paper abandoned any notion of passporting or mutual regulatory recognition as the model to underpin cross-border services to and from the UK. Instead it advocated for 'autonomy of decision making and the ability to legislate for [its]own interests' supported by expansion of 'existing autonomous frameworks for equivalence...to encompass a broader range of cross-border activities that reflect global financial business models and the high degree of economic integration'. It recognized explicitly, however, that 'this arrangement cannot replicate the EU's passporting regime'.

Given the legal fact the EU and the UK would have identical rule books for financial services at the point in time that Brexit completed, the UK's starting position for negotiations was that there should be immediate reciprocal recognition where existing EU regulations permitted equivalence decisions.

The financial services industry in the UK described the UK government's proposals as 'a real blow for the UK's financial and professional services

---

[28] UK Government, *The Future Relationship between the United Kingdom and the European Union White Paper*, July 2018.

sector'[29] by dropping the industry's (unrealistic) mutual regulatory recognition proposal before negotiations had even started.[30] The 2018 White Paper also failed to address significant industry and Bank of England concerns regarding contractual continuity for millions of financial contracts between UK-based companies and EU-based companies which would remain in force after the UK's planned exit date in March 2019 and whose legal enforceability was therefore uncertain. The Brexit wing of the Conservative Party saw the overall proposal as 'Brexit in name only'. And in EU capitals the proposals were viewed as 'cherry picking', with the UK seeking free movement of goods and capital but not services and people.

By November 2018, it was clear that the EU was not willing to contemplate anything more than existing, unilateral third-party equivalence mechanisms as the basis for ongoing cross-border financial services activities.

Firms, funds and markets operating in the EU under outbound passports from the UK spent much of the following two years leading up to the eventual end of transition on 31 December 2020 preparing for an assumed 'no deal' exit. This meant setting up permanent local operations within locally regulated subsidiaries onshore in the EU27 in order to be sure that they would be allowed to continue to serve their EU customers from 1 January 2021.

In November 2020, and before any trade agreement was certain, the UK unilaterally granted a number of equivalence decisions to facilitate the cross-border operation of relevant firms relying on EU passports to operate in the UK from 1 January 2021. In July 2018, the UK authorities had already legislated to permit EU firms and funds to continue to operate under existing permissions in the UK for a period of up to three years from the end of the transition period, that is from January 2021, the so-called temporary permissions regime (TPR).

The EU has not reciprocated either the TPR or the equivalence decisions granted by the UK, except in the time-limited case of clearing where an eighteen months' temporary equivalence decision has been made in favour of three UK centralized clearing platforms given the lack of capacity to replace this activity immediately within the EU.

---

[29] City of London, *Press Release from Policy Chairman Catherine McGuinness on White Paper*, 12 July 2018.
[30] TheCityUK, Press Release, *The Government Has Today Published a White Paper on the Future Relationship with the European Union*, 12 July 2018.

The impact of the Christmas Eve 2020 agreement

The agreement eventually reached between the UK and the EU on Christmas Eve 2020 to secure Brexit (the Brexit Agreement) did little more regarding financial services than commit both sides to use best endeavours to ensure that international standards to fight money laundering, terrorist financing and tax evasion and avoidance were applied in each territory. The so-called prudential carve-out was maintained permitting each party to go it alone so far as capital and liquidity rules for financial services firms are concerned.[31] In a declaration outside the treaty itself, both parties committed to agree a memorandum of understanding by March 2021 to establish a framework for regulatory cooperation to enable a durable and stable relationship between autonomous jurisdictions.

More revealing regarding the state of play in financial services than the Brexit Agreement itself was the language used in the EU's Q&A that accompanied its publication. The EU put the position clearly (emphasis added):

> As of 1 January, the **UK will no longer benefit from the principles of free movement of persons, free provision of services and freedom of establishment**.
>
> As a result, **UK service suppliers will lose their automatic right to offer services across the EU**. They may **need to establish themselves in the EU to continue operating**.
>
> Naturally, given that the UK will no longer be in the Single Market, all UK service suppliers . . . must abide by the domestic rules, procedures and authorisations applicable to the activities in the countries where they operate.
>
> [The Agreement] includes a **review clause** encouraging the parties to consider whether there are possibilities to improve trade in services and investment relations between the EU and the UK in the future – **except in the area of financial services . . .**
>
> The Agreement **does not include any elements pertaining to equivalence frameworks for financial services. These are unilateral decisions of each party and are not subject to negotiation.**

---

[31] UK Government, *Trade and Cooperation Agreement between the European Union and the European Atomic Energy Community, of the One Part, and the United Kingdom of Great Britain and Northern Ireland, of the Other Part*, 24 December 2020.

In the period leading up to the December 2020 deadline for the end of the transition period, EU and UK regulators had to operate in the same manner as firms and assume that there would be no meaningful deal of substance in relation to financial services. Since early 2019, EU regulators had continued to ratchet up pressure on UK-based financial services firms wishing to continue to do business with EU customers from 1 January 2021 to ensure that they had established substantially more than brass plate operations within continental Europe. Pressure was brought to bear consistently across relevant EU member states to ensure that permanent, viable operations of member firms were established within the EU.

Chief EU negotiator Michel Barnier could not have been clearer in addressing financial services firms and regulators at the Eurofi General Assembly in June 2020:

> we must look beyond short-term adaptation and fragmentation costs, to [the EU's] long-term interests:
> - Building our Capital Markets Union...;
> - Further deepening the Banking Union and;
> - Fostering the international role of the euro.
>
> And so, we will only grant equivalences in those areas where it is clearly in the interests of the EU; of our financial stability; our investors and our consumers.
>
> Furthermore, as you know well, in some areas – such as insurance, commercial bank lending or deposit-taking – EU law does not provide for the possibility to award equivalences that would grant market access to third-country firms.
>
> In these areas, if British firms want to provide services in the EU, they must ask for an authorisation in the EU. Or comply with all the national regimes of those EU Member States where they want to continue to be active.
>
> Nothing in the agreement we are negotiating will change this![32]

The EY Financial Services Brexit Tracker[33] estimated that as of 1 October 2020 some 7,500 financial services job had moved from the UK to continental

---

[32] Eurofi General Assembly, Remarks by Michel Barnier, 30 June 2020.
[33] EY, *EY Financial Services Brexit Tracker*, 1 October 2020.

Europe since the Brexit referendum with a further 2,800 new roles created for which hiring had been made or was being undertaken locally within the EU. Assets transferred totalled some £1.2 trillion as banks physically moved loans made to EU customers to entities set up within the EU. Thirty-six new insurance subsidiaries had been established in the EU and around thirty million insurance contracts had been transferred to subsidiaries there. The two largest banks in Ireland supervised by the Central Bank of Ireland by the end of 2020 were no longer AIB and Bank of Ireland but Bank of America and Barclays Bank Ireland as these US and UK-headquartered organizations chose Ireland as the location for their new EU banking headquarters.

No single centre in the EU has emerged as the destination of choice for relocating UK-established financial services businesses, with decisions made in favour spread across Dublin, Luxembourg, Frankfurt, Paris and Amsterdam depending on firm. Lloyd's of London has established its European base in Brussels at an estimated cost of £250 million for the process alone.

The short-term impact of Brexit on UK's financial services

The fact that there was a Brexit Agreement has been widely expected to reintroduce some degree of goodwill in the tone of the many ongoing discussions that remain to be had over the years ahead as the EU and the UK forge a new partnership. Part One, Title 1, Article COMPROV 1, of the agreement declares the purpose of the agreement to establish 'the basis for a broad relationship between the parties, within an area of prosperity and good neighbourliness characterised by close and peaceful relations based on cooperation, respectful of the Parties' autonomy and sovereignty'.

But as this chapter has illustrated, negotiations over the last four years have been characterized by tension and a mutual lack of understanding in forging any meaningful agreement and cooperation so far as financial services are concerned, even if cooperation between cross-border financial firm supervisors has remained more or less cordial. The desire of the UK government, the Bank of England and regulators to assert sovereignty in financial services rule making has resulted in an EU denial of available equivalence decisions except in the temporary decision in favour of UK centralized clearing platforms. The refusal by UK authorities to commit to an identical financial rule set to that of the EU going forward is inevitable and understandable, but this has led EU officials to ask how the UK rules are likely to diverge based on the suspicion that the UK tendency will be towards weakened standards in order to enhance the UK's relative competitiveness.

How this UK rule-making autonomy manifests itself in terms of divergence of financial services rule books is uncertain. At the annual City of London Mansion House event for financial services firms and their regulators in November 2020, Sam Woods, deputy governor of the Bank of England and chief executive officer of the Prudential Regulatory Authority, stated:

> The [UK] government proposes to move back to a more British style of regulation, with the rules made by regulators rather than set out in law . . . [That said,] we have no interest whatsoever in a race-to-the-bottom approach to financial regulation.
>
> Despite the fears sometimes articulated by politicians in the EU, we have absolutely no intention of weakening prudential regulation in the U.K. [However,] it is clear that neither the EU nor the UK wishes to be shackled in lockstep with the other.[34]

Many financial firms in the UK point to the gold-plating of prudential and conduct regulation in the UK since the British government is highly unlikely to seek to compete unfairly through deregulation. Capital and liquidity requirements are higher for most equivalent banks and insurance companies in the UK compared to the EU and the United States. The largest UK-established banks have been forced to legally separate their retail and SME banking activities from other businesses, so-called 'ring fencing', a unique and expensive exercise not replicated by the rest of Europe or the United States. Personal accountability of senior officers of financial institutions is defined under the UK's Senior Managers' Regime which codifies a regime, the contravention of which can lead to up to ten years imprisonment, far tougher than across the EU.

The relative size of the UK financial centre to the economy as a whole continues to be referenced by UK officials as the rationale for rules that are tougher than elsewhere. There would inevitably be tension between a future British government seeking a prospectus to continue to promote the UK as

---

[34] Bank of England, *Strong and Simple* – Speech Given by Sam Woods, 12 November 2020.

an internationally competitive financial centre to potential inward investors through deregulation and independent regulators led by an autonomous Bank of England, charged by law to maintain financial stability and promote market integrity and jealous to preserve those powers.

Nevertheless, the EU remains wary of the extent of possible future UK regulatory divergence. Brussels has insisted that the UK must wait until well after 1 January 2021 to learn what market access rights its financial services firms will enjoy in the EU in the future, rendering any such rights meaningless to businesses that have needed to plan how they can continue to service EU-based customers post Brexit for the two years leading up to the Brexit Agreement. Despite UK officials submitting answers to twenty-eight EU questionnaires to demonstrate how UK rules are identical to those in the EU for relevant parts of financial services for which equivalence awards are possible – the rules had to be identical explicitly as a condition of the UK's ongoing membership of the EU and through its transition to exit – the EU when announcing the Brexit Agreement stated:

> A series of further clarifications will be needed from [the UK], in particular regarding how the [UK] will diverge from EU frameworks after 31 December.
>
> For these reasons, the Commission cannot finalise its [equivalence] assessment[s] . . . and therefore will not take the decisions at this point in time. The assessments will continue.

The EU should be expected to monitor closely signs of perceived regulatory divergence by the UK. In a speech to the ISDA conference in early December 2020,[35] Robert Ophèle, chair of France's securities markets regulator, the AMF, contrasted the approach of the UK's Financial Conduct Authority (FCA) with that of European Securities and Markets Authority (ESMA) and the European Commission, urging the EU authorities to be faster and more pragmatic in support of its onshore financial markets, noting that the FCA had done just that in addressing derivatives trading and clearing in the context of Brexit. He highlighted comments by Andrew Bailey, then chief executive of the FCA,

---

[35] AMF, *Outlook for European Regulation,* Speech by Robert Ophèle, AMF Chairman – ISDA Conference, 2 December 2020.

who stated in 2019 that 'the UK regulatory system would evolve somewhat differently' after Brexit and that the FCA would 'take on board practical experience more rapidly', adding that UK regulation 'would be based more on principles'.

Ophèle also pointed to comments by UK chancellor Rishi Sunak made in late 2020 indicating that the '[UK] will use equivalence when it is in the UK's economic interests to do so'. Chair Ophèle went on:

> This definitely illustrates just how the UK will shape future financial market regulation domestically. It will become even more flexible with an ability to be agile and will have the strengthening of UK competitiveness at heart as provided by the FCA statutory objective.

Chair Ophèle was mistaken in pointing to an FCA statutory objective of UK competitiveness: in fact the third operational objective of the FCA is to promote 'competition' [between providers] in the interest of consumers.[36] Nevertheless, his observation highlights the determination with which the EU can be expected to look for evidence of UK political and regulatory behaviours, which may confer perceived unfair advantages to UK-based players.

Against this backdrop forward-looking equivalence determinations by the EU authorities in relation to the UK, when permitted under EU regulations, can be expected to be slow, bureaucratic, difficult to obtain and capable of withdrawal at short notice – as the Swiss Stock Exchange discovered at the end of June 2019 when the EU withdrew its permission for EU counterparties to trade stocks on the Swiss Stock Exchange by allowing its equivalence determination in respect of the Swiss Exchange to lapse because of a perceived failure to make progress on other, unrelated economic treaty matters between the two parties.

The EU is clear that awarding an equivalence determination is both a technical and a political process; it is unilateral and not subject to negotiation.[37] The UK lobby sought to persuade the EU to temper the unilateral nature of its equivalence regime through establishment of official fora to discuss and agree rule formulation and divergence. What emerged was one of a number of joint declarations made at the time of the Trade & Cooperation Agreement

---

[36] Financial Conduct Authority, *About the FCA*, 24 September 2020.
[37] Eurofi General Assembly, Remarks by Michel Barnier, 30 June 2020. https://ec.europa.eu/info/publications/speech-michel-barnier-eurofi-general-assembly_en.

that committed the UK and the EU to 'agree to establish structured regulatory cooperation on financial services', to be known as the Joint Declaration on Financial Services Regulatory Cooperation or memorandum of understanding ('MOU'). Though this was expected to be agreed by the end of March 2021, and though both parties confirmed at that time that the text had been agreed in principle, no MoU has as yet been formally agreed or published.

The EU Commissioner for Financial Services, Mairead McGuinness, has stated that the EU does not feel any pressure to rush decisions about financial services, whether in respect of the MoU or equivalence decisions in relation to UK financial services regulation. The best that can therefore be expected, assuming a political rapprochement which allows the MOU to be signed by both parties, is a forum where the UK and EU can discuss:

- regulatory developments and other issues of common interest
- the adoption, suspension and withdrawal of equivalence decisions
- market developments and financial stability issues
- enhanced cooperation and coordination including at international bodies

What seems certain is that the MOU will not be an 'agreement to agree' and will not fetter either party in terms of their independence with regard to regulatory, supervisory or other legal measures that each – unilaterally – considers appropriate. In the meantime, it seems that the EU will not resume assessing UK regulation from an equivalence perspective except on an emergency and temporary basis as in the case of clearing where insufficient EU-based infrastructure has yet been established to replace UK-based capacity.

We have already seen that an equivalence decision is not technically available for a wide range of underlying services, for example commercial banking and insurance broking, since it is not explicitly provided for in the underlying EU legal instrument regulating those activities.[38]

The non-binding declaration that accompanied the Brexit Agreement called on the UK and the EU to establish 'structured regulatory cooperation' allowing 'for an exchange of views and analysis relating to regulatory initiatives' and 'transparency and appropriate dialogue in the process of adoptions, suspension and withdrawal of equivalence decisions'. The declaration concluded that this framework for cooperation will include 'how to move forward with

---

[38] Ibid.

equivalence determinations between the Union and the United Kingdom, without prejudice to the unilateral and autonomous decision-making process of each side'. Despite the hopes of some that equivalence might become a more predictable and measured regime, few financial services businesses operating cross-border between the UK and the EU are likely to find the regime sufficiently predictable as a basis to organize their commercial activities. In assessing therefore what the potential impact of Brexit is on the UK-based financial services industry, we also need to consider the political doctrine of 'strategic autonomy' emerging for a wide range of products and services across the EU.

In September 2019, Bruno Le Maire, French economy and finance minister, addressed the 2019 Eurofi Financial Forum in Helsinki.[39] In seeking to kick-start stalled EU efforts to achieve CMU, he highlighted the need for the EU to 'do everything necessary to ensure [its] financial independence', stressing the importance of CMU to 'help us preserve our economic and financial sovereignty'. His verdict in respect of third-country equivalence regimes was that they should be reviewed 'to make sure that all existing equivalence regimes provide for the same level of investor and consumer protection' and 'to strike the right balance between open markets and the protection of legal sovereignty. We have been too swift in opening our markets and too shy protecting our legal sovereignty'. The verdict of market participants present that day, including me, was clear: financial market actors should not expect EU markets to be as open going forward.

This doctrine of legal and financial sovereignty for the EU continued to develop throughout 2020. European Council president Charles Michel addressed the Bruegel Institute in September 2020 in a speech entitled 'Strategic Autonomy for Europe – The Aim of Our Generation'. In an articulation of European collective autonomy, sovereignty and power, he itemized many areas of historic and forthcoming collective action, where Europe had been able or needed to strengthen its union and autonomy in the face of a rising 'global arc of instability' that had emerged around it. While recognizing the UK's choice in the Brexit referendum in favour of national sovereignty, he presented the

---

[39] Ministère de l'Economie et des Finances, Discours de Bruno le Maire, Ministre de l'Economie et des Finances, *The Future of the Capital Markets Union – Towards an Investment and Savings Union*, 13 September 2019.

choices that the UK now faced in the aftermath of Brexit as a dilemma in the following terms:

> What type of society do [the British] want? Would they rather maintain high standards? Or do they want to lower their standards, exposing their farmers and businesses to unfair, cut-throat competition from other parts of the world? The answer to that question will determine what level of access we can grant to our internal market.

He then pointed to a range of sovereign instruments available to the EU for it to pursue its sovereign agenda in pursuit of its own stability, standards and values including trade agreements, financial markets supervision, a digital agenda, the euro, sanctions and visas. AMF chair Ophèle's December 2020 ISDA speech,[40] referenced earlier, echoed some of these themes in the context of financial goals and markets:

> My idea of CMU is indeed to build a mature market for EU counterparts trading on EU platforms but firstly on EU currency denominated products. The creation of a strong EU market in euro-denominated derivatives from scratch is to be supported where possible, but trying to build up a GBP and USD derivatives markets [sic] in Europe with no critical mass of strong market players in these fields would be detrimental to European market players, without bringing any added value to the European market. Forcing them to hedge their positions in markets which by definition are less liquid than local markets of each currency would place them on an un-level playing field. . . . Regarding clearing services and more generally all post-trade infrastructures, the European Commission's aim is pretty clear: the goal is to ensure that the European Union has significant market infrastructures for all financial products issued by EU entities of those which are denominated in an EU currency. But also ensuring the implementation of this policy is appropriately phased in, in order to avoid triggering detrimental cliff edge effects.

Regarding the three UK clearing platforms for which the European Commission has adopted a time-limited eighteen months equivalence decision, he pointed to the likelihood that ESMA would conclude that at least some of these clearing services

---

[40] AMF, *Outlook for European Regulation*, Speech by Robert Ophèle, AMF Chairman – ISDA Conference, 2 December 2020.

are of such substantial systemic importance that they should not be allowed to be massively located outside the [EU] if they intend to provide services to EU firms. In the meantime, the European Commission expects EU industry to develop a clear process to reduce their exposures and reliance on UK CCPs. In the coming months the clearing services landscape within the EU may therefore evolve drastically, since some clearing operations may be relocated within the EU or to the UK.

Just before the Christmas Eve 2020 announcement of the Brexit Agreement, and independent of whether the Brexit Agreement would or would not be announced, EU financial services commissioner Mairead McGuinness referenced financial stability as a driving force in how the EU would respond to the 'logic of Brexit' and the assumed financial regulatory divergence that would follow:[41]

> I think some of the stakeholders or market participants believe that nothing will change. And we have been at pains to say, in every sector including the financial sector, that nothing will stay the same as it is now, and to prepare for change. . . . I know all the arguments that London is big, and we acknowledge that, and it has built up because it's been part of the European Union. . . . We are trying to take control of our system in a way that services our needs as Europeans, and also [ensure] that we're not vulnerable. So I think we need to look at that and be quite frank about it.

The political and regulatory signals from the EU are clear. The EU wishes to ensure strategic autonomy where it perceives potential vulnerability to its social, political and economic strategic interests. The EU sees cross-border financial services as strategic, particularly when it comes to Euro-denominated securities and the post-trade infrastructure that supports the clearing and settlement of all financial transactions on clearing platforms outside the EU by EU firms. Even the trading of shares of EU companies by EU counterparts has now forced on to EU exchanges, notwithstanding the cost in terms of best execution by prohibiting access to the most efficient and transparent pools of liquidity that may exist elsewhere.

Already Amsterdam has surpassed London as the European centre with the highest volumes of European share trading benefiting from an almost fourfold

---

[41] Sam Fleming and Jim Brunsden, 'EU Cannot Be "Captured" by City of London, Warns Financial Services Chief', *Financial Times*, 16 December 2020.

increase in volumes in January 2021 relative to December 2020, while volumes traded in London declined sharply.[42] Data published by IHS Markit showed that the trading of Euro-denominated interest rate swaps in London dropped from nearly 40 per cent of the total in July 2020 to 10 per cent in January 2020, with volume shifting to New York, Paris and Amsterdam. EU exchanges and New York in particular benefited with increases in share from around 10 per cent to 25 per cent and 20 per cent respectively for the same periods.[43] As EU regulators have refused to recognize UK exchanges as equivalent to date, so EU-based institutions have been forced to shift trading away to recognized exchanges within the EU or other third countries whose exchanges have been recognized as equivalent.

In securities clearing where temporary recognition has been granted in favour of three UK venues until June 2022, the EU in January 2021 made equivalence decisions in favour of US Securities and Exchange Commission regulated central counterparties.[44]

Giving evidence to the UK Parliament's Treasury Select Committee on 24 February 2021, Governor of the Bank of England Andrew Bailey warned that the EU risked a serious escalation in tension in its relations with the UK if it attempted to force the move of clearing of all Euro-denominated derivatives from London, particularly the three-quarters or so of current volumes undertaken by non-EU banks which Bailey predicted was 'where the debate is heading. . . . That would be very controversial and, would be a very serious escalation of the issue'.

There will be increased costs borne by EU savers, investors, corporates and governments in migrating onshore to the EU the financing, risk management and trading activities currently undertaken largely in London, but the EU perceives this to be a cost that must be borne[45] to further strategic autonomy and reduce vulnerability particularly to unfair competition that is likely to arise as the UK looks for ways to compete through lighter touch regulation.

As we have shown the quantum of activity at stake is significant for both the UK and the EU. Around one-third of total financial activity across the EU27

---

[42] Philip Stafford, 'Amsterdam Ousts London as Europe's Top Share Trading Hub', *Financial Times*, 10 February 2021.
[43] Philip Stafford, 'Fresh Blow for London as Euro Derivatives Trading Floods Out', *Financial Times*, 11 February 2021.
[44] Stefan Boscia, 'EU Opens Up to US Clearing Houses in Blow to City of London', *CityAM*, 16 February 2021.
[45] Eurofi General Assembly, 'Remarks by Michel Barnier', 30 June 2020.

plus the UK is undertaken in the UK. The most significant market dominated by UK-based firms are derivatives and foreign exchange trading, where over 80 per cent of total activity is concentrated in the UK and supported by the underlying infrastructure for such markets to operate efficiently. In asset management, over 40 per cent of total savings and pensions assets are managed from the UK, over half of European private equity fundraising takes place in the UK while until December 2020 a third of equities trading and a quarter of all IPO business was transacted in the UK.

As New Financial put it in their October 2020 report:[46]

> The UK is the largest [European] market in 80% of the financial sector metrics we looked at . . . Brexit means that the [EU] will be losing its largest market in the vast majority of the different sectors of banking and finance.

Brexit will inevitably continue to raise further barriers to the efficiency of cross-border UK–EU financial business at the expense of further existing jobs and tax revenues in the UK. Execution costs borne by governments, corporates and financial institutions, and therefore ultimately by investors and consumers, for financial products will rise in both the UK and the EU as markets fragment, liquidity reduces and some activity relocates beyond Europe as a whole to faster growing markets in North America and Asia.

Some have referred to these rising barriers as 'adding sand to the machinery',[47] others suggesting that the changes at stake are more significant. It seems to me that 'sand', with its implication of a little extra grit generating heat that needs to be overcome to maintain momentum, understates the efforts that are now required collectively across the British government, regulators and the industry for the UK to retain its global leadership position in financial services.

The asset management industry in the UK is dependent on the international convention that allows asset servicers operating in the jurisdiction of the end customer to delegate to specialist portfolio managers who decide how exactly assets under management should be invested. We have seen the quantum of Europe's assets under management managed by highly specialized managers covering assets located globally but operating in the UK. Any attempt by the EU

---

[46] Panagiotis Asimkopoulos, Manuel Haymoz and William Wright, New Financial, *Beyond Brexit: The Future of UK Banking & Finance*, New Financial, October 2020.
[47] Jonathan Ford, 'Future of the City: How London's Reach Will Shrink after Brexit', *Financial Times*, 9 December 2020.

to tackle this so-called delegation of portfolio management services to a third country like the UK would likely involve also attacking delegation to specialist managers of EU assets under management in the United States and Asia. There are very good reasons for offshore management of EU assets to continue, including access to the best and most specialized managers leading to better performance, and the economies of scale of pooled management leading to lower costs. But tackling delegation is a big unknown and one currently under review between ESMA, the EU regulator with competence to oversee asset management and the European Commission.[48] Any change would impact not only the asset managers based in the UK but also all the firms on whom they rely providing trading, broking, research, custody, clearing, administration, legal and accounting services.

Given the significant shift in activity that is already underway – £1.2 trillion of banking assets transferred to the EU from the UK together with 7,500 jobs so far – UK policymakers and regulators, working with the industry, will need to be imaginative, bold and rapid in resetting and promoting the UK as one of the world's great financial centres. But they will only do so if they are united in their desire to seek to retain and develop the UK's global position in the industry.

Some voices suggest that the reducing of the dependence of the UK on financial services and the perceived inequalities it accentuates could be an unexpected benefit of Brexit. Sir Paul Tucker, former deputy governor of the Bank of England, told the *Financial Times*:[49]

> I think we forget how alien London's extreme wealth appears to the rest of the country, and the social and efficiency problems caused by pricing people out of housing and diverting so many talented people into financial careers. It might be healthy for the UK if London was less dominant.

Throughout 2020 and early 2021, the British government was battling the Covid-19 pandemic and the heat of Brexit negotiations, and it had yet to articulate a bold vision that would reset the UK as a twenty-first-century global financial centre. Specific topics are under consideration without an overarching policy narrative to tie them together.

---

[48] Letter from Chairman Steven Maijoor to European Commission vice president Valdis Dombrovskis, ESMA, 18 August 2020.
[49] Jonathan Ford, 'Future of the City: How London's Reach Will Shrink after Brexit', *Financial Times*, 9 December 2020.

On 26 February 2021, the government-sponsored Independent Report on the UK Fintech Sector, led by Ron Kalifa OBE, reported highlighting the opportunity to create highly skilled jobs across the UK, boost trade and extend the UK's competitive edge over other leading fintech hubs. It set out a series of proposals for how the UK could build on its existing strengths, create the right framework for continued innovation and support UK firms to scale.[50]

A British-government-sponsored review, led by Lord Jonathan Hill (a former EU commissioner), on the competitiveness of the UK as a location to list the shares of companies is underway, even though in recent years this has not been a significant part of the balance of financial services trade in the UK's favour.

An HM Treasury review of Solvency II is underway which could lead to meaningful divergence in the prudential standards applied to UK-based insurance companies.[51]

An HM Treasury review of the architecture and substance of post-GFC financial services regulation in the UK has been initiated and welcomed by the UK-based industry.[52] There is, to date, little sense of any real political momentum to simplify substantially the burden of regulation and taxation on UK-based financial services firms. Regulators can be expected to resist any attempt by the government to include industry competitiveness as a statutory objective to which they should be held accountable.

The state of public finances does not bode well for the UK's Treasury being able to rebase taxation of financial services firms or offer tax incentives at an individual level to attract global leaders in the industry to base themselves in the UK. If anything, rising calls to reform capital gains tax in the UK could have wide-ranging consequences on businesses in general and undermine a core benefit for the principals of private equity firms to be based in the UK.

And while Robert Ophèle mistakenly assumed that UK regulators had a statutory duty to promote the competitiveness of the UK as a location from

---

[50] https://www.gov.uk/government/publications/the-kalifa-review-of-uk-fintech, February 2021.
[51] assets.publishing.service.gov.uk/government/uploads/system/uploads/attachment_data/file/927345/Solvency_II_Call_for_Evidence.pdf, October 2020.
[52] https://www.gov.uk/government/consultations/future-regulatory-framework-frf-review-consultation, October 2020.

which to undertake financial services,[53] they do not. They will need to have such a duty imposed on them, overseen through rigorous public scrutiny from the UK's Parliament, if the UK hopes to recover from the long-term impacts on its financial centre of its exit from the EU.

Medium-term impact of Brexit and other factors on London as the global financial centre

Writer and former banker Philip Augar predicted the decline of the City of London as a global financial centre in the late 1990s and early 2000s, particularly as the UK's indigenous merchant/investment banks were largely absorbed into global US and European firms.

By the end of 2020 he recognized that he had underestimated the power of the cluster effect that had endured, bringing together unique combinations of international talent in front and back office functions including digital and technological areas, as well as the legal, financial and compliance assurance skills readily available to support the UK's financial services ecosystem. He believes this cluster benefit will continue to act as a powerful factor supporting London but was cautious about the medium-term outlook:

> It is hard to read Brexit as a positive for the City of London if you peer forward 20 years into the future. It may not be a catastrophe, but it will place restrictions and frictions where there were none before.

Former Citigroup and Lloyds Banking Group chair Sir Win Bischoff, who chairs JP Morgan in Europe, pointed to these cluster benefits as a key source of the UK's competitive advantage historically, as well as the consequences of measures taken in other jurisdictions such as the US Interest Equalization Tax in 1963, which had driven capital markets business from New York to London. Though four of JP Morgan's eight global business heads were based in London at the end of 2020, he argues that London's pre-eminence will erode over time and that a continued relocation of EU-related financial activity to the EU will continue:

---

[53] Speech by Robert Ophèle, AMF Chairman – ISDA Conference, AMF, *Outlook for European Regulation*, 2 December 2020.

> The EU is a vital market for the world's largest firms and there is a very strong political view that it needs to be more self-sufficient in financial services. JP Morgan, and others like us, are under real pressure not to letter box in Europe and we will not do so.

Strong and competitive financial centres are already emerging within the EU, though no single centre has absolute leadership. In 2018 Olivier Guersent, then director general for Financial Services at the European Commission, predicted to me that Paris and Frankfurt would emerge as the parallel leading poles for EU financial services with satellites emerging in Dublin, Amsterdam and Luxembourg with particular concentrations of expertise.

As William Wright, managing director of capital markets think tank New Financial, put it at the end of 2020:

> Most large financial services players have executed their relocation plans in order to guarantee post-Brexit access to EU customers and markets. They can now afford to be relatively agnostic about the regulatory alignment versus divergence debate even though they would obviously prefer a single regime. Brexit is a sunk cost and firms will seek to generate shareholder returns from their EU establishments. These investments will not be reversed and are likely to promote greater comfort and familiarity in investing further within the EU as opportunities arise.

As the European business models of cross-border firms, and underlying markets, fragment, so the importance of regulatory cooperation and good relations on a supervisory level increase. Adam Farkas, former CEO of the European Banking Authority and CEO of the Association of Financial Markets in Europe, predicted an emerging close regulatory dialogue between EU and UK regulators, possibly on a more frequent basis than the current EU–US and EU–Japan models. He also pointed to the vital importance of international regulatory standard setters, such as the Basel Committee, IFRS, IOSCO and the FSB, as mechanisms for ensuring effective collaboration and consistency:

> The role of the Basel Committee is particularly critical in ensuring appropriate deference of regulators to and trust in each other's regulatory standards. My experience is that relations between the EU's Single Supervisory Mechanism and the Bank of England are excellent, though relations between the European Securities Markets Authority and its UK counterpart, the Financial Conduct Authority, have become more strained through Brexit negotiations.

Sébastien Raspiller, assistant secretary for the financial sector at the French Treasury, predicted:

> The development of Capital Markets Union in the EU will not happen overnight. But President Macron will continue to press for the EU's strategic autonomy.

Conclusion: Future competition in financial services between the UK, Europe and other world centres

Green finance and sustainable investing are recognized by many commentators as vital in driving future financial services activity and are likely to be areas where the UK and the EU compete vigorously. Sébastien Raspiller recognized the ambition of the UK to build on the platform of hosting COP 26 in Glasgow at the end of 2021 to establish an intellectual leadership that will attract investment in the UK. However, he commented:

> Green finance is as much a political and social project as it is technical, financial and regulatory. Many different visions and views on appropriate standards exist and the topic is politically critical for world leaders, citizens and many NGOs. European progress relative to an indifferent Trump-led US will probably erode under a far more engaged Biden administration keen to reassert its role as a global leader in many areas, and it will therefore be difficult for any jurisdiction to establish financial leadership.

Chris Cummings, CEO of the Investment Management Association in the UK representing the investment management sector, has said:

> Our industry's cross-border leadership position is built on excellence in complex areas of investment, for example multi-asset, target date and liability-led. We are well placed to develop expertise and leadership in the complex and emerging field of green and responsible asset management. But we are in a very competitive world and cannot be complacent. Asset management is a target industry for the EU, and for France in particular.

Both Cummings and his counterpart at the Association of British Insurers, Huw Evans, also emphasize the opportunities that digitalization, the application of artificial intelligence and other forms of financial technology represent in modernizing operating practices, improving risk management and lowering costs to make their respective sectors more competitive. Evans says:

> The draw of the UK as a global insurance centre was not the EU passport and single rulebook. Bigger forces than Brexit will define our future. In addition to the opportunities and threats of cyber and climate risks, the UK's financial technology success will help us to drive efficiency in how we insure risks to underpin our relative competitive position.

Raspiller also points to the role of BigTech and the fact that London has already attracted the European headquarters of Google, Amazon, Facebook, Apple and Microsoft:

> The so-called GAFAs will no doubt play a major role in how the financial services sector develops. Their investment will help UK-based financial services by virtue of this proximity.

Overall, Raspiller believes that London and New York will remain global financial centres, but they will not be as dominant as they have been over the last fifteen years.

Bischoff agrees, predicting the continuing growth of Hong Kong and Shanghai as global financial centres in which China will increasingly focus its financial ambitions and apply the financial services expertise it has derived through its presence in international markets like London and New York and through joint venture structures that it has permitted with global players in its domestic markets.

All agree that there are substantial opportunities available to the UK as financial services markets develop globally. While business models which see Asian-focused banks and insurers like HSBC, Standard Chartered and Prudential headquartered in the UK are now seen as accidents of history, many see the opportunities for the UK to develop global expertise that will continue to draw global investment and talent to the net benefit of the UK's economy and wider society.

They point, however, to the need for a new prospectus for the UK with an overarching and clear policy narrative from government, supported by regulators who are charged with including the UK's competitiveness as part of their statutory objectives against which they should be measured and held accountable. While applauding the efforts of Lord Grimstone, minister at the Department for International Trade, to promote the UK as a financial centre globally, the development and articulation of a coherent, integrated British government policy for financial services into which regulatory goals are explicitly connected are seen as vital.

In particular, the UK has yet to see a coherent and cohesive joining up of the Prime Minister's 'boosterism' vision with a regulatory approach explicitly focused on fostering and supporting innovation except on a piecemeal basis in fintech.

William Wright feels the UK needs a change of approach:

> Over the next 10 years, the EU will account for only 10% of total global growth in capital markets activity while Asia will account for 58% of that growth. The United Kingdom needs to recalibrate and tailor its policy to reflect these realities. . . . An EU regulatory framework for financial services that has to be codified in great detail to bind 27 member states is not the right model for the United Kingdom. And the United Kingdom will need to act with humility. Expecting fast growing markets to come to London may not be a successful strategy: we should think about exporting our expertise to those markets instead.

To many, the lack of a coherent and overarching vision to which the British government and regulators are working in lockstep remains the biggest risk to the UK's financial services pre-eminence. As Bob Wigley, chair of finance industry trade association UK Finance and author of the 2008 report for then mayor of London, Boris Johnson, entitled 'London, Winning in the Decade Ahead', puts it:

> Those who say today that 'only' 7500 jobs and $1.2trn of assets have moved to the Continent and that threats to London's dominance are overdone are missing the point. As it has taken centuries for London to establish its position as a leading global financial centre, so it will take a decade for the real impact of the loss of passporting to be felt.

Key determinants of the rate of drift to the Continent will include:

1. decisions by the European Union in relation to the asset management industry and how fast the buy side (which the banking industry serves) moves its centre of gravity away from London;
2. the ultimate decision on clearing when revisited by the European Union in 18 months' time; and
3. whether the British government creates, with industry help, a compelling vision for the United Kingdom as a leading global financial centre.

Wigley's proposal for the overarching competitiveness manifesto of government is clear and draws on previous policies from the last forty years, which have contributed to the UK's success. He says:

> We can reasonably assume that regulation will stay strong. What the industry needs then are some strong positive reasons for firms which have a choice to locate activities outside the European Union to locate them in the United Kingdom – including:
>
> 1. an internationally competitive aggregate rate of tax on financial services activities within the United Kingdom that is assured over the medium term;
> 2. continuing flexible labour laws to accommodate the necessary regular adjustments in a cyclical industry; and
> 3. the facilitation of labour mobility through the visa system.

Without these, the drift will accelerate and will likely meet the worst estimates which some have recently discounted. Any other policy initiatives may be helpful but ultimately these will drive the outcome.

Of the three, tax will be the long term driver. Here the British government would do well to focus on maintaining the long term size of the tax base from financial services and not focus on its short term potential to shore up its immediate fiscal shortfall.

Bibliography

AMF, (2020), 'Outlook for European Regulation', *Speech by Robert Ophèle, AMF Chairman – ISDA Conference*, 2 December.

Armakolla, A., Douady, R., Laurent, J-P., Molteni, F., (2017), 'Repurchase Agreements and the European Sovereign Debt Crises: The Role of European Clearing Houses', *Working Paper*, 6 October.

Asimkopoulos, P., Haymoz, M. and Wright, W., (2020), 'Beyond Brexit: The Future of UK Banking and Finance', *New Financial*, October.

Bank of England, (1989), 'London as an International Financial Centre', *Quarterly Bulletin*, 516–528. November.

Bank of England, (2016), *Monetary Policy Summary and Minutes of the Monetary Policy Committee Ending on 11 May 2016*, 12 May.

Bank of England, (2020), 'Strong and Simple', *Speech Given by Deputy Governor Sam Woods*, 12 November

Bank for International Settlements, (2019), 'Foreign Exchange Turnover in April 2019', *Triennial Central Bank Survey*, 16 September.

Bank for International Settlements, (2019), 'OTC Interest Rate Derivatives Turnover 1995–2019', 8 December

Benzie, R., (1992), 'The Development of the International Bond Market', *BIS Economic Papers No. 32*, January.

Boscia, S., (2021), 'EU Opens Up to US Clearing Houses in Blow to City of London', *CityAM*, 16 February.

City of London, (2018), *Press Release from Policy Chair Catherine McGuinness on White Paper*, 12 July.

City of London, (2020), *City History*, 19 June.

EU Directorate General for Internal Policies, (2017), 'Implications of Brexit on EU Financial Services', *Study for the ECON Committee*, June.

Eurofi, (2020), 'Remarks by Michel Barnier', *General Assembly*, 30 June.

EY, (2020), 'EY Financial Services Brexit Tracker', 1 October.

Financial Conduct Authority, (2020), 'About the FCA', 24 September.

Fleming, S. and Brunsden, J., (2020), 'EU Cannot Be Captured by City of London, Warns Financial Services Chief', *Financial Times*, 16 December.

Ford, Jonathan, (2020), 'Future of the City: How London's Reach Will Shrink After Brexit', *Financial Times*, 9 December.

Investment Association, (2020), 'Asset Management in the UK 2019 – 2020', *Investment Association Annual Survey*, 9, 19, 20, 104, September.

IRSG, (2017), *IRSG Report on Mutual Recognition – a Basis for Market Access After Brexit*, 11 April.

Kalifa, R., (2021), 'The Kalifa Review of UK Fintech', UK Government, February.

Maijoor, S., (2020), 'Letter to European Commission Vice President Valdis Dombrovskis', *ESMA*, 18 August.

Martin Arnold, (2016), "'Significant' Brexit Risk for 5,500 UK Groups Using EU Passporting', *Financial Times*, 20 September.

Mason, R., Walker, P. and Wintour, P., (2016), 'Boris Johnson Ridiculed by European Ministers After Prosecco Claim', *The Guardian*, 17 November.

Ministère de l'Economie et des Finances, (2019), 'The Future of the Capital Markets UnIon – Towards and Investment and Savings Union', *Speech by Bruno le Maire*, 13 September.

PwC for UK Finance, (2019), 'Total Tax Contribution of the UK Banking Sector', *A Publication Prepared by PwC for UK Finance, Fifth Edition*, October.

PwC and City of London, (2020), 'The Total Tax Contribution of UK Financial Services in 2019', *12th Edition*, January.

Roberts, R., (1992), *Schroders Merchants and Bankers*, Chapters 3 to 5, The Macmillan Press

Schenk, C., (2019), 'The City and Financial Services: Historical Perspectives on the Brexit Debate', *The Political Quarterly*, 90 (S2): 14, February.

Stafford, P., (2021), 'Amsterdam Ousts London as Europe's Top Share Trading Hub', *Financial Times*, 10 February.

Stafford, P., (2021), 'Fresh Blow for London as Euro Derivatives Trading Floods Out', *Financial Times*, 11 February.

Swiss Re Institute, (2020), 'World Insurance: Riding Out the 2020 Pandemic Storm', *sigma No4/2020*, 10.

TheCityUK, (2018), 'The Government has Today Published a White Paper on the Future Relationship with the European Union', 12 July.

TheCityUK, (2020), 'Key Facts About UK-Based Financial and Related Professional Services', April.

TheCityUK, (2020), 'Key Facts about the UK as an International Financial Centre', 7–9, 18, December.

UK Government, (2018), 'The Future Relationship Between the United Kingdom and the European Union', *White Paper*, July.

UK Government, (2020), 'Trade and Cooperation Agreement Between the European Union and the European Atomic Energy Community, of the One Part, and the United Kingdom of Great Britain and Northern Ireland, of the Other Part', 24 December.

UK Government, Department for Exiting the European Union, (2017), 'The United Kingdom's Exit From and New Partnership With the European Union', *White Paper*, 15 May.

Wyman, Oliver, (2016), 'The Impact of the UK's Exit from the EU on the UK-Based Financial Services Sector', 5 October.

Yorke, H., (2020), 'Exclusive Boris Johnson Interview: From Bruges to Brexit, This is the End of Our 30-Year Struggle', *The Telegraph*, 26 December.

Z/Yen, Long Finance and FS Club, (2020), 'The Global Financial Centres Index 28', September.

Part II

The UK and the World

6

The future of British trade policy

Minister Hands

Setting the scene

The United Kingdom's (UK) vote to leave the European Union (EU) will undoubtedly remain in the memories of those alive at the time for decades to come. After an energic and, at points, rather bruising referendum campaign, the result was a surprise to some. But on that sunny June morning as the country woke to the result, it was clear to most, whether you were on the Remain or Leave side, that the UK's future and direction were undeniably different to the day before.

The implications of the result were seismic, and the engines of government needed to respond accordingly and quickly. Looking back to the pace at which this change occurred was striking – from the resignation of the Prime Minister, a subsequent leadership election in the Conservative Party, followed by an incoming administration of Theresa May, in the space of just nineteen days.

As perhaps the biggest peacetime policy initiative in British history, one of the first tasks of the May government was to decide how Brexit should be coordinated and consider whether the current machinery of government was sufficient to support the UK's orderly departure from the EU and fully grasp the opportunities ahead.

Clearly there was already existing expertise and experience within government. We had the institutional relationship between the UK and the EU led by United Kingdom's Representation to the European Union (UKREP), the diplomatic channels between the UK and EU27 member states through the Foreign Office, and UK Trade & Investment (UKTI) that supports British exporters and takes measures to make the UK attractive to overseas investors. But it was judged that the breadth and depth of EU Exit demanded more than minor departmental tinkering, which is why on 15 July 2016 the Department for Exiting the EU (DExEU) was created alongside the Department for International Trade (DIT). DExEU was to focus on planning and supporting EU Exit negotiations while also securing a future UK–EU relationship. DIT would develop, coordinate and deliver a new UK trade policy, including preparing for and negotiating free trade agreements (FTAs) and market access deals with non-EU countries, and planning to take up an independent seat at the WTO.

On that day I received a call from the Prime Minister who invited me to be Minister of State, working alongside Liam Fox as Secretary of State for International Trade. I agreed the offer quickly. I recognized then that this was a vital position in government to help shape how the UK would trade and engage with the rest of the world.

While both DIT and DExEU were created simultaneously, and in response to the same event, it is fair to say that political and media attention was largely focused on the immediate chronology of EU Exit: when the government would trigger Article 50 to commence formal negotiations, what the UK's negotiating objectives would be, whether there was political will to support these objectives in Parliament and Brussels, and how any agreement would be ratified and when.

The fact that these questions were largely, though not exclusively, for DExEU and No 10 Downing Street to answer had considerable advantages for DIT. It gave the department the opportunity to engage in extensive planning and consultation about the nature of the UK's trade policy going forward, along with the space and time to recruit the right people and in the right numbers to support these aims. With the creation of DIT, existing functions across government were brought together: UK Export Finance, the Defence & Security Organisation, the GREAT Campaign and UK Trade & Investment. The department inherited about 2,500 staff, including around 1,250 based in 108 locations overseas or in regional teams. As of January 2021, there are over 5,100 working in the Department for International Trade, of whom over 1,500 are based overseas in 119 countries. The department now includes:

- *Global Trade and Investment* responsible for driving growth in the value of UK exports and supporting investment into and out of the UK.
- *Trade Policy Group (TPG)* responsible for delivering the best international trading framework for the whole of the UK to maximize global trade and investment opportunities.

- *The GREAT Campaign* working with government departments across Whitehall to raise the profile and reputation of the UK abroad.
- *UK Export Finance (UKEF)*, founded in 1919, the world's first export credit agency.
- *Overseas Staff and HM Trade Commissioners*, responsible for supporting UK exports and investment across the world, divided into nine regions.
- *Strategic Capability* in the Ministerial Strategy and Global Strategy Directorates that fuse trade, economics and foreign policy, and place the day-to-day work of the department on a long-term strategic horizon
- *Trade Remedies* capability, which will become the Trade Remedies Authority with the passage of the Trade Act.

The Trade Policy Group started with fifty staff from the Department of Business and has grown to over 900 today. It includes trade negotiations capability, which delivers continuity agreements, new free trade agreements and economic partnerships agreements (EPAs). TPG also includes bilateral trade relations capability to tackle individual market access barriers directly. We have also re-energized the centuries-old Board of Trade with advisers from academia, business and public life.

My contribution will focus on defining this policy and giving an account of UK trade policy in action.

An independent trade policy

The ability to pursue an independent trade policy is a clear and exciting opportunity, but to capitalize on this opportunity effectively requires more than just eager anticipation and goodwill. In the four years since its inception, the Department for International Trade took a consultative approach to carefully planning and ambitiously pursuing the UK's economic interests at home and abroad.

The UK's historic and current prosperity has relied on the strength of its global networks, diverse trading relationships and an abundance of inward and onward investment, inputs and ideas. The success of UK future trade policy is therefore not a 'nice to have' or an optional extra within a broader macroeconomic picture but is instead an active and integral ingredient to the UK's future prosperity.

Trade has always been crucial to our success, and this was true even during the UK's membership of the EU. The key difference, however, is that our trade policy can now be exclusively tailored to meet the needs of every nation and region of the UK, rather than balanced against the diverse and competing interests of twenty-seven nation states. Our positions were developed with support from public consultations, specialist Trade Advisory Groups and the Board of Trade. The fruits of these efforts are already visible, with the promise of more to come. In addition, we are committed to transparency and working closely with Parliament to enable effective scrutiny of our trade agenda and to ensure that parliamentarians, UK citizens and businesses have access to information on trade negotiations. We will continue to keep Parliament updated on negotiations as they progress, including close engagement with the International Trade Committee in the House of Commons and the International Agreements Committee in the House of Lords.

HM government's ambitions on trade policy

The UK's independent trade policy can be best divided into two interdependent core elements: vision and strategy. A vision is a statement of values and aims, which are translated into specific objectives. Strategy is the art of organizing our capabilities to deliver on these objectives in accordance with our values.

In terms of vision, the government under Prime Minister Boris Johnson regards trade as more than the material exchange of goods and services, but also as an arena in which our values are both expressed and realized. This has been termed as a 'values-driven and value-generating' trade policy. If we are to be driven by these values, we need to be clear about what they are. On this we are unequivocal; our values are about respect for sovereignty, democracy and the rule of law combined with a fierce and unwavering commitment to high standards, environmental protection and human rights. A values-driven and values-generating trade policy includes a commitment to free and fair trade, and to strengthen rules-based international system. Often the term 'value-free' is used to describe a highly rational or objective determination of a situation. Yet in the context of UK trade policy, the opposite is true. Our trade policy will not be free of values but driven by them. We have learnt from the twin errors of values-free globalization and protectionism. We pursue an entirely rational and objective vision of a values-driven, value-generating trade policy which shapes how the world should be.

This means working to reform the multilateral system and deepening partnerships through preferential trade agreements in FTAs and WTO plurilateral agreements. Closer bilateral and regional partnerships create the alliances we need to help reform the WTO. We first prioritize as partners our friends and family of democratic nations with whom we share these values and high standards. Ultimately, as we trade with old friends and new partners in pursuit of UK prosperity, we do so confident in the knowledge that freest trade is the fairest trade and overall makes for a freer, fairer and more prosperous world. We are well on our way to securing the manifesto commitment of 80 per cent of UK trade through FTAs within three years of leaving the EU.

Global trade priorities

I would like to give some further insight into the UK's trading priorities, which will play a prominent role across all FTA negotiations. The UK's priorities on the global stage are fourfold. First, we want to boost economic resilience by boosting resilient supply chains. Second, we want to provide new opportunities for globally competitive UK firms by liberalizing trade in services. Third, we want to retool the global trading system to accommodate technological change, particularly the impact of digital trade. And finally, we want to use trade as a vehicle for driving clean growth. These four priorities help inform the key policy areas in which the UK will be ambitious including digital trade and the environment.

First, digital trade is a hugely valuable asset to the UK economy, forming a crucial part of the government's levelling up agenda and our economic recovery from the pandemic. Our services-driven economy places us at the centre of online transactions from across all sectors and our knowledge economy, supported by some of the world's most well-respected universities, means that we provide an ideal base for technology-driven organizations and those that rely on them for their business needs. With the onset of big data, artificial intelligence and the internet of things, the UK will be pursuing trade provisions which are modern and ambitious enough to foster continued innovation while ensuring citizens and consumers have appropriate protections. This will support our overall vision to lead the world in digital trade, creating an export-driven global digital economy that encourages innovation and investment, enables business of all sizes to succeed across borders and works for everyone.

Second, we are consistently clear there we do not need to choose between pursuing ambitious trade agreements on the one hand and ensuring environmental protections on the other. The UK has a long-standing commitment to uphold high environmental standards, and our negotiation teams are focused on securing strong sustainability provisions with key trading partners, drawing upon existing FTA precedent to enhance cooperation on areas such as biodiversity, forestry and supply chains. The UK's presidency of COP26 provides a unique opportunity to showcase our global leadership on climate change. As part of this, we can boast that our outset approaches to FTAs with the United States, Japan, New Zealand and Australia have committed to provisions to trade in low-carbon goods and services, supporting R&D and innovation in sectors such as offshore wind, smart energy systems, low-carbon advisory services and energy from waste.

Multilateral reform

The UK is endowed with some key strategic advantages. We have seats on all the world's major multilateral bodies, from the WTO and the IMF to the G7 and the G20, along with a permanent seat on the UN Security Council, and we take a leading role in the Commonwealth comprising some 2.4 billion people. Crucially, we not only enjoy numerous opportunities to make the case for free, fair and open trade but also have influence within these key institutions to make our vision a reality. Nowhere is a strong voice in favour of free, fair and rules-based international trade needed more than in the WTO.

If the effectiveness of the WTO is judged on its three key functions – negotiations, transparency and dispute settlement – then there is considerable and urgent need for improvement. The challenges presented by Covid-19 coupled with the rising threat of protectionism only make this situation all the more acute. It is therefore timely that the UK has now reclaimed its independent seat at the WTO and can be an avid and effective champion of genuine reform.

The UK has always been a firm supporter of the WTO, and, despite its faults, it remains the bedrock of the international trading system, guaranteeing the baseline of our trading relationships. Since 1995, the WTO has seen countries cut their import tariffs by two-thirds, which is testament to its long-standing contribution to free trade and global prosperity. Nevertheless, in a time of unprecedented uncertainty and instability, members of the WTO should be providing the dependability that brings confidence to businesses and consumers. After all, there is no rival or alternative organization on which to focus our efforts so it is incumbent on the UK to work with partners to ensure the WTO is fit for the challenges of the twenty-first century.

Since regaining our independent voice we have actively argued for higher ambition on key WTO issues at the Australia-hosted WTO Informal Ministerial Meeting and at the Saudi-led G20. We have co-sponsored a number of proposals and worked with like-minded members to advance UK priorities at the WTO. These include a proposal to improve transparency among WTO members, joining the 'Trade and Environmental Sustainability Structured Discussions' (TESSD) and adding the UK's name to initiatives aimed at using global trade policy to help tackle Covid-19.

We look forward to building on this momentum in 2021, including through the UK's presidency of the G7. We want to see trade restrictive practices rolled back and develop rules relevant to the modern global economy on issues such as digital trade in health care and environmental protection. We also want to ensure a fully functioning, two-tier compulsory, binding and impartial multilateral trade dispute settlement system and find a permanent resolution to the impasse of the Appellate Body. The 12th WTO Ministerial Conference will be a key milestone in advancing many of these issues.

The UK Global Tariff (UKGT)

We have also taken unilateral steps to promote free trade. For the first time in almost fifty years, the UK has created its own Most Favoured Nation (MFN) tariff policy, tailor-made for the UK economy. On 1 January 2021, the UKGT replaced the EU's Common External Tariff (CET) as the UK's MFN tariff schedule, almost doubling the number of tariff-free products relative to the EU, with just under 50 per cent of products now being tariff-free. The UKGT is simpler and easier to use than the EU's CET and includes unilateral liberalizations in several areas, including key inputs for manufacturing industries, goods not produced in the UK and the removal of so-called nuisance tariffs below 2 per cent.

Additionally, the UK's Global Tariff has liberalized a list of the 'Green 100' environmental goods to promote the deployment of renewable energy generation, energy efficiency, carbon capture and the circular economy through recycling and reducing single-use plastics. The UK Global Tariff is designed to support the government's wider ambitions for free trade agreements and our multilateral ambitions for the WTO.

Continuity agreements

I have previously mentioned the creation of two departments, DExEU and DIT, in the wake of the UK's decision to leave the EU. While much of the political drama was concentrated on the Article 50 negotiations, DIT ministers and officials were in the meantime quietly focused on ensuring that the agreements the UK was party to by virtue of its EU membership would continue to apply following the UK's departure, whatever the terms of that departure. This was a hugely important undertaking. It was about ensuring that businesses and consumers could enjoy continuity in their trading relationships, and make decisions and preparations for the future with confidence that there would be no cliff-edge at the end of the transition period. The programme was therefore focused on ensuring that UK businesses could get the same preferential tariffs, the same market opportunities and legal certainty for our world-leading services sector, the same chances to compete for government contracts, the same protections for our intellectual property and access the same other benefits of these agreements as they had while the UK was part of the EU.

Despite suggestions in some quarters that this undertaking was beyond the UK's capability, within two years the UK has secured trade agreements with sixty-three non-EU countries, covering £217 billion of total UK trade in 2019. This is a phenomenal achievement; no other country in history has negotiated trade deals with so many countries simultaneously. It is testament not just to the dedication and tenacity of UK officials around the world but also to the clear recognition from our global partners that trade with the UK is valuable and worth retaining and building on. If the scale and success of these continuity agreements surprised some, it was also suggested in those same quarters that the UK could only hope to replicate deals that the EU had negotiated and that we had little chance of being able to secure 'British-shaped' agreements. The UK–Japan Comprehensive Economic Partnership Agreement (CEPA) is the strongest indication yet that this pessimistic scepticism is misplaced.

The UK–Japan CEPA was signed by the Secretary of State Liz Truss and Japan's foreign minister on 23 October 2020 and is now in force. It gives legal certainty for our trading relationship with the world's third largest economy, is the most powerful symbol so far that the UK has retaken its place as an independent trading nation and offers a glimpse of what we can achieve outside the EU. The economic benefits of this agreement are even more encouraging. While the agreement secures the current £30 billion worth of trade between Japan and the UK, our analysis also shows that in the long run, the UK–Japan CEPA could increase bilateral trade by £15.7 billion and increase UK workers' wages by £800 million (compared to 2019 levels). What is crucial, however, is that this agreement not just achieves continuity and promising economic opportunities but also goes beyond what the EU was able to negotiate with Japan. The CEPA includes new provisions in digital and data on the free flow of data, a commitment to uphold the principles of net neutrality and a ban on unjustified data localization, as well as financial services provisions that allow the free flow of financial data, transparency on licensing procedures and enhanced regulatory cooperation between UK and Japanese authorities (such as HM Treasury and the Financial Services Agency of Japan).

It expands Japan's mobility offer, specifically on the scope of the intra-corporate transferee category. We have agreed on more liberal rules of origin, which remove certain restrictions contained in the EU–Japan Economic Partnership Agreement for sugar confectionary, biscuits and cakes. There are improvements in intellectual property rights, alongside a new provision on geographical indicators (GIs), that may allow more world-famous British products to receive protected recognition in Japan such as Scotch beef, Welsh lamb and English sparkling wine. Altogether this demonstrates how genuine bilateral trade negotiations with just two partners in a room can enhance the scope and bespoke quality of FTAs to the clear advantage of the businesses and consumers in the UK and Japan alike. This agreement has given additional momentum to other ongoing negotiations around the world.

New FTA negotiations

The UK–Japan CEPA gives a flavour of only what the UK can achieve. But the UK's trade policy is not just focused on securing and enhancing existing trade agreements but also securing new and quality agreements with old friends and new partners alike who the UK has never enjoyed formal trade agreements with before, until now. That is why we have embarked on an ambitious programme of free trade agreement negotiations in order to become a truly Global Britain. We aim to secure FTAs with countries accounting for 80 per cent of current UK total trade within three years of leaving the EU. While this target may appear ambitious, it is not only achievable but will serve to strengthen and accelerate our recovery from Covid-19. The pandemic has seen the reassertion of protectionism within the global trading environment, but we are clear one of the best antidotes against this unwelcome trend is to agree new FTAs to provide economic security at home and opportunities abroad.

The obvious place to start this endeavour is the United States. No two countries do more with each other than the UK and the United States. We are each other's closest allies with links at every level of society, culture and the economy, and a new free trade agreement would allow this relationship to grow even more. It is important we build upon our close trading relationship and resolve outstanding issues affecting producers and consumers on both sides of the Atlantic such as Section 232 tariffs and the Airbus and Boeing disputes. As two global economic leaders, an FTA would provide certainty that we can work together in building back better, leading the world in showing that cooperation and free trade are crucial to a global recovery. As the UK's biggest single trading partner, it is little surprise that analysis shows that the US deal we are seeking is expected to benefit every region and nation of the UK, delivering improved access for businesses, more investment, better jobs and higher wages. An ambitious deal could increase UK's GDP in the long run by £3.4 billion. Furthermore, the UK would be the largest economy the United States has ever signed a comprehensive bilateral trade agreement with.

It goes without saying that the NHS is not and never will be for sale, in this trade deal or any other. High standards are an essential component of the Global Britain brand, and we remain firmly committed to upholding our high environmental, food safety and animal welfare standards outside the EU.

At the time of writing, we have held five rounds of negotiations with the United States. We are in a good position to move forward with the Biden administration, and we look forward to discussions with the new United States Trade Representatives (USTR) in due course. In the meantime, our negotiations with Australia and New Zealand are making promising progress. Our nations share strong historical and familial ties, and rank among our closest allies. An ambitious, wide-ranging free trade agreement with Australia and New Zealand can help deliver the things that our people care about – better jobs, higher wages, greater choice and lower prices. These will be entirely progressive FTAs, equipping us to face the challenges and opportunities of the twenty-first century. Furthermore, both Australia and New Zealand are at the cutting edge of trade policy globally and are key players in the Indo-Pacific region. FTAs with both countries will assist the UK's pivot towards this dynamic area of the world. This will help diversify our trade, make our supply chains more resilient and make the UK less vulnerable to political and economic shocks. This economic security is important at a time of increased turbulence and uncertainty in the world.

The deal we have achieved with Japan, the deals we are confident of striking with Australia and New Zealand, and the existing continuity agreements with Canada, Chile, Mexico, Peru, Singapore and Vietnam pave the way for the UK's next step in its independent trade policy – the Comprehensive and Progressive Agreement for Trans-Pacific Partnership (CPTPP).

On 1 February 2021, we submitted our notification of intent to begin the Comprehensive and Progressive Agreement for Trans-Pacific Partnership accession process. This is the first formal step towards accession before formal negotiations start later in the year.

CPTPP countries accounted for £111 billion worth of UK trade in 2019, and the 2016–19 annual growth in UK trade with CPTPP member countries was 8 per cent a year. Trade is already increasing with these markets and joining CPTPP now will help boost UK's trade with these economies, bringing more opportunities for the UK, its economy and people. As the CPTPP removes tariffs on 95 per cent of goods traded between members and reduces other barriers to trade across four continents, UK businesses would only be set to benefit. To give just one example, the UK automotive manufacturers exported £3 billion worth of cars to the eleven CPTPP countries last year. Joining this trade block would therefore provide an invaluable support for an industry that employs 164,000 people in the UK and which overall could support an industrial revival in the UK.

Accession to the CPTPP would also diversify our supply chains and, as mentioned earlier, this would provide additional economic security in uncertain times. But crucially as part of our trade strategy, UK accession would help us secure our future place in the world and advance our longer-term strategic interests by placing the UK at the centre of a modern, progressive network of free trade agreements with dynamic economies.

Conclusion

I hope this outline of the work of the Department for International Trade has given a useful insight into the UK's trading priorities for the years ahead. For a department of relative youth, I am proud of how much it has accomplished over just four years and excited about what it can achieve in the future. Leaving the EU has already opened up many promising and enriching opportunities for the UK, and we stand ready to grasp them. We have reclaimed our place in the world as a truly independent and outward-looking trading nation.

So as the UK enhances its trading ties with long-standing friends and global partners, we can be confident that our values-driven and values-generating trade policy will project and protect our principles around the world while creating more jobs, greater choice, lower prices and overall prosperity for the peoples in every nation and region of the UK.

Bibliography

Hancké, Bob, Lauren Mathei & Artus Galiay. *Dancing in the Dark: What Brexit Means for UK-EU trade & UK Industry*. London School of Economics, July 2021

MacKenzie, Baker. *The Realities of Trade after Brexit*, 2017.

Nicolaides, Phedon A. & Thibault Roy. Brexit and Trade : Between Facts and Irrelevance. *Intereconomics*, 52(2) (2017): 100–106.

The Future of UK Trade after the UK-EU Trade and Cooperation Agreement : An Overview of the Implications of UK-EU TCA for UK Trade. Burges Samon, 2021.

Trade after Brexit. London: Institute for Government, December 2017.

7

Brexit and the 'special relationship'

Lord Robin Renwick

As the British ambassador to the United States in the 1990s, I banned any use in or by the embassy of the term 'special relationship' as it carried with it too much nostalgia and a mistaken assumption that the Americans, more often than not, could be expected to agree with us, come what may. The relationship, in reality, has been marked not only by many common actions but also by some fierce disagreements. The Americans, unsurprisingly, two and a half centuries after the Declaration of Independence, are unimpressed by British (and French) suppositions that, as Harold Macmillan put it, they may be more vigorous and powerful, but we are older and wiser than they are. They have seen too many examples of folly on our side of the Atlantic to take this seriously.

The reality or otherwise of the 'special relationship' was analysed in a book I published about the United States and Britain in peace and war, *Fighting with Allies* (Biteback 2018). The title was a quotation from Churchill who, dismayed at Roosevelt's failure to understand Soviet intentions in 1945, declared in exasperation that 'There is only one thing worse than fighting with allies and that is having to fight without them' – a thought that deserves to continue to be taken seriously today. In another moment of frustration, Churchill exclaimed that 'The United States can be relied upon to do the right thing in the end, having first exhausted the available alternatives!'

I always tried to persuade my colleagues and, with less success, the political class in Britain, to describe it more accurately and less sentimentally, as an *especially close relationship*, as incontrovertibly it is, above all in defence, the sharing of intelligence and nuclear cooperation. The spectacle of American and British forces fighting together in successive crises since the Second

World War, from Korea to Afghanistan, has led Americans and Britons alike to conclude that we are each other's closest and most dependable allies.

Lyndon Johnson was outraged at Harold Wilson's refusal to contribute even 'a platoon of bagpipers' to the Vietnam War and Tony Blair never recovered from his ill-fated support for George W. Bush in Iraq. But the United States remains the only ally that can give Britain decisive support in any major or even relatively minor conflict, as proved to be the case in Bosnia and the Falklands War. For all his magnificent rhetoric, Churchill knew that without the United States, the war against Germany was not actually winnable. On hearing of the attack on Pearl Harbour in December 1941, Churchill that night 'slept the sleep of the saved and thankful', in the conviction that victory now was certain.

Post the war, in 1949, Churchill's greatest ambition was realized in Article V of the North Atlantic Treaty, with the signatories agreeing to provide mutual assistance in the event of an attack on any one of them, committing the United States, for the first time in its history, to help defend its allies in Europe against any such attacks. The intent was in future to *deter* such aggression, the United States, as Montgomery put it, having turned up only at half-time in two world wars.

From that point of view, NATO today has claimed to be the most successful alliance in history. When Donald Trump raised doubts about it, he was reminded of the separation of powers in the US Constitution, as his fellow Republican, the Senate majority leader, Mitch McConnell, appeared on the steps of the Capitol to declare: 'NATO *is* important and the Russians (under Putin) are *not* our friends.' Joe Biden is a long-standing supporter of NATO and will seek to lay to rest any doubts about the continuing US commitment to the alliance.

The relationship between the United Kingdom (UK) and the United States has always been more important to Britain than to the United States. Yet, with the exception of Jeremy Corbyn, representing the strong undertow of anti-Americanism on the left in Britain, it has enjoyed bipartisan support on both sides of the Atlantic. Tony Blair was an American-style politician, who tried and failed to turn the Labour Party into a British version of the US Democratic Party. When, during the Falklands War, I called on Senator, now President, Joe Biden, I was greeted with the words: 'Don't give me that crap about self-determination for 1800 islanders. We are going to support you because you are British!'.

The supposedly 'special" relationship frequently has been declared defunct by the British press, only to display a Lazarus-like tendency to survive innumerable changes of President and Prime Minister. Richard Nixon and Henry Kissinger were astonished to find that Edward Heath, having negotiated Britain's entry to the European Economic Community, wanted deliberately to downgrade the relationship with the United States to demonstrate Britain's European credentials. This was not supported by his Foreign Secretary, Sir Alec Douglas-Home, who did his best to contain the damage, or by his other colleagues and nor has such an attitude ever been adopted by any subsequent British prime minister.

Ever since, the disparity of power between the United States and its European allies has increased exponentially. The smallest of the US armed services, the Marine Corps today has more planes than the RAF, more ships than the Royal Navy and more men under arms than the entire British (or French) armed forces. Yet, in engaging US forces in any conflict, Congress will always want to know whether US allies will participate, as Britain and France did in the war to liberate Kuwait.

Margaret Thatcher, who got on well with Mitterrand ('he likes women, you know', as on one occasion she observed to me!), was impressed that France, alone among the Europeans, 'had the stomach for a fight'. President Sarkozy's decision to take France back into NATO structures has transformed the defence relationship with the United States. Successive US defence secretaries, notably Robert Gates, who served in that position under both George W. Bush and Obama, have concluded that NATO has become a two-tier alliance, with only Britain and France capable of offering effective support in any serious conflict.

Beyond the extremely close defence relationship which, almost uniquely, extends to the interoperability of British and American forces with joint real-time battlefield intelligence, the United States and Britain are by far the largest investors in each other's countries, with Britain to date having received the lion's share of US investment in Europe, for reasons of language and because Britain post Thatcher has been perceived as more business friendly than many other European states. But the other great attraction for American companies investing in Britain has been tariff-free access to the wider European market, which was imperilled by Brexit but has now been preserved.

The ties of history, language and culture and the myriad personal connections, including within the political class, also have contributed to what often have been similar attitudes in world affairs. That said, prolonged exposure in Washington and elsewhere in the United States convinced me that many of my compatriots, including in the press and many politicians, understand the United States a good deal less well than they think they do.

Those who continue to imagine that the United States resembles us more than it does find it hard to understand that when governments change in Washington, 8,000 jobs change, not around 200, as in Britain, causing chaos for months after the election. The fascination exerted by New York and Los Angeles tends to obscure the fundamental differences in outlook and values between them and the mainly far more conservative myriad 'fly over' states in the mid-West and the South, with telling political effects, including Donald Trump being elected as the result of a white revolt. Hillary Clinton's pollster confirmed to me that she polled behind Trump in all categories of white voters, irrespective of age or income.

Most Americans do not have passports. While *l'Etat providence* is seen by many in Europe as the solution to our problems, many Americans harbour a distrust of government and frequently vote for deadlock in Washington, so that it can do less harm.

So much for the 'specially close' relationship as it has existed until now. Re Brexit, how did we get to the position we are now in?

When we negotiated the Fontainebleau agreement in 1984 reducing by nearly two-thirds the British budgetary contribution to the European Community, this appeared to have laid to rest the principal grievance about British membership of the EC. The Single European Act opened up the European market in services, the main strength of the UK economy. (The resultant mutual recognition of professional qualifications has been a casualty of Brexit.) There was wide support in Britain for the single market, so obviously beneficial to the member states. But there never was support for the much more integrationist ambitions of the Brussels institutions.

The UK's ill-judged attempt to link sterling to the Deutschmark in the European Exchange Rate Mechanism ended ignominiously on what became known as 'Black Wednesday'. But the British economy thrived once sterling was permitted to float freely against other currencies, in accordance with the principles of Adam Smith. Twenty percent smaller than that of France at the time, it is estimated to be slightly larger than that of France today.

After this experience with the ERM, there was never much likelihood of Britain joining the euro. When it was launched, the Bundesbank told me how dismayed they were that Chancellor Kohl had ignored their advice in permitting what they described as the 'Club Med' to join. Yet the euro, thanks especially to Mario Draghi, has proved remarkably resilient, albeit at a heavy cost to the economically weaker member states. As Donald Trump and many others have pointed out, the euro has been of enormous benefit to Germany by lowering the cost of its exports.

The British were strong supporters of the enlargement of the European Community to help consolidate democracy in the newly free countries in Eastern Europe – one of the truly great achievements of the EC. But the further integrationist steps in the 1992 Maastricht Treaty were close to the limit of what the House of Commons would accept. When it came to the European Constitution of 2004, the Labour government felt obliged to promise to submit it to a referendum. As a result of strenuous lobbying, the title eventually was changed. The new treaty otherwise remained essentially the same, but the government of Gordon Brown declined to submit it to a referendum, which they knew that they would lose. As I observed in Parliament at the time, this was a question not of the government losing the confidence of the people but of the people losing the confidence of the government.

For by this time a dangerous gap had opened up between officialdom in Britain, concerned not to be 'left out' of European integration and the sentiments of much of the electorate, who were allergic to it. It also was evident that an effect of enlargement had been further to increase the powers of the Commission, no longer finding it necessary to pay as much attention to the views of individual member states, except in the cases of Germany and France.

This since has culminated in the European Union (EU), at the instance of Chancellor Merkel, requiring *by majority vote* all member states to accept tens of thousands of the refugees or economic migrants who had arrived mainly in Greece, Italy or Germany which, despite a ruling against them by the European Court of Justice, Poland, Hungary and the Czech Republic have flatly refused to do.

Yet Brexit still could hardly have been more of a close run thing and could have been avoided with even a modicum of flexibility on the part of the EU. Concerned at the rise of the UK Independence Party and in an effort to paper over the differences in the Conservative Party, David Cameron, a Prime Minister more interested in tactics than in strategy, promised a referendum not on any specific measure but on the principle of Britain remaining in the EU, which he was far too confident of persuading the British people to vote to do.

Cameron failed to campaign across Europe, though he could have found allies in arguing for the Commission to be more responsive to the views of member states and their electorates and less intent on hyper regulation. Instead he embarked on a pseudo 're-negotiation' which yielded no credible results.

Because of a relatively successful economy and an exceptionally generous non-contributory benefits system, the UK had been acting as a magnet for migration from Eastern and Southern Europe – and, thanks to a more enterprise friendly environment, from France. London was acknowledged by the future president Macron to have become the sixth largest French city, ahead of Bordeaux and Strasbourg, with 250,000 French citizens officially believed to be living there and the real numbers much higher than that. The French in London are sufficiently numerous to elect their own representative to the French National Assembly.

Five million EU citizens currently are living and a high proportion of them are working in the UK and will be able to continue to do so post Brexit, though there will be much tougher criteria in future to qualify for employment in Britain. The nearly one million Polish workers and other EU migrants have made a huge contribution to the British economy, albeit doing so in part by holding down wages. In the year preceding the referendum, the UK experienced *net* immigration of 600,000 people, half of them from within the EU. Romanian beggars became a familiar feature of London street scenes.

Yet the Brexit outcome could hardly have been a more close run thing and could have been avoided with a modicum of flexibility in Brussels. Cameron sought to secure the agreement of the Commission that a country experiencing a surge in migration from within the EU could seek temporary relief from full freedom of movement. This was rejected in Brussels. An appeal to Merkel was rejected by her. In doing so, they made it probable that the Remainers would lose the vote. An intervention by Obama, obviously prompted by Cameron, in favour of the UK remaining in the EU did not help either.

Until the eve of the referendum, Cameron had hoped that Boris Johnson would not campaign to leave. Johnson famously drafted two documents, the one setting out the case to remain, the other to depart. But ever since serving as the *Daily Telegraph* correspondent there in the 1980s, Johnson had been a sceptic about the workings of Brussels. In declaring for Brexit, he was doubtful about his chances of winning, but his calculation seems to have been that, in any event, this would enhance his chances of succeeding Cameron in due course as the Conservative Party's leader.

Having declared for Brexit, he and others waged a very effective populist campaign, including promising that Brexit would be a relatively easy and painless process, based on the continuing community of interest with the EU and the large trade balance in its favour. There was a deliberate failure to judge the intensity of the likely reactions in Brussels or the disruption liable to affect long-standing existing trading relationships and industrial supply chains. The struggle through four years of negotiation to reach a new agreement with the EU owed much to the Hotel California ('You can check out, but you can never leave') mentality in Brussels, but gave definitively the lie to the supposed ease of exit promises made in the Brexit campaign.

In the event, the Brexiteers won by just 52 per cent of the votes to 48, with a clear majority of younger voters opting to remain. An immediate effect of the referendum was a 10 per cent slide in the value of sterling. There followed a complete failure of nerve by the Remainers who, despite having won 48 per cent of the votes, failed to unite behind demands for a second referendum once the terms of an exit were known. But contrary to many expectations, the British economy, until coronavirus, continued to perform better than most others in Europe, with unemployment remaining at 4 per cent.

As for the terms on which, at the end of the year, Brexit will take place, it never was realistic for the Commission to imagine that having voted to leave, the British would agree thereafter to be bound forever by the several thousand existing EU laws and regulations *and by future EU regulations* and the continuing jurisdiction of the European Court of Justice. In pursuit of the goal of a 'soft' Brexit, preserving UK access to the European market, Theresa May and her chief negotiator accepted just that, plus the proviso that henceforth, no exit would be possible from this arrangement without the agreement of the EU. As a former British negotiator with the EU, it would have been inconceivable for me to recommend such an outcome nor did there appear any chance of getting it accepted by Parliament. And so it proved, as it was voted down decisively three times in 2019.

The European Commission is a hyperactive regulatory machine, which naturally has seen the promulgation of new regulations as enhancing its own power and that of 'Europe' vis-à-vis the member states. The last British commissioner, Lord Hill, found that the word 'deregulation' was not allowed to be used in Brussels – it was permissible only to talk in terms of 'better regulation' – and the concept was *verboten* too. Many of this flood of regulations have been beneficial and necessary, but one does not have to be a Brexiteer to worry about plenty of other cases of regulatory overkill and the bureaucratization of the European economy.

Above all, the Commission failed to comprehend that this dense network of regulation favours larger companies, with their serried ranks of lawyers and accountants, at the expense of the smaller companies Europe wide, on whom the bulk of job creation depends. This, plus the deflationary effects of membership of the currency union on the southern member states, has been one of the factors behind the persistently high levels of unemployment and weak economic growth in important parts of the EU. There has been near to zero economic growth in Italy over the past decade.

Brexit created two potential nightmares within the Brussels institutions. The worst was that one or more other member states might be tempted to follow the deplorable British example. This encouraged the Brussels authorities to try to make the exit terms as unattractive as possible *pour décourager les autres*. The other fear has been that a Britain post Brexit no longer subject to EU regulations might function as a dangerous competitor, a sort of 'Singapore on the Thames'. Among the member states, France under President Macron was the most adamant about the need for no concessions to the British.

In reality, there was never going to be a Singapore on Thames, as support does not exist in Britain for the Singapore social model. As the eventual outcome showed, much of post Brexit regulation in Britain will resemble that in Europe, including the setting of some equally ambitious environmental targets and similar labour standards. But the whole point of Brexit was for Britain no longer to be governed largely from Brussels but by its own legislators and regulators.

The final phase of the Brexit negotiations unfolded like an episode of Kafka and the theatre of the absurd. The Commission appeared agitated about the supposed risk of massive UK state aids to industry, despite the fact that for the last four decades Britain has been far more parsimonious about such aids than, for instance, France or Germany. Johnson decided to fight to the death for the UK fishing industry, which accounts for 0.1 per cent of GDP, while being unable to negotiate any protections for UK financial services, which the EU declined to discuss. This was mirrored by Macron demanding no concessions to the British on fish or in any other respect. The EU kept declaring that all concessions must come from the UK. The financial markets to the end proved unwilling to believe that an agreement so clearly in the interests of both sides would not be achieved. The main business organizations throughout Europe lobbied for one, though they have not always proved to be very influential in Brussels.

It was only in the last month, then in the last week of the negotiation, that there was an outbreak of common sense, with Johnson sensibly staging a hasty climbdown over fisheries. He ended with a mere 25 per cent reduction in the EU catch from British waters, phased in over five-and-a-half years, while UK fisherman have lost out because of new controls preventing them selling much of their catch to the EU. The negotiation should rather have concentrated on phasing out the Dutch and Danish mega trawlers causing damage to the environment and fish stocks as they hoover up vast quantities of fish. At the end the two sides were arguing about £60 million worth of fish, regardless of the fact that no agreement which, until the eleventh hour, Johnson believed he was heading for would have imposed huge costs and disruption on the rest of the UK economy.

The near-term consequences would have been chaotic, with vast queues of lorries held up in Kent as they attempted to cross the Channel, custom controls liable to cause nightmarish delays, the disruption of industrial supply chains, permanent damage to the UK automobile and aerospace industries and all agricultural producers facing extremely high European tariffs.

The consequences undoubtedly would have also been negative for the car manufacturers and many other exporters in Europe, given the huge trade balance in favour of the EU. For the UK, after China and the US, is the EU's largest trading partner. Far from being a zero-sum game, this was one in which all the participants risked ending up as losers.

On the hugely more important issue of the so-called level playing field, both sides gave some ground. The EU side had to drop its insistence on the right to adopt 'lightning tariffs' automatically in response to divergences of standards they did not like, any role for the European Court of Justice in resolving disputes and the notion that assistance administered by the European Commission did not constitute state aid.

The British had to accept an independent arbitration mechanism, binding on both sides, to judge whether any challenged divergences or government aids constituted unfair competition. They also had to accept a high degree of convergence with EU regulation, in particular on the environment, workers' rights and social standards. The Johnson government could find substantial measures of deregulation challenged by the Commission as constituting unfair completion, though that would fall to be judged by independent arbitration. It also had to undertake not to withdraw from the European Convention on Human Rights, which is not part of the EU. It is this convention, or rather British judges' interpretation of it, which has been used to prevent the deportation of migrants brought by people traffickers to the UK and of a number of convicted rapists and murderers.

Despite the agreement being 1,264 pages long, with only one day allowed to debate it, the agreement was approved by Parliament, with the Labour leader, Sir Keir Starmer, insisting that his party must support it, the alternative being no deal. He also ruled out the possibility of the UK rejoining the EU.

As, despite tariff-free trade, the UK is no longer a member of the single market, the outcome is far from being frictionless trade, with customs documents required for goods heading for the EU and, predictably, the French authorities being especially difficult about these. This was bound to result in near-term disruption as many UK businesses were not prepared for this and the computerization intended to speed things up was not yet in place. There are permanent new checks in relation to rules of origin, all agricultural and food exports, product safety and the movement of plants and animals. On the British side, these checks will not be applied until July and are likely to be less aggressively applied thereafter. The effect will be permanently to impede UK food and agricultural exports to the rest of Europe. British professionals will no longer have the right to work in the EU. Nor, even when most of the coronavirus restrictions fall away, will UK citizens find it quite as easy to visit the EU.

Most importantly of all, the agreement did nothing to resolve the future relationship between the EU and the key financial services sector of the UK economy. To reduce the dominance of London in European financial services has been the long-standing ambition of the Commission, and the new commissioner for financial services, Mairead McGuinness, has vowed that in financial services 'nothing will remain the same'.[1]

Nevertheless, from a British perspective, this was a much better outcome than that achieved by Theresa May and was greeted with relief on both sides of the Channel. In common with the Europeans, the British people by now had had enough of Brexit: they wanted it to be over and done with. The decision of Sir Keir Starmer to require his party to support the agreement reflected that reality. With Nigel Farage, founder of the UK Independence Party, backing the agreement, ultra Brexiteers were left isolated and with no leverage, the huge Covid-induced blockages at the border having helped to convince many that the alternative would have been a great deal worse.

Michel Barnier, as the EU's chief negotiator with Britain, starting with an impossibly rigid mandate, never gave up on the possibility of an agreement, even after being called to order by President Macron. When, in the dying days, Ursula von der Leyen as President of the Commission took over the negotiation, she made a real effort to overcome the outstanding issues. Boris Johnson, until a very late stage, believed that no agreement was the likeliest outcome, but nervousness about the domestic political fallout that would have resulted from further severe disruption to an economy already enfeebled by Covid kept driving him back to negotiate.

Von der Leyen and Barnier expressed relief at the agreement but dismay at the finalization of this divorce. With good reason, for there were no winners in this outcome. For the EU is about to lose its (marginally) second-largest economy, and one of the most competitive, with unemployment roughly half the rate of that prevalent in the EU. Europe's share of world trade and world output, which was 30 percent in the 1960s, has been shrinking steadily since then and, post Brexit, will be closer to 10 per cent henceforth.

The loss of the UK as the second largest net contributor to the expanding EU budget will sharpen the arguments in Brussels over future EU budgets

---

[1] Refer to Stephen Jones (Chapter 5): 'The Impact of Brexit on the Future of the UK's Financial Services'.

between the more vulnerable EU states clamouring for more support and the 'thrifty' northern member states who are going to have to pay for it. President Macron, in pursuit of his ambition of 'more Europe', has tended to side with the southern member states.

The European Central Bank's quantitative easing programme has entailed the ECB buying huge amounts of government debt, including from countries the Bundesbank regards as barely creditworthy. But preserving the EU and preventing any further haemorrhaging is a fundamental interest for Germany. Angela Merkel therefore joined with Macron to announce their support for a euro 750 billion EU programme of grants and loans in support for the member states most affected by coronavirus, to be financed by borrowing on the capital markets directly by the Commission on a hitherto unprecedented scale, with Merkel declaring that this was necessary to 'save Europe'.

This agreement has been hailed, rightly, as an exceptional display of European solidarity, though Germany will continue to resist any further moves towards the mutualization of EU countries' debt. But the manner in which the decision was taken, by France and Germany, with the other EU members being invited to agree, was indicative of the way the EU is liable to function in the future.

As for Britain, there is no reason the UK economy should not continue to prosper post Brexit, provided government policies remain pro enterprise. But our departure will have resulted in a permanent loss of influence in Europe and beyond, as our partners elsewhere all attached importance to the influence we could exert within the EU.

The prospects for future cooperation with the EU suffered an extraordinary mini crisis as the UK raced ahead with a mass vaccination programme, while the EU lagged embarrassingly far behind, due to the Commission's insistence that they must place orders for the bloc as a whole, with extraordinary delays in doing so. Ursula von der Leyen overreacted furiously to being advised that the amount of vaccines the Commission had ordered from the UK/Swedish company Astra/Zeneca would have to be cut back for some time due to manufacturing problems, banning the export of vaccines produced in the EU, with the Commission also demanding controls on the Northern Irish border to prevent a leakage of vaccines! Having infuriated the British and Irish governments and got a terrible press, the Commission back-tracked to some degree, though still embargoing vaccine exports from the EU and continuing to lag far behind with the European vaccination programme. The contrast between the UK's relative success and France's problems in that regard provoked some remarkable displays of Anglophobia from President Macron and his ministers.

What then will be the effect on Britain's relationship with the United States?

Donald Trump supported Brexit and regarded Boris Johnson as a kindred spirit. Unrealistic hopes were generated of rapid agreement on a new US–UK trade agreement. This incipient honeymoon was marked by two serious disagreements. It was not only Trump but the entire US intelligence community who were dismayed at the Johnson government's decision to allow the Chinese telecom provider Huawei to play a key role in the future British 5G network. Huawei was created by the Chinese People's Liberation Army. There was no doubt that it would have to obey intelligence sharing directives from the Chinese government, a consideration that led France to exclude the company from its 5G networks. The contention that its role in Britain could be circumscribed to protect sensitive defence and intelligence data was not accepted by the Americans, who started considering withdrawing from Britain US surveillance aircraft gathering and transmitting real-time war zone intelligence from their base at RAF Mildenhall. As this would have compromised a core element of the US–UK relationship, the UK government back-tracked hastily from its position on Huawei.

The UK government deplored Trump's decision to withdraw from the Iran nuclear agreement and joined in a combined effort with France and Germany to indemnify their companies from violations of the new US sanctions against Iran, an effort that proved futile as no major international companies were prepared to imperil their interests in the United States by continuing to trade with Iran.

The Johnson government also made clear its disagreement with Trump's denialism about climate change. These and some other sources of friction will now be reduced, with the Biden administration reversing Trump's positions on climate change and Iran, though given Iran's continuing disruptive behaviour, the attempt to revive the nuclear agreement may encounter some serious problems.

The Johnson government, meanwhile, engaged in a fresh Defence Review, the outcome of which is important to the future relationship with the United States. The Royal Navy is commissioning two new aircraft carriers, which will enhance the ability to project power. France has a single aircraft carrier; no other European country has this capability. US–UK cooperation over the UK nuclear deterrent, which is not just 'special' but unique, remains as close as ever.

But the budgetary pressures resulting from no real increase in defence expenditure for many years left the RAF short of front line aircraft and, to the dismay of the US military, the British Army down to 70,000 men. The Americans, therefore, have strongly welcomed Johnson's decision to increase the defence budget to well above the NATO target of 2 per cent of GDP, to a proportion higher than that of France and twice that of Germany. The beneficiaries will be the Royal Navy and the RAF, with a further reduction in the size of the army and the United States sceptical about British claims that the UK would still be able to field as highly capable a fighting force at the level of an armoured division, as it was able to do in the liberation of Kuwait and the Iraq War.

The defence relationship will remain extremely close and 'special' in terms of command and interoperability, but the British suffered in both Iraq and Afghanistan from trying to do too much with limited forces and will need to avoid making the same mistakes again.

Both the new president and Nancy Pelosi, Speaker of the House of Representatives, historically have been supportive of the close relationship with Britain. They both were good friends and colleagues when I served in the British Embassy in Washington as they were to some of my successors. But neither will prove to be a sentimentalist. The UK will be judged in terms of what we can contribute and the dialogue with Europe henceforth will be conducted primarily with the German Chancellery.

Boris Johnson had to overcome initial mistrust in the Biden administration, given his close relationship with Trump, who he took it upon himself to describe as 'a great leader'. Biden and his foreign policy advisers are not fans of Brexit, which they see as likely to diminish Britain's influence in the world and especially in Europe, where the United States had counted on Britain to keep helping to tie together Europe and the United States and to contain trade disputes and other divergences.

Americans would never agree to 'share' or cede sovereignty themselves and nor does the US foreign policy establishment have a high opinion of the Brussels institutions. Biden's Secretary of State, Anthony Blinken, said that it was not for the United States to tell the UK whether to stay or leave, but Britain's exit from the EU was negative for the United States. The pro-European sentiments of the Biden team were dented by the EU scrambling deliberately to push through a new trade agreement with China just days before Biden took over, with no discussion of Chinese abuses, including over Hong Kong, and by the German president's assertion that his country must proceed with the Nordstream gas pipeline from Russia as compensation for the Second World War!

But the Prime Minister's exchanges with the new president have been friendly. Johnson is instinctively pro-American and provided he is able to avoid further complications over Northern Ireland, he is likely to be able to establish as good a relationship with Biden and his team, as John Major was able to do after, initially, a sticky start with Bill Clinton. On the major issues vis-à-vis China and Russia, Biden will find him more on the same wavelength than other Europeans.

Biden made clear his concern that the Good Friday peace agreement on Northern Ireland could become a 'casualty of Brexit' and that any trade agreement with the UK would be contingent on 'preventing the return of a hard border'. Even in the event of a no agreement Brexit, the UK had no intention of reintroducing controls at the Northern Ireland border and the Irish government did not wish to do so either. To avoid doing so, Johnson had to over-rule the representatives of the Protestant majority there and accept that Northern Ireland will remain within the European single market, resulting in customs barriers between the province and the rest of the UK. Attempted rigid enforcement by the European Commission of controls on the export of food and plants to Northern Ireland from elsewhere in the UK caused some serious shortages, leading the Johnson government unilaterally to insist on extending transitional arrangements. An effect of Brexit to date has been to increase political tensions in the province, with some violent demonstrations by elements of the Protestant community there.

The United States under Biden and the UK will continue to explore the possibility of an eventual new free trade agreement. This was never going to be without some difficult negotiation and new trade agreements are not a priority for the Biden administration, which has had to promise to emulate Trump in putting 'America First'. The Americans will seek to insist that a new agreement must improve access for US agriculture to the UK market. The British response has been to emulate the EU in pretending that US chlorinated chickens constitute a health risk, for which there is no scientific evidence. British consumers eat chlorinated vegetables every day. Nevertheless they do constitute a serious threat to British farmers whose natural poultry costs more. The British will have to protect their farm industry from larger and more efficient American producers and cannot give ground anyway because of the common tariffs on agriculture they will have to maintain with the EU.

They also have vowed to protect the National Health Service from US involvement. They will be concerned about the myriad 'Buy America' provisions at every level of government in the United States, now further reinforced in a protectionist move by Biden. The EU will be extremely concerned that tariff cuts between Britain and the United States should not have a knock-on effect on them. So a potential new 'free trade' agreement, which still would be beneficial in many respects, including in relation to cross investments and financial and other services, is liable to take years to negotiate and would be likely to have to remain limited in scope.

Beyond that, Scotland voted to remain in the EU, resulting in demands for another independence referendum, which the British government (and the Labour opposition) will resist and a surge in support for independence, notwithstanding the fact that Scotland remains heavily subsidized from Westminster. The US administration would regard its doubts about Brexit as well and truly justified if it appeared to render more likely eventual Scottish independence.

So, apart from the obvious loss of British influence in Europe, what else especially risks being lost post Brexit?

The departure of a major member state, and one of the only two with serious defence capabilities, is not going to help the EU's standing in the world. As for the UK, Dean Acheson in the 1960s annoyed the British by declaring that Britain, having lost an empire, had not yet found a role. Britain ever since has seen its role as being to keep helping to tie together Europe and the United States and to avoid transatlantic drift towards a less cooperative relationship, which would be liable to inflict more damage on Europe than on the United States.

The turning inward of the United States started not under Trump but under Obama, who resented advice from and the attitudes of the US foreign policy establishment, which his advisers were in the habit of describing as 'the Blob'. Rejecting explicitly the notion of the United States as the 'indispensable nation', his favourite mantra in the discussions within the White House about overseas policy was 'Don't do stupid shit', by which he meant 'let's not get involved militarily in other people's quarrels'.

Like most Americans, he regarded Syria as a problem for the Europeans. Having declared a 'red line' against the use of chemical weapons by the Syrian regime, his failure to uphold it opened the way for adventurism by Putin in Syria and Ukraine. Donald Trump, egged on by his daughter, did take action, with Britain and France, in response to a further chemical weapons attack. Obama in turn dismissed the Islamic State as merely like a 'junior varsity team' and proved very hesitant about the effective use of force against them even when they started beheading Americans. He approved the raid to kill bin Laden, but otherwise did not want to risk US special forces on the ground in support of the Kurdish and other allies. That was reversed by Trump's Defence Secretary, General Mattis, who, with the Iraqi and Kurdish forces, put a swift end to the 'Caliphate' in Iraq and Syria. The Trump administration also helped to broker the recognition of Israel by the United Arab Emirates.

But Trump conducted his entire election campaign on the theme of 'America First' and showed that he meant it. He depicted Germany, with its very low defence spending and exports favoured by a relatively weak euro, as enjoying a free ride at the expense of the United States. In response to the prospective imposition by France of a tax on revenue in France from the US digital service companies, Trump threatened drastic retaliation. Following a World Trade Organization ruling against the subsidies for Airbus, a finding against US subsidies to Boeing has triggered partial retaliation by the EU.

European countries, including Britain, all would like to impose taxes on the enormous profits the US digital companies are making in Europe and more effective regulation of them, a cause now being espoused also in the United States. Both the further US tariffs and French digital taxes having been put on hold, the Biden administration and the EU will need to try to seek convergence on the regulation and taxation of the US digital companies.

This is not going to be an easy discussion and this short-term truce is a vast distance from where we ought to be. Britain for decades has campaigned in Europe for a transatlantic free trade agreement, with zero tariffs on manufactured goods. European efforts in that direction have been half-hearted, due to fears of intensified US pressure to open up the European market in agriculture. France has been most opposed to any further reduction in transatlantic tariff and non-tariff barriers, contending that no agreement would be possible with any country that did not sign up to the 2017 Paris Agreement on Climate Change. Even with Biden now reversing the US position on climate change, it will be hard to overcome the lack of any real appetite in Europe for new trade opening measures, which so far has left the planned Transatlantic Trade and Investment Partnership dead in the water.

When it comes to the defence relationship, Biden will be more diplomatic than Trump about the failure of the Europeans to make more of a contribution to their own defence. But it is a serious aberration that three-quarters of a century after the Second World War, Germany should be spending so little on its own defence, while the poor state of equipment and readiness of its armed forces have become a national scandal. The UK, having unwisely cut defence spending under Cameron, declaring Russia no longer to be a threat, nevertheless has remained one of the few European allies to meet the modest NATO target of defence spending at the level of 2 per cent of GDP and is now pledged to exceed it. Germany has refused to consider meeting such a target at any point in the foreseeable future.

President Macron bizarrely chose the anniversary of the armistice that ended the First World War to talk of the need for Europe to create its own army 'to protect us vis-à-vis China, Russia *and even the United States.*' Amid the many justifiably derided statements of Donald Trump, it is hard to think of one much sillier than this or that could have caused more indignation in the United States. Ursula von der Leyen and Angela Merkel also have endorsed the idea of a 'European army'. This despite the fact that there is no appetite whatever in Europe to make the sacrifices, of both budgetary and sovereignty, to give Europe the capacity really to defend itself, which will remain a mirage in the absence of any serious contribution from Germany.

The danger is obvious of creating the illusion rather than the reality of 'European defence'. The German defence minister, Annegret Kramp-Karrenbauer, upset President Macron by declaring the obvious in November

2020, namely that 'Without America's nuclear and conventional capabilities, Germany and Europe cannot protect themselves'. She added that the French idea of 'strategic autonomy' for Europe nurtured the illusion that European security could be achieved without NATO and the United States. Europeans need to be careful what they wish for. Do they really wish Congress to start embracing the idea that Europe should indeed assume responsibility for its own defence?

A further element of sanity will be introduced into this debate by the East Europeans who, without exception, believe that all that has deterred Putin from seeking to regain control of the Baltic countries has been the United States and Article V of the NATO treaty.

It will take at least a decade after Brexit to determine whether, in economic terms, it can be judged to have been a success or failure. The likely effects on the hugely important UK financial services industry are analysed in Chapter 5 by Stephen Jones. As he observes, it may appear extraordinary that while both sides were prepared to go to war over fisheries, the UK's most important industry was left out of the negotiation entirely. The Bank of England and others supervising the financial services industry in Britain remained resistant to close alignment with EU regulation. The Governor of the Bank of England, Andrew Bailey, has declared that it is not in Britain's interest to become a 'rule taker' from the EU in financial services. If that was the condition for being granted 'equivalence' by the EU in financial services regulation, the price was too high. For the ambition must be to ensure that the UK remained globally competitive, with far more of the growth in the sector in future likely to come from Asia than from the EU and the main competitive threat continuing to come from New York. But it was naïve for the governor then to complain about the EU seeking to bring Euro derivatives trading under its control.

Brexit has ended the 'passporting' of the provision of financial services into the EU, and the trading of euro shares has moved predominantly to Amsterdam. No serious discussion of the regulatory issues has yet been engaged, though the Chancellor, Rishi Sunak, has unilaterally opened the UK capital markets to EU competition.

This epitomizes the contrast between the more market-based attitudes in London and the determination of the EU Commission now to pursue the French-inspired autarchic goal of 'strategic autonomy' in the provision of financial services into the EU, which they will seek to insist must in future be managed from within the Union.

This will be to some extent illusory as international banking increasingly is dominated by the five major US banks. JP Morgan has displaced Deutsche Bank as the pre-eminent bank in Germany. The European banking system is far more fragmented and in several countries more fragile than that in the United States.

So Brexit undoubtedly will inflict damage on the financial services industry in the UK. The effects to date have been the reallocation by the major banks of vast amounts of regulatory capital into the EU plus the transfer so far of several thousand high value jobs, though with more to follow. The Commission will oppose the creation of purely 'letter box' subsidiaries in the EU and is seeking to require the vast Euro derivative operations to be managed from within the EU. The London-based financial institutions will face continuing pressures to enhance their presence in the EU.

Nevertheless, the former head of the Bundesbank, Axel Weber, has pointed out that London will remain the premier financial centre in Europe. The major US banks all have based their transatlantic headquarters there. The main beneficiaries of reallocation so far have been Frankfurt and Dublin. The attractions of Paris for the most part have not proved sufficient to overcome the deterrent effect of French labour laws, but Amsterdam has become far more seriously competitive with London in share trading.

The principal activities of the major banks are by their nature truly international. A high proportion are conducted electronically. If the EU did seek to ban the sale of investment products managed from Britain into Europe, this would be very disruptive for the UK industry, but also damaging to European savers and investors and bizarre, as it could not, without a trade conflict, be applied to funds managed from the United States which, unlike the UK, has been granted 'equivalence' in regulation to the EU. If counterproductive measures are adopted, the migration of business is more likely to be to New York than to Europe.

Brexit, therefore, is likely to check the hitherto rapid expansion of the UK financial services industry and could reverse it, but unlikely to imperil London's position as the pre-eminent financial centre on this side of the Atlantic. The plethora of smaller companies in Britain operating in this sector are not going to miss the unending hyper-bureaucratic regulation emanating from Brussels, with the first Market in Financial Instruments Directive (MIFID 1) being followed post-haste by the still more onerous MIFID 2, though the essence of UK regulation will remain similar to that in Europe. If the effect of Brexit is to lighten, or at any rate to avoid increasing, the bureaucratic burdens on the smaller companies in all sectors of the British economy, there will be a more convincing economic case to be made for Brexit.

I do not, therefore, believe in apocalyptic forecasts about the effects of Brexit on the UK financial services industry or on London, which will remain by far the most dynamic and truly international city in Europe. The city has been described by one of the immense galaxy of European students who studied there as 'seething, international, colourful, the epitome of modernity' and as 'the source of an inner freedom that I've kept to this day'. Her name was Ursula von der Leyen.

The former governor of the Bank of England, Lord Mervyn King, is not alone in believing that UK economic growth is likely in due course to resume, post the far greater damage inflicted by coronavirus, at roughly the same rate as before. The recovery from the economic effects of coronavirus will be led by the United States and China. The EU and Britain will take longer to recover. The more the EU tries to shield itself from international competition by following the Colbertist agenda of protectionism, 'strategic autonomy', autarchy and *dirigisme*, the more ground it will be likely to continue to lose vis-à-vis the more dynamic economies in the United States and Asia. If that does turn out to be the direction in which the EU is heading, there will be a stronger case to be made about the decision to leave.

What the Americans admire most is success. If the UK pursues more business-friendly policies and sensible regulation, there is no reason the UK economy should not continue to outperform those of many members of the EU. The Macron reforms having been very limited to date, it quite possibly will continue to surpass that of France. How the British economy fares post Brexit will have a very important bearing on the future health of the relationship with the United States.

Britain, in due course, is going to find itself in a series of further negotiations with the EU. It is important that, on both sides, these should be conducted more cooperatively and more rationally than was the case until the last weeks of the withdrawal negotiation. Five million Europeans currently are living in

Britain – more than the population of several EU member states. The most important benefit of the agreement reached should have been to avoid the distrust, antagonisms and recriminations that would have resulted from a 'hard' Brexit and to provide a better basis for cooperation in the future, though that has yet to prove to be the case.

It was, for Britain, the best outcome that could have been achieved. The same can be said from the European perspective too. It is due to be reviewed in four years' time. The post agreement relationship to date has been described by the British negotiator, Lord Frost, as 'more than bumpy' with, obviously, faults on both sides. The future Partnership Council needs to be used not just as a mechanism for resolving disputes but to deepen future cooperation between the UK and the EU, the risk being obvious that, otherwise, the two sides may continue to drift further apart. There are many challenges we will need to continue to face together, including the common threat of terrorism and the tidal wave of attempted migration from outside Europe. It is time to rediscover what we have in common, for we should now move beyond what has divided us.

The Americans, post Brexit, will be sceptical about British ambitions to continue to play much of a role in the wider world. But they will attach importance to what may be a still closer economic relationship and to Britain remaining a viable defence ally. The relationship may appear superficially to be almost as close as ever. Whether Britain will have as much influence in Washington as it did when we were consulted by the Americans on every major European issue is another matter. The fiasco of US withdrawal from Afghanistan will affect relations with the White House so long as Biden is President, but the institutional defence, nuclear and investment relationships are strong enough to ensure that an especially close relationship will endure.

Bibliography

Bartlett, C.J. *The Special Relationship : A Political History of Anglo-American Relations since 1945.* New York: Longman, 1992.

Baylis, John. *Anglo-American Relations since 1939 : The Enduring Alliance.* Manchester: Manchester University Press, 1997.

Coughlin, Con. *American Ally: Tony Blair and the War on Terror*. London: Politico's, 2006.

Dumbrell, John. *A Special Relationship : Anglo-American Relations in the Cold War and After*. Houndsmill : Macmillan, 2001.

Renwick, Robin. *Fighting with Allies: The U.S. and Britain in Peace and War*. London: Biteback Publishing, 2017.

8

Choppy waters

The future of the Entente Cordiale after Brexit

Sophie Loussouarn

Until the fall of Napoleon Bonaparte, Britain was France's historical foe, and there has been a lack of historical understanding between the two nations going back a long way. The enemy of Great Britain was the France of Louis XIV during the War of the Spanish Succession, the France of King Louis XV during the Seven Years' War and the France of Louis XVI assisting the American revolutionaries. From the seventeenth to the mid-eighteenth centuries, the French used the Jacobites to destabilize Britain; in the late eighteenth and early nineteenth centuries, they used Jacobins; and then there was Bonaparte.

The United Kingdom (UK) and France have a colonial past and have had their voices heard on the world stage. Britain has always tried to prevent the domination of the Continent by a single power. Yet the natural ally for France in Europe has always been Britain. Franco-British relations go back to the Battle of Hastings (1066) and William the Conqueror, the Hundred Years' War, the Crimean War and the Entente Cordiale. France and Britain have thus been rivals and allies for a long time.

Yet French became the official language of England; the Court, diplomacy and the embryo of civil service. In the end the English language triumphed, although not until the fourteenth and fifteenth centuries, but it was an English heavily influenced by French. An important factor must have been the fact that a French dynasty – the Plantagenets – reigned over England from Henry II to Richard III (killed 1485; this date conveniently ends the Middle Ages in England).

There has been a long saga of mutual hatred. The French Revolution was a traumatic event for the British who were afraid it might spread to Great Britain and damage British institutions.

In 1830, King Louis-Philippe brought France and Britain together. The word 'Entente Cordiale' was coined by French foreign secretary François Guizot, who inspired King Louis-Philippe in his speech where he referred to 'a true friendship' and a spirit of 'entente cordiale' in September 1843 when he entertained Queen Victoria at the Château d'Eu in Normandy. Queen Victoria also referred to the same expression before the British Parliament in February 1844. As Lord Clive summed it up in his speech in the House of Commons:

> The situation of those two countries was in many respects so similar – they were separated by so short a distance, that there was scarcely anything which could injuriously affect the one without injury in the same degree to the other. But he could conceive no assurance of the friendly feeling existing between the two nations more strong than that conveyed by Her Majesty's recent visit to France, by the cordial manner in which she was received by the Sovereign and by the people of that country, and by the equally cordial greetings which awaited her on her return amidst her own subjects.[1]

At first the Entente Cordiale was 'a cordial good understanding', as the then British foreign secretary the Earl of Aberdeen said in October 1843. The Entente Cordiale was later sealed by King Edward VII on 8 April 1904 as an alliance meant to counter the aggressive tendencies of the German Empire. It was the work of the French ambassador in London Paul Cambon (1843–1924) and the British foreign secretary Lord Landsdowne from 1900 onwards. The Entente reflected the British and French claims over Egypt and Morocco. France kept Morocco whereas the UK controlled Egypt. For more than a century, representatives of the French Republic and the British Monarchy thus entertained each other, during state visits in Paris or in London. On 23 April 1914, King George V and Queen Mary came to Paris to celebrate the tenth anniversary of the Entente Cordiale.

France and the UK went to war together in 1914, 1939 and 1956. Britain and France fought together hand in hand. During the First World War, a secret treaty was signed between the UK and France in 1916 – the Sykes–Picot

---

[1] *Hansard*, House of Commons debate, 1 February 1844, Vol. 72, c. 42.

Agreement – which divided the Ottoman Empire into areas of British and French influence. The Sykes–Picot Agreement thus allocated to the UK control of southern Israel and Palestine, Jordan and southern Iraq while France was to control south-eastern Turkey, northern Iraq, Syria and Lebanon. The Treaty of Versailles was signed on 28 June 1919 and went into effect on 10 January 1920. It was a major contributory factor to the outbreak of the Second World War. During the two great wars, France and the UK came closer together. During the darkest hours, Sir Winston Churchill fought alone against the German enemy as France had surrendered to Germany in 1940. The Fall of France in 1940 was unexpected. It was an economic defeat for the UK which had its supplies reduced. The UK came to depend on the empire. The year 1940 was a moment of catastrophic defeat which transferred power to the United States. Had France remained in the war, Britain and France could have countered the German attack and could have marched on Berlin. Instead, Britain turned to the United States. The UK took part in the Yalta Summit and became a permanent member of the Security Council of the United Nations after the war. Yet the UK refused to join the European Community for Coal and Steel in the 1950s and the Common Market when the Treaty of Rome was ratified in 1957.

Britain and France understand their mission in a different way. The French and the British have always had different conceptions of Europe. France and Britain approached negotiations with Germany in a different way owing to wartime and historical experience as Queen Victoria was related to most European leaders through her own family connections and through her children's marriages. The UK then tried to join the Common Market in the 1960s during Macmillan's and Wilson's premierships, but it was vetoed twice by President de Gaulle in 1963 and 1967, arguing that the British would never cut their ties of dependency to the United States and would maintain their links with the Commonwealth. De Gaulle was not wrong when he perceived this. Before Brexit, much of the Franco-British relation was about the European Union (EU). How is President Macron viewing Brexit? He wanted the UK to stay in the EU when he first met Prime Minister Theresa May in June 2017 after being elected President of France. President Macron believes France is central to the Western world's culture.

Brexit has revived tensions between France and the UK which are underpinned by centuries of rivalry. The UK officially left the EU on 31 January 2020 and remained in the single market and the customs unions for a transition period until 31 December 2020. In February 2020, President Macron declared that he did not want Brexit to succeed. Since March 2020, the spread of Covid-19 has delayed negotiations, but a deal was reached at the last minute on Christmas Eve before the end of the transition period on 31 December 2020. What will come out of the Entente Cordiale after Brexit? The best way to understand the current French approach is to go back to the past starting with the origins of the Entente Cordiale to Jean Monnet's vision of Europe, moving on to de Gaulle's position, before we come to the immediate reactions to the 2016 referendum on British membership of the European Union.

The origins of the Entente Cordiale: From an informal relationship to a diplomatic alliance

Following Wellington's defeat of Napoleon at Waterloo on 18 June 1815, it became clear that Great Britain and the France of the restored constitutional monarchy had numerous common interests, which merited close and frequent consultation. This circumstance led to the development of the informal Entente Cordiale. The Château d'Eu was the focal point of the meeting between Queen Victoria and King Louis-Philippe on 2 September 1843. The Queen's voyage to Eu sealed the *rapprochement* between France and Britain from 1843 to 1845. Queen Victoria set foot on the French territory at Tréport, where she was welcomed by King Louis-Philippe and his family with 'God Save the Queen'. Prince Albert was one of the greatest supporters of the Entente Cordiale together with Queen Marie-Amélie who did her utmost to maintain the friendship between France and Britain in spite of the quarrels over Tahiti and the Spanish alliances. Louis-Philippe's eldest daughter who married Leopold, first king of the Belgians, played her part in facilitating the meeting between the Queen of Great Britain and the French king in Eu. Queen Victoria was entertained in the Galerie de Guise on the first floor of the Château d'Eu, which featured numerous family portraits of Louis-Philippe's family. It was the setting for concerts given by singers of the French Opera. On the first evening of the Queen's visit a concert was given by the director of the King's Music, Auber. On the second evening, a French horn player entertained them. On the final day of the Queen's visit, King Louis-Philippe and Queen Marie-Amélie had arranged a picnic in the Forest of Eu, where servants had set up marquees and a huge table together with camp stools. The King himself presided over the picnic for fifty people. Queen Victoria and Prince Albert left Eu at 6.00 am. The Queen thoroughly enjoyed her first trip abroad with the French royal family, and it played a great part in improving the relationship between the British and the French.

In October 1844, King Louis-Philippe and Prince Albert inaugurated the train which took the King of the French to Windsor Castle to strengthen the Entente Cordiale. King Louis-Philippe and his son, the Duke of Montpensier, visited Queen Victoria and Prince Albert who introduced them to their four children. Royal visits carried on at Frogmore House, Eton, Hampton Court and Claremont.

Louis-Philippe first used the expression 'Entente Cordiale', but Napoleon III made it more of a reality. He constantly, however, endangered it by foreign adventures which did not meet with British approval and annoyed Queen Victoria. One of the preoccupations that the Queen, at least, nurtured was that Napoleon III had designs on Western Germany, her 'second homeland', and indeed this seems to have been the case.

The Marquess of Dufferin and Ava (1826–42) greatly improved Franco-British relations during his time in the embassy in Paris, but he had to retire after being posted in Paris for five years on account of his poor health. Dufferin's successor, Sir Edward Monson (1843–1909), faced a growing Anglophobia after Fashoda, which brought France and Great Britain to the brink of war. President Emile Loubet hosted King Edward VII's state visit in May 1903 to seal the Entente Cordiale. Its aim was to maintain peace. On 8 April 1904, the Entente Cordiale put an end to the conflicts between Britain and France and paved the way to their diplomatic cooperation against Germany. This diplomatic alliance was to last for thirty years. It was the apex of the policy of French foreign secretary Theophile Delcassé, who served at the Foreign Office from 1898 to 1905 and tried to secure alliances with France and Russia.

According to Article 4 of the Declaration between the UK and France respecting Egypt and Morocco:

> The two Governments, being equally attached to the principle of commercial liberty both in Egypt and Morocco, declare that they will not, in those countries, countenance any inequality either in the imposition of customs duties or other taxes, or of railway transport charges. The trade of both

nations with Morocco and with Egypt shall enjoy the same treatment in transit through the French and British possessions in Africa.²

Yet France was not completely ousted from Egypt. France remained the junior partner in the Suez Canal Company and French remained the official language of Egypt and Sudan into the twentieth century.

Following the Algeciras conference of 1905, the British and French general staffs had held regular and close consultations. General, later Field Marshal, Sir Henry Wilson played a great part in promoting this closer military relationship with France. After the Agadir crisis in 1911, cooperation between the Admiralty and the War Office was established to enable the smooth transport of the British Army to France. In 1912, Sir John French became Chief of the Imperial General Staff and started discussing aspects of a possible war between France and Germany and a British intervention by sea or land. In 1914, Sir John French was appointed Commander-in-Chief of the British Army and the whole expeditionary force was sent to France under his command after the council of 5 August 1914.

Ambassador Monson was replaced by an old crony of King Edward VII, Sir Francis Bertie (1844–1919), who incidentally was a friend of Marcel Proust. Ambassador Bertie was posted to Paris during the First World War, which had a great impact on the Entente Cordiale with the role of Sir John French from 1914 to 1915 and Field Marshal Douglas Haig, Commander-in-Chief of the British Army on the Western Front from 1915 to 1919.

Haig was on good terms with the French leaders, Clemenceau, Joffre, Foch and Poincaré, and spoke excellent French. So he was able to talk directly to them in French and not through an interpreter, as happened with Sir John French. This made a great impression on the French leaders, who welcomed the new spirit of helpfulness inspired by a genuine desire for real cooperation with the allies.

In 1914, Britain had unflinchingly answered the call to defend its ally across the Channel. The bitter struggle on the Western Front against a powerful and supremely efficient military force lasted over four years and was finally brought to a close by the resolute determination of the French and the British working together.

---

² Great Britain, Parliamentary Papers London, 1911, Vol. CIII, Cmd.5969.

As the Germans advanced on Paris in early September 1914, Ambassador Bertie withdrew to Bordeaux along with the French government. He later returned to Paris. Whereas France was the major battlefield where blood was shed and numerous soldiers killed or maimed, Great Britain was spared invasion but it was bombed, mainly by airships. British cities on the east coast suffered, including London, Hull and Edinburgh. There was also naval bombardment of some coastal towns, notably Scarborough. The British had always believed that they were safe inside their island and that the Royal Navy could always protect them from every threat. This led to calls for the creation of the Royal Air Force, which became a reality in April 1918, with Churchill's and Lloyd George's support.

The collapse of the Ottoman Empire in 1918 led to the Western control of Mesopotamia. Britain's Empire proved vital for waging the Great War. In May 1916, diplomats Sir Mark Sykes and François Georges-Picot concluded a secret agreement delineating British and French spheres of influence in most of the Ottoman Empire. Sir Mark was very familiar with the Middle East and Arab culture as he had travelled with his father to the Ottoman Empire from an early age and had published his first book, *Through Five Turkish Provinces*, as an undergraduate. He became honorary attaché in the British Embassy in Constantinople, which led him to publish his *Report on the Petroliferous Districts of the Vilayets of Baghdad, Mosul and Bitlis*. He entered the House of Commons and became part of several committees about the future of the Ottoman Empire. He was aware that an agreement on the Middle East required French involvement and started negotiating with François Georges-Picot who was a staunch nationalist. The two men played a great part in shaping the modern world.

At the Versailles Peace conference, American president Woodrow Wilson and his fellow statesmen, Clemenceau and Poincaré, together with British prime minister Lloyd George pored over maps of Europe trying to work out its new frontiers in the elegant Hôtel de Murat in the Rue de Monceau. The First World War made it clear to France and Great Britain that their status in the international order had diminished. The Treaty of Versailles in 1919 was different from the Congress of Vienna in 1815. Prime Minister Lloyd George was aware of Britain's growing dependence on the United States for its peace and security and of the importance of the British Empire. After the First World War, British Liberals, especially Sir Edward Grey, favoured the League of

Nations to avoid the failure of democracy and shape world affairs. In February 1922, Britain recognized Egypt as an independent sovereign state.

During the 1930s, there was growing instability in Western Europe and there was extensive collaboration between France and Britain. There were regular contacts between the officials of the two countries, and there was systematic intelligence sharing. The state visit of King George VI was thus the embodiment of the ties uniting France and Britain. King George VI and Queen Elizabeth spent three days in Paris from 19 to 21 July 1938, after the abdication of Edward VIII who married Wallis Simpson. There was a state dinner hosted by President Albert Lebrun and his wife for King George VI and Queen Elizabeth. On 21 July 1938, a lunch was held at the Château de Versailles for 280 guests with the most exquisite dishes and wines. Finally on 21 July 1938, King George VI was invited to the French Foreign Office. Throughout the centuries, French cuisine has always played a crucial role in diplomatic negotiations. During President Lebrun's reciprocal state visit to London in 1939 a few months before the outbreak of the Second World War, the French president addressed both Houses of Parliament in Westminster Hall, speaking of 'the rare privilege of unreserved friendship which exists between France and Britain'. He was also entertained at a banquet in the Durbar Court of the Foreign Office, which included a performance of the balcony scene from *Romeo and Juliet*. A reception was also held at the French Embassy in London for King George VI and Queen Elizabeth.

In July 1940, after France surrendered to Germany, Prime Minister Winston Churchill wondered whether Britain could survive without France in Europe and without the support of its colonies against Germany and Japan which had closed the road to Burma:

> In these summer days of 1940 after the fall of France we were all alone. None of the British dominions or India or the colonies could send decisive aid, or send what they had in time. The victorious, enormous German armies, thoroughly equipped and with large reserves of captured weapons and arsenals behind them, were gathering for the final stroke. Italy, with numerous and imposing forces, had declared war upon us, and eagerly sought our destruction in the Mediterranean and in Egypt.[3]

---

[3] Winston Churchill, *Their Finest Hour, The Second World War*, Volume II. 1949. London: Penguin, 2005, Volume II, 225.

There were close links between Winston Churchill and Léon Blum and on 14 July 1939, Churchill attended the National Day parade in Paris. Léon Blum and Paul Reynaud were great friends of Sir Winston who was very perceptive. There was a system of close cooperation between France and Britain, but there was a fundamental shift after France surrendered to Germany. The Second World War was very different from the First World War, and the shape of the Franco-British relations changed. From the Battle of Britain in 1940 to the German invasion of the Soviet Union in 1941, the British Empire fought alone against Germany; all its allies had been defeated. During the Second World War, France was occupied by the German Army. At the time, a seal was fixed to the embassy before December 1941 and rooms were filled with diplomats' furniture. The British Embassy's ballroom was requisitioned by the German Information Division and the British ambassador Sir Ronald Campbell (1883–1953) left Paris on 10 June 1940 and joined the French government at the outbreak of the war. He asked the American ambassador in Paris, William Bullitt, to take charge of British interests and British property in Paris and any parts of France.[4] When Paris fell on 14 June 1940, Americans assumed responsibility for Britain's diplomatic relations and assets in France. The French and British governments had different approaches and Vichy had a long rivalry with Italy.

Once General de Gaulle had been accepted as Leader of the Free French, Churchill made great efforts to accommodate him. Part of the residential complex of Dolphin Square was vacated to provide offices for the French government in exile. In St James's, an elegant stucco house belonging to the Crown Estate, became de Gaulle's official residence. His statue now stands outside it. It was within walking distance of No 10 Downing Street and Buckingham Palace. Prior to that, however, de Gaulle had been brutally humiliated by British officers inferior in rank to himself and refused broadcasting facilities. These slights, together with the memory of Fashoda, which had blighted his schooldays, caused him to regard the UK askance for ever afterwards. De Gaulle always had a curious relationship with Churchill, and Britain could never decide whether they wanted France to remain an active partner in the Middle East. Then from 1943 to 1944, the Resistance could support military

---

[4] The National Archives FO 371/243326.

operations and Lille, Amiens and Bordeaux played a major part in supporting Britain.

The war years were fraught with difficulties and the British Empire fought ruthlessly against Germany. The Second World War was pivotal in the relationship between France and Britain, and the towering personalities of Charles de Gaulle and Sir Winston Churchill cast a long shadow. After the Liberation of Paris, Sir Alfred Duff Cooper (1890–1954) was posted to Paris, where he played a major part in negotiations between France and Britain.

Monnet's supranationalism and Britain's refusal to join a customs union

Monnet, one of the founding fathers of the European project, was himself a British civil servant during his wartime exile from France. The Anglo-French coordinating committee was chaired by Jean Monnet, who never understood why Britain did not join the European Community for Steal and Coal in the early years ascribing it to 'the price of victory – the illusion that you could maintain what you had without change'. Nevertheless, he laid the cornerstone of today's EU with a plan for a European federal authority in coal and steel. It was one of the landmarks of the century. The implications go well beyond Europe as Monnet was the champion of a Europe united by free trade.

The Cold War and the Marshall Plan changed the entire context of French policy to Germany.

Customs union was in the air. The fear of Stalin also led to the Congress of The Hague in May 1948, which launched the European movement. On 18 April 1948, Jean Monnet wrote to Prime Minister Robert Schuman, who was negotiating on wheat for France in Washington. The aim was to exorcize the demons of the past. Monnet and Schuman wanted to rule out a new invasion of France from Germany. In a prophetic speech following the signing of the statutes of the Council of Europe on 5 May 1949, Robert Schuman declared:

> We are carrying out a great experiment, the fulfilment of the same recurrent dream that for ten centuries has revisited the peoples of Europe: creating between them an organisation putting an end to war and guaranteeing an

eternal peace.... The European spirit signifies being conscious of belonging to a cultural family and to have the willingness to serve that community in the spirit of total mutuality, without any hidden motives of hegemony or the selfish exploitation of others.

Jean Monnet's solution reached its highest expression in the Schuman Plan. The Schuman Plan was a laconic declaration on 9 May 1950 that France and Germany agreed to pool their coal and steel industries and invited other nations to join them in a supranational body that would regulate the production, sale and distribution of these natural resources. By 1950, Britain was widely believed to have a veto on European integration. Monnet broke with the past with supranationality. The British refused to commit themselves to a supranational High Authority.

Why did the British think a closer union was not a good thing for them? 'A political federation limited to Western Europe is not compatible with our Commonwealth ties, our obligations as a member of a wider Atlantic alliance, or as a world power', as the Labour government put it. There seems to have been a consensus between all the parties on this issue.

The draft treaty made clear provision for a single market in coal and steel of all the member states. Customs duties, subsidies, discriminatory and restrictive practices were all to be abolished. Monnet was a leader in whose person was incarnated the spirit of European solidarity. He thought of a European Coal and Steel Authority as a source of peace. He was trying to ensure against the German dangers. Monnet was the architect not the politician, and Monnet's prime invention bore the name of Prime Minister Schuman. Monnet had become Mr Europe. He stressed that six parliaments had established 'the first European community, merging part of its members' national sovereignty and subordinating it to common interest'.

There was interest in Whitehall in a common market in steel with the Six, but the British steel industry was strongly opposed to it. Association materialized only later in different circumstances. Monnet's involvement was more direct in the association agreement with Britain. He handed over to René Mayer the presidency of the High Authority from 10 June 1955 to 1958. René Mayer had been Foreign Secretary and finance minister after the Second World War and had presided over the Department of Munitions from 1939 to 1940.

France's conversion to the Common Market had little to do with competition or with industry. Negotiations began in earnest in September 1956. The Treaty of Rome was signed on 25 March 1957. It was widely expected that the Common Market would lead to economic rather than political union. The seeds of the Franco-German reconciliation were planted at the root of today's EU.

On 9 April 1957, President de Gaulle invited Queen Elizabeth II for her first state visit in France at the Château de Versailles. On 10 April 1957, there was an informal lunch at the Château de la Celle Saint-Cloud after Queen Elizabeth II's visit to the Renault factories in Flins.

Yet, in 1957, Britain refused to ratify the Treaty of Rome thus keeping apart from the EU because the UK was in favour of a free trade area instead of a customs union. It is a long-standing maxim of Britain's foreign and trade policies: 'Free Trade good – Tariffs bad!' The empire was adapted to constitute a free trade area within which goods and services could be freely exchanged, on terms decided by Westminster and Whitehall. It was entirely in keeping with this long-standing policy that the UK promoted the creation of the European Free Trade Agreement founded by the Stockholm Convention in 1960. Britain was therefore unable to influence the development of European institutions.

De Gaulle's reluctance towards the UK and his veto to its membership of the EU in 1963 and 1967

The new communities were only five months old when a legal coup d'état in France on 1 June 1958 brought Charles de Gaulle back to power, and he was to be in command for fifteen years. Macmillan's appointment as Prime Minister in 1957 was also a major turning point, and the Entente Cordiale was developing in the backchannels of Whitehall.

De Gaulle's attitude to the Common Market was much more favourable than to the European Community for Steel and Coal. President de Gaulle believed in Europe from the Atlantic to the Urals. He wanted to free Europe from the American hegemony as he wanted Europe to play the role of a third pole of global power and even acquire a central role in the new system, the holder of the balance between the American and Soviet spheres of influence. Throughout the Fifth Republic, France has had a very haughty attitude towards the UK. President de Gaulle believed Britain would remain close to the United States because of the transatlantic alliance and was afraid it might endanger the European project. He was convinced that leadership in Europe should come from within Europe:

> This leads us to implement the Economic Community, to trigger a regular consultation in the political field, to make sure that others among whom Great Britain would not lead the West towards an Atlantic system which would be incompatible with a European Europe.[5]

France, which had been ruined by the Second World War and had been saved from German annihilation by Great Britain and the United States, had now become the leading power of the European Community and sounded indifferent towards its former ally.

British prime minister Harold Macmillan tried to negotiate with Europe and the Commonwealth instead of relying on the transatlantic relationship only, but President Kennedy shared Macmillan's global framework whereas de Gaulle and Adenauer focused on Europe. Macmillan believed in interdependence and thought that Britain and America were acting as 'An inner core working in unison gradually extending by example and influence their own harmony and confidence to all the free world'.[6] In his diary, Harold Macmillan underlined the reluctance of the French government towards Britain as it had refused to join the Common Market: 'The trade negotiations with France drag on – as the French intend. Meanwhile, the discrimination against the United Kingdom and the 11 Europeans not in the Treaty of Rome has begun.'[7] The UK tried to set up the European Free Trade Agreement to compete with the Common Market: 'For if we cannot successfully organise the opposition group – Scandinavia; Denmark; Switzerland; Austria etc – then we shall undoubtedly be eaten up, one by one, by the 6.'[8]

According to President de Gaulle, geography, the British Empire and the belief in a customs union accounted for Britain's position towards the Common Market:

---

[5] Charles de Gaulle, *Mémoires d'Espoir, Le Renouveau, 1958-1962*. Paris: Plon, 1970, 182. Personal translation.
[6] Dwight D. Eisenhower Library, Abilene, KS, Whitman File, International Series, Box 23: memorandum of conversation, 23 October 1957, 'Closer US-UK Relations and Free World Cooperation'.
[7] Peter Catterall, *The Macmillan Diaries, Volume II, Prime Minister and After, 1957-66*. London: Macmillan, 2011, 186.
[8] *The Macmillan Diaries*, Ibid., 231.

Whether Great Britain was staunchly opposed to this endeavour, how would one be surprised, taking into account its geography, and therefore its political life, it never admitted to see the Continent united or to merge with it. One can even say to a certain extent that for eight centuries, all European history can be summed up in this. As for now, our neighbours across the Channel were meant for free trade.[9]

The UK ratified the European Free Trade Agreement with Scandinavian countries, Portugal, Switzerland and Austria. When Prime Minister Harold Macmillan became aware of the economic success of the Common Market, he applied for membership of the EU in 1961 in order to increase Britain's wealth and strength. He had fought in the First World War at the Battle of the Somme and was a friend of Jean Monnet.

On 3 July 1961, visiting Metz, de Gaulle said, 'Britain must enter the Common Market without posing conditions.' This was reminiscent of Monnet's style. The major stumbling block was the Commonwealth and British agriculture. Prime Minister Harold Macmillan was aware of France's changing position towards Britain: 'It seems clear that there has been a change in French opinion. They now seem really to want us in Europe – but will they pay our price?'[10]

British politicians were still divided over the EU, and membership was very controversial, as Macmillan recorded in his diary: 'The internal political situation about Europe is interesting. In both Government and opposition parties there are three groups – the keen partisans of our joining the Six; the keen opponents; and the doubtfuls.'[11]

Harold Macmillan gave an insight into de Gaulle's strained relationship with the UK when it came to its membership of the EU:

De Gaulle was very avuncular, very gracious, very oracular, and very unyielding. He would take all the plums – tripartism, new arrangements in NATO, and help with the techniques of missiles and bombs (other than the actual nuclear content) with cavalier profligacy. But when it came to giving anything in return – e.g. Britain's desire to enter Europe on reasonable terms, having regard to Commonwealth and British agricultural structures – then the General was in his most austere and Puritan mood.[12]

---

[9] De Gaulle, Ibid., 198–9. Personal translation.
[10] *The Macmillan Diaries*, Ibid., 386.
[11] *The Macmillan Diaries*, Ibid., 386.
[12] *The Macmillan Diaries*, Ibid., 391.

On 5 August 1961, the British government applied to enter the Common Market under Article 237 of the Treaty of Rome. Prime Minister Macmillan agreed with President de Gaulle on almost everything: a political Europe, anti-federalism, economic planning. Yet Macmillan felt de Gaulle's hatred and distrust of the UK, as he remembers in his diary:

> His pride, his inherited hatred of England, his bitter memories of the last war; above all, his intense vanity for France – she must dominate – make him half welcome, half repel us, with a strange 'love-hate' complex. Sometimes, when I am with him, I feel I have overcome it. But he goes back to his distrust and dislike.[13]

President de Gaulle was ruthless. On 14 January 1963, he gave a press conference to denounce Britain and oppose her entry into the Common Market. He vetoed Britain's first application to join the EU in 1963 on the ground that Britain was 'insular, maritime, linked through her exchanges, her markets, her supply lines to the most diverse and often the most distant countries'. According to President de Gaulle, Great Britain had different economic structures and was unwilling to comply with the European Economic Community. He wanted Britain to accept all the conditions of the Six. De Gaulle's veto on Britain in 1963 marked the watershed between the first half of his presidency and the second half of political trench warfare. France was afraid of destroying European unity. On 28 January 1963, the French government gave orders to the Dutch and Belgian foreign ministers and asked that negotiations be brought to an end. It was a major blow to Edward Heath who had negotiated with the Six.

In 1967, the British Labour government to make sure the country's claims to enter the European Community could not be ignored renewed the request to join. President de Gaulle again cast a veto. Yet the world had changed. President de Gaulle's decade at the helm had legitimized the state bureaucracies in their visceral rejection of outside interference. Britain had to wait until President de Gaulle left the Elysée Palace to join.

Edward Heath, the most European British prime minister, negotiated Britain's membership of the European Community with newly elected President Pompidou who supported British entry into the Common Market but insisted that the UK must accept the Common Agricultural Policy.

---

[13] *The Macmillan Diaries*, Ibid., 431.

Pompidou was President de Gaulle's Prime Minister at the time of the first French veto in 1963.

Britain duly entered the Common Market with Denmark and Ireland on 1 January 1973. It was a long-delayed fulfilment for Jean Monnet, yet he would have preferred Britain to join alone. The ties that bound the UK with the European Community were less firm than those of other countries. Britain saw itself as the champion of a Europe of nation states which came together voluntarily to make the business of the world easier to conduct. As Europe moved towards 'an ever closer union, the tensions grew'.

When the Falklands War broke out, President Mitterrand understood that the honour of the British nation was at stake and that international law should prevail over the use of force. On 3 April 1982, President Mitterrand was the first Western leader to phone Prime Minister Margaret Thatcher expressing his support to the UK after Argentina's invasion of the Falklands on 2 April. The Falklands War was a climax in the Franco-British relations, and President Mitterrand was determined to back Britain against Argentina.[14] During his state visit to the Ivory Coast on 23 May 1982, President Mitterrand reasserted France's support to Britain:

> Our solidarity to Great Britain must never be questioned. It is our first duty. Yet France must try as much as it can to maintain its friendships, its interests and this historic community which binds her to Latin America. France will always be in favour of peace and against the infringement of the law. France will do its utmost to stop the fighting as soon as possible. But we will not surrender to either Britain or Argentina. We will fight for the restoration of peace which is a pillar of French foreign policy.[15]

As Margaret Thatcher wrote in her diary: 'I was to have many disputes with President Mitterrand in later years, but I never forgot the debt we owed him for his personal support on this occasion and throughout the Falklands crisis. France used her influence in the United Nations to swing others in our favour.'[16]

But the picture of harmonious cooperation is not unqualified. During the Falklands War, the French defence industry continued to assist Argentina even after the war had begun. Behind the scenes, actions were speaking louder than

---

[14] Jacques Attali, *Verbatim I*, 270.
[15] Archives, Institut François Mitterrand, 7 March 2010.
[16] Margaret Thatcher, *The Downing Street Years* 1993. London: Harper Collins, 2011, 182–3.

words. In what would appear to be a clear breach of President Mitterrand's embargo, a French technical team mainly working for a company 51 per cent owned by the French government stayed in Argentina throughout the war.

The French ambassador in London, Emmanuel de Margerie was vitriolic in his condemnation of the British military action. He clearly detested Margaret Thatcher. In a stinging memo dated 7 April 1982, the ambassador described the British prime minister as 'Victorian, imperialist and obstinate'. He went on to add that she had a 'tendency to get carried away by combative instincts'. In another document entitled *The Falklands: Lessons from a Fiasco*, senior French official Bernard Dorin accused Britain of 'superpower arrogance' and claimed the country had shown 'profound contempt for Latinos'. Sir John Nott, defence secretary at the time of the Falklands crisis, later commented: 'We asked Mitterrand not to give assistance to the Argentinians. If you are asking me: "Are the French duplicitous people?" the answer is: "Of course they are, and they always have been."'

There was good understanding between President Mitterrand and the Iron Lady on the Falklands, their attitude to Gorbachev and on the Channel Tunnel. But there were antagonisms between the two countries over the European budget, the Common Agricultural Policy and German reunification. The disagreements between Thatcher and Mitterrand over Europe mattered less than their mutual understanding. The first Franco-British Summit took place in London on 10 September 1981, a few months after Mitterrand's election as President. Margaret Thatcher reasserted the importance of the EU for Britain but underlined the problems of the Common Agricultural Policy. She wanted her money back, as she constantly repeated. Mitterrand felt that she did not share the values of the European Community, but he praised the commercial genius of Britain and called for cooperation between the two countries in computer engineering. This summit saw the beginning of the Channel Tunnel project, which ended Britain's isolation as an island and linked it to continental Europe.

Margaret Thatcher and President Mitterrand managed to sign the treaty leading to the construction of the Channel Tunnel on 12 February 1986. Margaret Thatcher was very enthusiastic for this quasi-Napoleonic project. The treaty was the outcome of negotiations between Margaret Thatcher and Mitterrand, which took shape at the Franco-British Summit on 30 November 1984. It was signed in the Cathedral chapter house of Canterbury with their foreign secretary Geoffrey Howe and his French counterpart Roland Dumas. It boiled down to four principles: the technical criterion, the improvement of passenger transport between Europe and Great Britain, the improvement of economic relations on either side of the Channel and finally environmental protection.[17] The British prime minister and the French president met in Paris on 20 July 1987 to exchange the ratified treaties. It was a great political achievement for Margaret Thatcher and François Mitterrand.

The British contribution to the EU was the major obstacle between Margaret Thatcher and François Mitterrand. Mitterrand warned against the increase of the European budget by 10 per cent during a meeting with the Iron Lady, but she would not accept the Athens agreement in 1983 and wanted to renegotiate the treaty. The Iron Lady wanted her money back and she wanted to get 1.25 billion pounds a year whereas Mitterrand agreed to 1 billion pounds.

A compromise was reached and the British prime minister got a 65 per cent rebate, but the Iron Lady had underestimated the links between Mitterrand and German chancellor Helmut Kohl. As Margaret Thatcher wrote in her diary: 'The rebate I had won had limited our net contribution from rising to a totally unacceptable level; but several of our Community partners now wanted to cut or eliminate it.'[18]

The British prime minister tried to convince the French president that Anglo-French cooperation was essential and that defence cooperation should be developed. During Iraq's invasion of Kuwait in August 1990, Margaret Thatcher, George Bush and François Mitterrand rallied together and adopted resolution 600 at the United Nations to condemn Iraq and declare embargo against Iraq and Kuwait. On her last visit to Paris, the British prime minister discussed the issue with President Mitterrand on 20 November 1990. She was keen to stop Saddam Hussein and was willing to send troops, whereas Mitterrand was reluctant to send more soldiers to Kuwait.[19] That was to be their last meeting. Margaret Thatcher admits that her disagreement with the French 'never led to ill-feeling'. She was opposed to political union but European Monetary Union was a greater threat to Margaret Thatcher. Europe would always be a stumbling block in Franco-British relations, yet the Iron

[17] Mathieu Monot, 'Eurotunnel: Dernière Manche Franco-Britannique', *Lettre de l'Institut François Mitterrand*, n. 39, 8.
[18] Margaret Thatcher, *The Downing Street Years*, 728.
[19] Jacques Attali, *Verbatim II*, 1200.

Lady was keen to rebuild an Anglo-French entente as a counterbalance to the German influence.[20] When Margaret Thatcher left Downing Street in 1990, President Mitterrand paid tribute to her and said that 'she had played a historic role in Great Britain and in Europe', he meant it as he greatly admired her for her courage and determination. In the end, the socialist President was sad that she resigned in the Conservative leadership contest and welcomed John Major with mixed feelings: 'she was an opponent but she had a vision. After all, I got on very well with her.'[21] President Mitterrand respected Margaret Thatcher and reciprocally she held Mitterrand in high esteem. Two days after leaving the British Embassy in Paris, Margaret Thatcher had to resign from the premiership.

Euroscepticism started to burgeon within the UK, and the Maastricht Treaty drove Britain further apart from the EU. That is precisely the reason why when Tony Blair became Prime Minister, he wanted the UK to be at the heart of the EU not on the sidelines as it had been from 1992 to 1997. He was in favour of the enlargement of the EU. He believed that Europe was to do with the modern world and that Britain had to be involved in economic decision-making: 'Britain needed Europe in order to exert influence and advance its interests.... It was a practical question of realpolitik.'[22] On 11 November 1998, to celebrate the eightieth anniversary of the Armistice, President Chirac and Queen Elizabeth II inaugurated Sir Winston Churchill's statue in Paris. A lunch was hosted with Champagne Pol Roger Cuvée Sir Winston Churchill to pay tribute to the Prime Minister of Great Britain who led his country to victory against Germany. To celebrate the centenary of the Entente Cordiale, a dinner was hosted by his Excellency the President of the French Republic and Mme François Mitterrand for Her Majesty Queen Elizabeth II and His Royal Highness the Prince Philip, Duke of Edinburgh, at the Elysée Palace. The dinner started with broccoli soup, foie gras and quail with mushrooms, cheese and Le Chambord as a dessert. The dinner was served with exquisite wines such as Château d'Yquem 1990, Château Mouton Rothschild 1958 and Dom Perignon Champagne 1995.

---

[20] Margaret Thatcher, *The Downing Street Years*, 815.
[21] Jacques Attali, *Verbatim II*, 1205.
[22] Tony Blair, *A Journey*. London: Hutchinson, 2010, 533.

The Saint Malo declaration signed in December 1998 by Prime Minister Tony Blair and President Chirac created a successful military partnership between the two countries in response to the armed conflict in Kosovo. This led to a deep strategic defence relationship which weathered many storms.

A few years later, addressing both Houses of Parliament, President Sarkozy delivered perhaps the warmest homage to Britain delivered by any post-war French leader on 17 June 2010. He declared the birth of an Anglo-French axis as a force for progress in Europe and the world, on issues ranging from climate change and nuclear power to UN reform and the war in Afghanistan. Differences over the EU and past rivalries, he said, could be overcome:

> In the name of the French people, I have come to propose to the people of Britain that together we write a new page in our shared history, that of a new Franco-British brotherhood – a brotherhood for the 21st century. If the UK and France together want more justice, the world will be more just. If the UK and France struggle together for peace, the world will be more peaceful.

The impact of Brexit on the Entente Cordiale

Former socialist prime minister Michel Rocard once wrote in *Le Monde* that Britain should leave the EU before the spirit of the EU disintegrates:

> There is between you and us continental Europeans a misunderstanding which is becoming vicious. There is boundless admiration for your great history. You invented democracy and human rights three centuries ago, you mastered the world, by sea with your Navy and finance. You do not like Europe, that is your right and this is quite understandable. You entered the European Market forty two years ago, but it was a misunderstanding.... You should leave before breaking the Union. There was a time when elegance was synonymous with British. Let us rebuild Europe. Recover your traditions and we will hold you in high esteem.[23]

Boris Johnson led the campaign to take Britain out of the EU. Many French politicians may have rejoiced at Britain's vote for Brexit as they disagreed with

---

[23] Michel Rocard, "Amis Anglais, sortez de l'union européenne mais ne la faites pas mourir !", *Le Monde*, 5 juin 2014.

Britain's vision of Europe, its attempts at cherrypicking, its flexible labour market and free circulation of capitals.

When Emmanuel Macron won the election in May 2017, he voiced his dream of leading the EU. President Macron is in the wake of the gaullist tradition of an intergovernmental EU. His proposal of European integration goes back to the concept of Jean Monnet's supranationalism. President Macron believes that France is central to the world's culture, and he appears as the champion of the enlightenment values. During his first meeting with Prime Minister Theresa May at the Elysée Palace in June 2017, President Macron said to the British prime minister that the doors of the EU were still open if the UK wanted to remain. President Macron welcomed the UK to stay in the EU as France and the UK needed each other. There was a meeting between Prime Minister Theresa May and President Macron at the Fort de Bregançon, the summer residence of the French president, on 3 August 2018. Yet President Macron rejected the Chequers Plan like Chancellor Merkel and the twenty-seven EU countries because it questioned the integrity of the single market. His inflexibility in the Brexit negotiations led to the fall of a British government.

France wanted to find an agreement between the EU and the UK, but not at all costs and three outstanding sticking points remained on 5 December 2020, less than a month before the end of the transition period: fisheries, level playing field and governance. France wanted to reach an ambitious deal but was keen to protect its interests and refused to yield on demands for post-Brexit fishing rights in British waters. For France and its supporters, especially the fishing nations of the Netherlands, Denmark, Belgium and Spain, continued access to British waters was the price the UK had to pay for continued tariff-free access to the EU's single market after the transition period ended on 31 December 2020. Fishing is a symbolic issue for both French and British fishermen even though fishing only represents 0.1 per cent of the GDP. According to the French European minister Clément Beaune: 'The British want access to the single European market without constraints for their social, environmental or health standards, which is unacceptable. For our part, we are ready to put in place a system in which a divergence of standards would be allowed but beyond which corrective measures would be taken.' In the early 1990s, the former chairman of Peugeot Jacques Calvet compared the UK to a 'Japanese aircraft carrier off the coast of Europe' because of the investment of Nissan, Toyota and Honda in the British car manufacturing industry. President Macron was frightened by unfair competition from exporters across the Channel.

It is rare to find a European policy these days on which the German chancellor, the French president and the prime ministers of Hungary, Italy and Poland agree. Brexit is the exception. The unity of the twenty-seven countries of the EU has never faltered before the breakout of Covid-19. The twenty-seven countries of the EU have remained united in their approach to the Brexit negotiations.

The eleventh-hour deal is unprecedented because it is the first time a member state of the EU has left the customs union and the single market. The Brexit negotiations are not only about the future relationship with the UK but also about the future of Europe and what it means to be a member of the EU. The Union's most important asset is its single market and the customs union. The deadline of 29 March 2019 was not respected by Theresa May's government. The UK got an extension until 12 April and 31 October 2019. France accepted the postponement of the withdrawal of the UK from the EU until 31 October 2019, which required the UK to hold elections to the European Parliament. Theresa May lost control of Parliament, the unity of her Cabinet, the support of her political party and the support of most voters, and she had to resign on 24 May 2019 as head of the Conservative Party yet remaining Prime Minister during a transition period until the election of the new Tory leader on 23 July 2019. Theresa May was replaced by Boris Johnson as Prime Minister. He managed to reopen negotiations in Brussels and achieved a deal on Thursday 17 October 2019. Yet the House of Commons voted the Letwin amendment on 19 October by 322 votes, that is to say, a majority of sixteen MPs. The Letwin amendment asked for an extension to the vote of the deal until the technical arrangements were clear. It was an insurance policy to make sure the UK left with a deal. It meant that the Prime Minister had to write a letter asking for another extension from Brussels. After bitter and endless negotiations between the UK and the EU27, British Brexit negotiator Lord Frost and Michel Barnier reached an agreement in Brussels on 24 December 2020, and on 1 January 2021 the UK took back control of its finances, laws and borders and began a new chapter in its nation's history. Northern Ireland remains in the UK customs union as well as in the single market for goods. There will not be a physical border between Northern Ireland and the Republic of Ireland in order to maintain the Good Friday Agreement.

President Macron was coveting the jobs in London's financial sector and his administration also tried to lure London-based bankers to Paris. Yet this failed with the weekly rebellion of the yellow vests and apart from JP Morgan most banks have sent a few bankers to Frankfurt but London may remain the European financial centre for the next few years. President Macron also tried to attract UK-based car manufacturers to France and organized a private dinner party at the Elysée Palace in 2019 for the heads of Renault Nissan, Vauxhall and Jaguar Land Rover to attract them to France which he is trying to make more business friendly. This charm offensive was an attempt to attract car companies that were nervous about the uncertainties created by Brexit. On 28 June 2021, President Macron organized a lunch with chairmen of major companies at Versailles Palace to entice them to choose France. The chairman of JP Morgan has sent 400 traders to Paris. Yet London remains the first financial centre in Europe ahead of Amsterdam, Paris and Frankfurt. So far, Brexit did not lead to the UK's economic demise but British customers have bought 16.3 per cent more from the rest of the world. Brexit has thus been a big loss for the French economy, which is down £3.3 billion since 2016 because of the 12.7 per cent drop in sales to British customers, according to a report published by Brexit Facts 4 EU.org.[24]

President Macron wants to use his presidency of the EU from 1 January 2022 to turn French into the language of the EU, yet English is likely to remain the working language in the foreseeable future, as most EU members do not learn French as a foreign language at school. French remains the most popular foreign language taught in British schools, but it looks set to be overtaken by Spanish by 2030, or earlier, if current trends continue, according to the British Council Report by Ian Collen, *Language Trends 2020: Language Teaching in Primary and Secondary Schools in England*. Overall, there is still a long way to go to return to the figures of 2005. French is declining in popularity as a foreign language in British schools from 250,000 in 2005 to 125,000 in 2020. At A level, Spanish entries have increased by almost over 5 per cent from 2018, overtaking French as the most popular language for the first time since A levels began.

Defence cooperation between France and the UK remains crucial for both countries, and they value bilateral defence and security ties as the only two substantial military powers in Western Europe. France and the UK are both

---

[24] 'The EU's biggest losers, as the "Treasure Island" Brits choose to buy "non-EU"', *Brexit Facts 4.eu*, 1 August 2021.

members of the Security Council of the United Nations and they are nuclear powers. The Lancaster House Treaty for defence and security cooperation was signed at Number Ten on 2 November 2010 by Prime Minister David Cameron and French president Nicolas Sarkozy. It led to the sharing and pooling of materials and equipment including through mutual interdependence, the building of joint facilities, mutual access to each other's defence markets and industrial and technological cooperation. It created a new framework for exchanges between the UK and French armed forces on operational matters and has led to the two military powers working seamlessly together. They are fighting against terrorism. French troops are deployed in the Sahel and France is grateful for the support of the UK in Africa. In Iraq progress has been made and France and Britain are fighting alongside. As threats to Europe have intensified, Europeans have had to develop their strategic autonomy. The Franco-British rapid reaction force reached full capacity late in 2020, able to deploy 10,000 men on land, sea and air in combat operations. France's new commissioner Thierry Breton is in charge of defence industry and space and presides over a European Defence Fund to boost research in defence industry. France has no other such tight arrangement with any other country and felt betrayed by the AUKUS partnership reached between the UK, the United States and Australia on 16 September 2021. Australia cancelled the £72.8 billion contract with France for twelve conventional diesel-powered submarines in order to invest in nuclear-powered boats more suited to combat Chinese expansionism in the Indo-Pacific region. The pact is a long-term security partnership in which Britain will share with Australia the technology garnered over half a century of running a nuclear-powered submarine fleet. The AUKUS deal has therefore damaged the Entente and the security pact between France and the UK. It was a national humiliation for France and a personal blow for President Macron who signed the original France–Australia deal as finance minister during President Hollande's term in office. The peacetime relations between the two countries have never been so icy.

Conclusion

In a nutshell, Brexit has complicated the fraught relations between France and the UK. France does not want the UK to block the EU and to cherrypick bits of the single market. France does not want to change the rules of the EU even for an ally such as the UK. President Macron has been unflinching and has tried to marginalize Britain as a power in Europe. For France, compromising on core European values would have been impossible. France believes in a sovereign Union and France is not in favour of federalism. France is working at strengthening the EU to face the challenges of the twenty-first century such as migration, digital transformation, cybercrime, terrorism and pandemics like Covid-19. Covid-19 has slowed down negotiations and has brought the EU27 closer together.

Brexit is a very complex issue, which has weakened the European fabric and which leaves Europe vulnerable to the populists. The deal reached on 24 December 2020 was good news for both the UK and France. A no-deal Brexit would have cost billions of euros to France in the next decade. Yet tensions remain between France and the UK especially on fishing and the Northern Ireland Protocol as could be seen in the bilateral meeting between President Macron and Prime Minister Boris Johnson during the G7 in Cornwall on 12 June 2021. Macron wants the British people to 'honour their word to the Europeans and the framework defined by the Brexit agreements' and hinted Northern Ireland was not part of the UK, whereas Boris Johnson declared Britain was a single country and he was ready to trigger Article 16 of the Protocol, suspending the terms of the agreement if the EU failed to change its position on the issue of Northern Ireland. Besides President Macron suggested that the EU was better off without the UK: 'The EU demonstrated in the last four years that it is a political entity not just an economic entity. . . . We can have certain interests and values we can pursue together and not be blocked by another partner.'

At a time when Brexit will change the way the UK interacts with the rest of Europe, it is important to remember and celebrate the strength and the depth of the links between the two countries.

Bibliography

Attali, Jacques. *Verbatim II. 1995*. Paris: Robert Laffont, 2011.
Blair, Tony. *A Journey*. London: Hutchinson, 2010.
De Gaulle, Charles. *Mémoires d'Espoir, Le Renouveau, 1958–1962*. Paris: Plon, 1970.

Macmillan, Harold. *The Macmillan Diaries, Volume II, Prime Minister and After, 1957–66*, ed. Peter Catterall. London: Macmillan, 2011.

Reynolds, David. *The Long Shadow: The Great War and the 20th Century*. London: Simon & Schuster, 2013.

Rocard, Michel. Amis Anglais, sortez de l'union européenne mais ne la faites pas mourir!. *Le Monde*, 5 June 2014.

Sacre, Jean-Maurice & François Bertin. *Invitation à l'Elysée: 150 ans de Tables présidentielles*. Rennes: Editions Ouest France, 2011.

Sykes, Christopher Simon. *The Man Who Created the Middle East: A Story of Empire, Conflict and the Sykes-Picot Agreement*. William Collins, 2016.

Thatcher, Margaret. *The Downing Street Years. 1993*. London: Harper Collins, 2011.

Védrine, Hubert. *Les Mondes de François Mitterrand: A l'Elysée 1981–1995*. Paris: Fayard, 1996.

Brexit and the German position

Jochen M. Richter

Introduction

This analysis aims to shed light on the process and consequences for Germany following the decision by the United Kingdom (UK) to leave the European Union (EU). The author will quote several sources including from the EU institutions. However, none of the opinions expressed represents the views either of the institutions or of the German government.

This chapter considers three aspects which, in the author's opinion, are still evolving. Why? The date of Brexit taking effect has passed and so has the agreed transition period. In the author's view, however, Brexit is still a moving target. In the meantime, a whole series of analyses is available, mostly addressing the reasons why Brexit got most votes, and its consequences. Only a few publications provide a comprehensive view of the German position.

The first aspect concerns the process. Disbelief was a regular reaction from the moment Prime Minister David Cameron announced the referendum until its outcome. During the subsequent negotiation phase, Germany was defending a strictly rule-based approach. Provided the situation required it, German pragmatism prevailed. Germany (and the EU) hoped that the UK also wished, in the end, to avoid crashing out. A particular focus will be on an important issue: When did Brexit start? Moreover, did Germany miss the early warning signs? The author argues that the starting point of the process leading to Brexit goes back to the time when Margaret Thatcher became Prime Minister.

The second aspect is Germany's loss of a strategic partner. The immediate association is the area of foreign and defence policy. However, there are other elements of equal importance. The UK consistently held a high-ranking position in implementing EU laws, especially in economic matters. In budgetary discussions, the UK was often the country which was able to send conciliatory messages helping to reconcile different camps. In the context of the 2020 multi-annual budget discussions,[1] those camps were the 'frugal four' and the 'friends of cohesion'. Germany, as holder of the Council presidency, had to deal almost alone with their incompatible positions. Beyond budgetary matters, the UK had a particular relationship with some Eastern European countries that had proved to be helpful in the past.

The third aspect relates to the future. The ongoing coronavirus crisis has exposed the difficult choices Germany has to make. The French demands for more Europe, particularly favouring shared economic policies, are for Germany still difficult to accept. Nevertheless, Germany is also increasingly uneasy about following the strict line of the 'frugal four', seeing the risk of further dividing lines between EU member states. The latter is also true for its relations with Italy and Poland. The author wonders what concept Germany holds for the future. Can an admittedly so far successful approach of 'wait and see' really work mid-term or long-term?

Early warning signs

'Brexit' is a word adopted by those who campaigned for and were strongly in favour of the UK leaving the EU. Along the way, many, including Germany, were almost convinced that in the end, the well-known British attitude of being reasonable would prevail, and voters would see the damage such a decision would potentially create. Disbelief that the referendum could be successful was mostly the reaction, also because opinion polls pointed to a positive outcome. Like many observers who followed the preliminary results until after midnight, the author went to bed assuming, with a sigh of relief, that the worst was not going to happen. Well, we all know of the nasty surprise the following morning.

Though it is established knowledge, one cannot often enough stress the division within the UK. England and Wales voted Leave, but London,

---

[1] Multiannual Financial Framework 2021–2027.

Northern Ireland and Scotland voted Remain. One might ask how united was and is the UK?

Middle England by Jonathan Coe provides enough examples of a divided country. Reading it was yet another trigger for my reflections on whether this phenomenon is not something that has built up over time. Moreover, were there early warning signs? If so, could Germany have influenced the process that, at a certain stage, irreversibly took the direction of Brexit? After all, the two conservative parties[2] had strong ties over many years.

As stated at the beginning of this chapter, in my view Brexit had its starting point with Margaret Thatcher becoming Prime Minister. Of course, one could also argue that the different visions about Europe started much earlier. Brendan Simms reminds us of the failure of the meeting in May 1948 at The Hague, where the British foreign secretary Ernest Bevin said 'no to a complete political union'.[3] The same author points to the incompatible visions at the Messina meeting in June 1955.[4] One cannot conclude this brief historic review without mentioning the events of June 1975. The governing Labour Party organized a referendum on EEC membership resulting in a clear majority in favour of staying. However, this campaign and debate 'divided the country, the parties and even families'.[5]

This was the starting point of a much larger divide that in my view initiated a process that led to the Brexit referendum.

Margaret Thatcher launched her campaign in the hostile environment that was the basis for her 1979 election success. Furthermore, the global changes due to international developments (second oil crisis and Russian invasion of Afghanistan) during that election year created a polarization of positions in Europe. Moreover, the French initiative in 1984 aimed at fostering a European defence policy under the auspices of the Western European Union ran counter to Margaret Thatcher's focus that the EU should predominantly be a free-market economy.

Germany's reunification and the forced end of British membership of the ERM[6] in September 1992 following the Black Wednesday events

---

[2] Germany's CDU and the British Tories.
[3] Brendan Simms, *Europe*, p. 399.
[4] The conference assessed the progress of the ECSC and, deciding that it was working well, proposed further European integration. Britain, not being a member, tried to push for a looser free trade association.
[5] Brendan Simms, *Europe*, p. 465.
[6] European Exchange Rate Mechanism.

merely increased the feeling that the UK was never on the same page. The 1997 announcement by Gordon Brown of the 'five economic tests' that would determine whether the UK would (ever) become a member of the Eurozone was thus almost a logical consequence.

In this context let me quote the former German EU ambassador Dr Dietrich von Kyaw: 'A glorifying view of Britain's past and hatred of Europe and its Institutions, was Prime Minister Margaret Thatcher's baseline in all negotiations. Against advice, Chancellor Kohl agreed the British rebate hoping to ease this situation. But Margaret Thatcher's fear of a Germany that was "economically too strong" and now reunified, prevailed.'

Summarizing the above, let me quote an extract from an article in the *Neue Züricher Zeitung*:

> When Prime Minister Margaret Thatcher was forced to resign because of the dispute over Europe, it emerged that the cards had to be put on the table. Next, her successor, John Major, came under increasing pressure from opponents of the EU. For them, *Brussels* was the reincarnation of the hegemon one must fight. David Cameron's failed attempt to tame these internal forces by means of another referendum finally paved the way to what is now becoming a reality: Britain's EU membership will soon be an episode of history.[7]

These were in my view early warning signs of a gap that was growing. Why should Germany have seen coming what culminated in the 2016 referendum?

As mentioned previously, the German and British conservative parties had especially good ties and engaged in regular exchanges. By way of example, the following are all taken from a series of articles published in 2005 on the twentieth anniversary of British-German Parliamentary Meetings[8] in Cadenabbia, highlighting the many aspects of that missing joint European vision.

An article by Angela Merkel calls for strong EU institutions. She wrote this in view of the difficult ratification process of the constitutional treaty. She favoured strong EU institutions to enable not only the single market but equally a joint security policy.

---

[7] https://www.nzz.ch/meinung/ein-teil-europas-und-doch-separat-ld.1537067#back-register
[8] Hartmut Mayer/Thomas Bernd Stehling, German-British Relations, 2005, Konrad Adenauer Foundation.

Michael Howard's contribution can be read as a reply: he almost exclusively stresses the economic cooperation issues. This follows the logic of his February 2004 speech in Berlin, entitled 'A New Deal for Europe'.[9]

David Curry's article reminds us of the complex UK situation. He underlines the challenge presented by Tony Blair's failure to deliver on his 1997 promise 'to reconcile Britain to an unequivocal engagement in Europe', while Peter Müller addresses Germany's challenges in relation to integration and migration. In contrast to today's situation, Peter Müller portrayed his country's cautious approach and recognized a much more progressive UK position back in 2005.

Finally, in line with Margaret Thatcher's position, Douglas Hurd's contribution sheds light on the UK's fear of German economic predominance.

The year 2005 marked another step that created hectic diplomacy at EU level. When David Cameron became Tory party leader, his moderate agenda faced criticism from internal hard-liners. A visible sign was the exclusion on 7 June 2005 of MEP Roger Helmer from the still joint group EPP-ED.[10] While Mr Helmer's exclusion triggered the break-up of the joint faction later on, there was more at play. Helmer was part of a small but vocal group that insiders in the European Parliament called the H-group (Roger Helmer, Daniel John Hannan and Christopher Heaton-Harris). An inside source explained how influential this group must have been, pointing out 'British members voted in plenary regularly for more extreme positions despite EPP-ED compromise proposals'. As is well known, in the end the British Tories left the EPP-ED group, which thereafter became the EPP again.

Another Parliament source recalled a gathering in Cadenabbia[11] in summer 2013 of young members from the German and British conservative parties. The commemorative publication from this event points, on the one hand, to some common European goals and, on the other hand, states the British criticism of too much Brussels interference. As a high-ranking official of Parliament added, 'Having been present at several of these German-British meetings, it

---

[9] https://www.theguardian.com/politics/2004/feb/12/conservatives.uk
[10] The group of the European Peoples Party (EPP) made earlier a concession to the British Tories and therefore gave itself a new name, called EPP-ED. The ED addition representing the British members was a concession by the EPP leadership.
[11] Former summer residence of Konrad Adenauer in Italy, today a meeting place of the Konrad Adenauer Foundation.

became increasingly difficult to have discussions that remained factual rather than emotional.'

Given the German struggle to keep Britain on board, one could have expected that Germany would take a tough position after the referendum's outcome. However, during the negotiation process thereafter, Germany never showed any signs of wishing to punish the UK for its decision. In addition, in contrast to several public statements by the French authorities, Germany kept its pragmatic approach.

Before looking at some examples, let us recall that the EU's founding spirit in 1957 was one of a 'membership to the European Economic Community that was entered into for an indefinite period. For eternity, in other words'.[12] The Lisbon Treaty, signed in December 2007, introduced Article 50 and thereby Paul-Henri Spaak's invention of the infinite duration of membership no longer existed. Article 50 provides for a withdrawal procedure, allowing any member state to leave the EU in accordance with its own constitutional rules. It is hugely ironic that Sir John Kerr, a UK member of the Convention for an EU Constitution, is alleged to have come up with the idea that later became Article 50. As is well known, Sir John himself was not at all in favour of the UK leaving the EU.

I think it is safe to say that nobody expected that any member state would invoke Article 50. Berlin was probably the least prepared as it was an unwritten rule within the German Chancellery that the potential British departure was not to be discussed. This was in line with Commission president Jean-Claude Juncker's promise to Prime Minister David Cameron not to interfere in an internal affair of the UK. In my view, this non-interference created a huge challenge for Germany.

As expected, Chancellor Angela Merkel called the result the day after the referendum a 'blow to Europe'. At the same time, she was in favour of a calm and prudent reaction in line with what I call 'German pragmatism'. The sound bites from Paris were quite different. President Hollande expressed the desire to take decisive action. He accordingly announced an early meeting with Angela Merkel to prepare initiatives that he defined as a 'European leap forward'.

However, Germany did not sit on its hands. Upon invitation by the German president Frank-Walter Steinmeier, on 25 June 2016 the foreign ministers of

---

[12] Luuk van Middelaar, *Alarums and Excursions: Improvising Politics on the European Stage*.

the six founding members met in Berlin. The discussions resulted in agreeing to a nine-page document entitled 'A Strong Europe in an Uncertain World'.[13] Steinmeier, in his statement to the press, called on the EU to avoid any retaliation towards Britain. Furthermore, Germany coordinated a meeting with the Dutch government to which the Netherlands invited the Nordic EU members.

To illustrate how complicated this German positioning was, let me quote some examples that Luuk van Middelaar lists in his book I referred to before.

- Council president Donald Tusk, Parliament president Martin Schulz, Prime Minister Mark Rutte for the rotating presidency and Commission president Jean-Claude Juncker issued a very business-like declaration expressing regrets about the referendum result but showing respect for the decision of the voters. However, later in the day Martin Schulz called it a scandal that Cameron wanted to postpone issuing the Article 50 letter until October. That same evening, Jean-Claude Juncker stressed in another interview the urgency of receiving such a letter from London.
- Berlin saw the need to orchestrate a weekend meeting at the end of June to agree a joint EU position: no negotiations without notification.[14]
- Moreover, there was still the question of the (immediate) consequences, best described by the following triangle of events. The EU was preparing to celebrate the sixtieth anniversary of the Rome Treaty in March 2017, knowing that London would not and, of course, could not be present. Meanwhile France, Germany, Italy and Spain came back to the previously sketched out idea of a Europe of different speeds. Finally, let us remember that elections were due in Germany and France during 2017.

The loss of a strategic partner

Was Brexit just a difficult member leaving the EU – some even adding bitterly 'finally'? This view seems supported by my earlier description of the voting behaviour of the conservative British MEPs, the break-up of the joint group and so on. Moreover, Council representatives can give plentiful examples of complex if not impossible negotiations with the UK.

---

[13] Reuters News from 25 June 2016.
[14] Luuk van Middelaar, *Alarums and Excursions: Improvising Politics on the European Stage.*

However, from my own time in the EU institutions, especially in the cabinet of Internal Market Commissioner Frits Bolkestein, I recall the UK as a tough but fair negotiating partner. The former commissioner often said, 'They fight until the very last moment but, once they agree to a compromise, they stick to it and implement the laws.'

The 2020 Internal Market Scoreboard states that

> The UK is now under the EU average deficit and one of 12 Member States that has achieved the 0.5% proposed target. Nevertheless, it transposed 19 of the 23 Single Market-related directives (83%) due to have been transposed in the 6 months prior to the cut-off date for calculation (1 June–30 November 2019). This shows that the UK could monitor the timely transposition of directives even better.[15]

Furthermore, the UK transposed EU laws into national law faster than the EU average (around five to six months in comparison to eleven months as the EU average).

Yet was there more to worry about? As stated earlier, the increasing perception was that London was almost constantly on the brake. As the 'ever-closer union' became more and more reality, the British side increasingly rejected the further planned steps towards integration.

In my view, with Brexit Germany has lost a strategic partner in several areas. Of course, the UK was on Germany's side as regards many economic questions, be it free trade or budget discussions. The 90-hours-long discussions about the next multi-annual financial framework[16] were a clear example of the missing British voice. Germany had to keep the role of arbitrator as it held the rotating Council presidency. While all concentration was on the so-called frugal four, the moderate but clear British position was absent. Notably, for Germany, as an exporting nation, the UK market is and remains of economic importance. Whatever an agreement would look like, this is unlikely to change.

Beyond economics, there is another area where the loss is already quite visible. For decades, the UK was for Germany an ally and fully reliable partner,[17] especially in defence and security affairs. Of course, I hear those

---

[15] https://ec.europa.eu/internal_market/scoreboard/performance_by_member_state/uk/index_en.htm
[16] July 2020 Council negotiations for the Multiannual Financial Framework 2021–2027.
[17] This was reinforced by Commission president Von der Leyen's speech on 24 December 2020 praising the UK as a 'trusted partner'.

reminding us of the clear division between Germany and the UK over the Iraq War. Yet, this was one of the very few exceptions. Moreover, in the context of the United Nations, Germany could regularly appreciate that it had two European countries with veto powers. Most often, as a former ambassador said, the British position was one of moderation and reason.

The lasting conflict between Greece and Turkey about exploration rights in the Aegean Sea is another example where Germany is missing British support within the EU context. France's unequivocal support of Greece did not necessarily make the overall situation any easier. Germany's ambiguous position is already drawing criticism of not wishing to endanger the migration deal with Turkey rather than the country having assumed the role of honest broker.

Looking at defence cooperation, a joint paper by the Royal United Services Institute (RUSI) and Konrad Adenauer Foundation (KAS) of May 2012[18] addresses the already mentioned dispute regarding the Iraq intervention. 'The British-German defence relationship has been defined, rather, by a lack of trust in the political atmosphere, legal and constitutional obstacles to co-operation, and differences in strategic culture and attitudes towards the use of force.'

The paper, however, points also to the potential prospects of cooperation in stating 'Germany and the UK subscribe to the idea of NATO as a regional alliance with a global horizon'.

In line with this more positive outlook, there was agreement in October 2018 between Defence Secretary Gavin Williamson and his German counterpart Ursula von der Leyen for a deepened defence cooperation between these two countries. The UK representative stated on that occasion, 'Although we are preparing to leave the EU, our commitment to European security is resolute. The statement signed today strengthens UK-German ties and bolsters the defence of two key NATO partners. This is an alliance we both hold dear.'[19] In discussing the prospects, I will return to this point.

To sum up these considerations, let us take a brief look at the balance of power in the European Parliament. Has Brexit changed anything for

---

[18] https://www.kas.de/en/single-title/-/content/britisch-deutsche-verteidigungszusammenarbeit-in-der-nato by Lisa Aronsson and Patrick Keller.
[19] https://www.gov.uk/government/news/uk-deepens-defence-cooperation-with-germany#:~:text=In%20an%20era%20of%20evolving,the%20Defence%20Secretary%20reaffirmed%20today.&text=The%20statement%20signed%20today%20strengthens,of%20two%20key%20NATO%20partners.

Germany's significance in Parliament? Purely mathematically, it seems that German members have a slightly stronger position. Before Brexit, Germany had 96 of the 751 seats (then 12.8 per cent). Post Brexit, Parliament shrank to 705 members with Germany keeping its 96 seats (now 13.6 per cent).

This is probably too simplistic a reading. Leaving aside the question whether more seats held by German members[20] would automatically mean stronger influence, the real question is about converging political convictions. In an exchange with a Parliament representative, I learnt

> It is about very fundamental political tendencies and ideas. Concepts of Europe, of the state of society and economy, of solidarity and responsibility, of relevant issues in foreign, security and neighborhood policy, etc. In all these issues there are first party-ideological dividing lines. However, beyond that there is also a basic national consensus. In this House, the UK MEPs in the mainstream parliamentary groups tended to belong to the traditional allies of the Germans on most of the above-listed issues, sometimes even across parliamentary groups. Because of the departure of the British, the *common sense* has shifted in many factions and the Germans might feel this. As suggested above, the Germans, seen in isolation, might have gained in proportion, but they have lost a strong ally. In my opinion, the Eastern Europeans and the Southern Europeans benefit from a relative increase in importance.

What does this mean for the future?

Prospects

The UK after Brexit

The negative effect of a very emotional campaign in the UK is openly demonstrated hatred, especially towards Eastern Europeans, many often living in the country for several years. As a British friend explained, the feeling of losing its international importance as a former nation of empire combined with a more and more complex mixture in societies and cultures were important

---

[20] There were times in the previous legislature one could hear unofficial *complaints* about a 'total control by the Germans' because there was a German president of Parliament, three and later even four political groups were headed by Germans plus various Committee Chairs and both Secretary-General and Deputy Secretary General were German.

triggers for the Leave vote. It is an unanswered question how the UK will deal with this situation. Migration, whether more restricted or not, will remain a factor for the good functioning of many sectors of society. But relevant laws set clear restrictions.

The economic consequences right after Brexit took effect remained somewhat limited and probably blurred by the effects of Covid-19. Meanwhile they became more visible with a serious lack of truck drivers and many service jobs pending to be filled. But 'cheap labour' from across Europe is no longer available and society might face further challenges.

The rather sidelined British Parliament will have to rediscover its role. Some already saw a constitutional crisis emerging during the partly chaotic discussions of the Brexit laws. The developments over the recent past with Prime Minister Boris Johnson casting doubt over the obligation to adhere to the signed exit law indicate a repetition of what happened previously.

None of the British political forces now seems to question Brexit. An article in Politico end 2020 summarized the situation well. Following the confirmation of Ed Davey as leader of the Lib Dems, the leadership of all three main political parties either is explicitly in favour of or at least won't fight Brexit.

Brexit as a negotiation process

For a long time, the negotiations for the future relations between the EU and UK were seemingly going nowhere. I would point to the following challenges.

Red lines in negotiations are a commonly used instrument, but they constitute at a certain stage an obstacle if there is no exit strategy. The complex issue of a mutually recognized level playing field is probably never agreeable for the UK but is indispensable for the EU. Moreover, the importance of fishing rights has for a long time been underestimated, though it is practically more for emotional than purely economic reasons. Experts state clearly that it is non-negotiable for the UK. Nevertheless, neither France nor Spain can afford for the UK to declare in the end a one-sided victory.

In the autumn of 2020, a new attempt was expected at aiming to solve the migration issue. Even if such a proposal to reform the EU asylum system were to find agreement among EU member states, the UK will not be part of such changes. Recent events have exposed the fragility and importance of the sea border between France and the UK. Besides this, Gibraltar remains another sticky issue. Germany's Council presidency did not bring any solution to these conflicting yet important issues.

Insiders also predict a push to clarify and regulate the data flow between the EU and the United States. The question remains, where will this leave the UK? A similar argument goes for the ambition to reduce the influence of the GAFA. One wonders whether there is a risk that the UK might become a new battleground.

Regarding the financial markets, it is worthwhile noting that the importance of the euro seems to be on the rise. While it is too early to claim that the European currency has effectively the potential to overturn the leading role of the dollar, the UK's currency will be ever more in the shade of such developments. Yet, for the near future London will still outrank many other financial hubs as being one of the most important marketplaces in the world. However, green financing of investments in Europe is getting a clear momentum. Related market access and regulation will happen without considering the interests of the UK.

Defence cooperation

Alberto Cunha[21] wrote in his research paper of July 2020 about the prospects in this area. The title reads 'Post-Brexit EU Defence Policy: Is Germany Leading towards a European Army?'

While the paper points to the well-known obstacles, like the constitutional boundaries, especially for Germany, it rightly suggests that 'The EU, in particular Germany, will have to accept that an increasingly important role at a global level potentially entails painful costs[22] and risks, and has to determine which ones can be tolerated and which are unacceptable'.

The paper suggests, as a potential answer to increasing US isolation and the loss of the British contribution to EU defence cooperation, the following way forward. 'If France and Germany convince the rest of the EU members that they must strengthen their own defence capacity to gain greater autonomy

---

[21] Member of the European Foreign Policy Research Group and Centre for German Transnational Relations.
[22] According to the German industry and trade organization DIHK, about 750,000 employees are depending on export from Germany to the UK 1607088662815 (800×800) (licdn.com).

from Washington, the evolution of the CSDP can accelerate significantly in the medium term.'

The key question remains this: Is there a willingness to incorporate the UK's defence capacities? In that sense another paper[23] points out that 'This partnership[24] may not garner the level of attention enjoyed by the bilateral defence relationships between France and Germany or between the UK and France, but its success will have an impact on the ability of all three countries to shape the future of European defence'.

A kind of conclusion

By summer 2021 some aspects of Brexit are clear.

Earlier I referred to the German pragmatism in relation to the Brexit process. However, London was hoping until the very end of negotiations that Germany would finally give the British side what they need to call the result their own success. The level of trust on both sides is thus important. From what is known, I would not be surprised if both were to claim at least that the other side failed to understand its own needs.

From a German perspective, Brexit is still very much regrettable. The costs will be high, particularly for the UK but also for Germany. Independently of the previously stated economic interest in the UK market, today Poland is a more important trade partner for Germany than the UK. It seems that especially small and medium-sized companies in Germany are retreating from the UK market.

Former ambassador Dr von Kyaw defined the situation as follows. He recalled negotiations with London where he met Boris Johnson while he was working as a journalist. 'Prime Minister Johnson today perfectly copies the hatred for the EU that I experienced myself in the negotiations with Margaret Thatcher. Sadly, he keeps on nurturing British people's feeling of a diffuse loss of pride, fostering their unqualified rejection for all that is foreign while promising a

---

[23] Michelle Shevin-Cotzee, *An Overlooked Alliance: A Case for Greater UK-German Defence Cooperation*.
[24] Between Germany and the UK.

glorious economic future.' One wonders, if not worries, what might happen if his supporters realize that such promises will remain unfulfilled.

On a global scale, the relations with the United States require a careful analysis even though the confirmation of President Biden seemed to have eased some aspects. The pull-out from Afghanistan was another sign how the US line is regularly misread. Second, any kind of normalization of the complex situation with Russia is out of question following Chancellor Merkel's confirmation of Alexei Navalny's poisoning. Her last visit to Russia was without any tangible result. Third, the EU and, most importantly Germany, must define the balance between economic interests and the many other opposite goals regarding China. The meanwhile published German strategy 'Indo-Pacific Guidelines'[25] is a good start. It might even serve as a basis for an EU position. What does this mean for the geopolitical role of the EU? For which ambitions is Germany ready to engage and how would it bring the public along?

The question has recently arisen whether there would be any prospect for the UK to return to the EU. One of my sources replied:

> The current government is not only very ideological; it still tries to sell Brexit as a victory. The discussions in the UK about the handling of Covid-19 gives a flavour of what people are likely to see happening. Furthermore, those in leading positions use their previous media experience and diffuse their populist views using social media. Therefore, it is more likely to take a generation and certainly, a change in political class before any rapprochement is realistic. Of course, only if the EU is then in good shape and ready for it.

In the interest of both countries and the entire EU, one can only hope that this time will be shorter rather than longer.

Epilogue

Earlier I was questioning the prospect of a deal by stating that Germany would provide the UK the leverage needed to call any deal their success. As a kind of Christmas gift both sides effectively made a deal, though its implementation will be *ad interim* due to outstanding ratification by Parliaments on both sides.

---

[25] https://www.auswaertiges-amt.de/blob/2380514/35e5c739e1c9a5c52b6469cfd1ffc72d/200901-indo-pazifik-leitlinien--1--data.pdf

Was Germany in any way instrumental in ensuring that a deal could still be struck in time? I think it is fair to say that the general circumstances, especially yet another twist of the Covid crisis – a more infectious mutation of the virus that was identified first in the UK and the closure of the borders between France and the UK – gave the talks another dynamic.

Yet, the stickiest point was apparently to find an acceptable agreement on fisheries. It not only became a symbol for the UK's independence but led also to big fears, especially in France. To that extent it was very important that close contacts between Berlin and Paris ensured that the top priority remained what Chancellor Merkel had already defined at the October 2020 Council meeting: 'We want a deal, but obviously not at any price. It must be a fair agreement that serves the interests of both sides. This is worth every effort.'[26]

Recent events such as the end of the military intervention in Afghanistan, the outstanding trade deal between the United States and UK, supply shortages in the UK but also in the EU and the ongoing migration question will soon set the focus on how future relations in foreign matters and military cooperation – including NATO – will shape and which role the UK wishes and the EU will allow the UK to play.

The result of the German general elections in September 2021 are favouring a coalition under the leadership of the Social-Democrats. Any coalition, even in the more unlikely event of the CDU forming the government, will be influenced by the two other partners, Greens and Liberals. While no party programme went much further than expressing regret about Brexit and calling for good relations with the UK, the real questions are the following. What general position will a future government take in relation to the EU? Will Germany (have to) leave the lead to France? Of course, provided the next French president continues to keep up the ambition of President Macron. Will a new German government actively address the issue of the (social) costs of what is called 'the green deal'. Will a German government take a different stance on trade relations given a possible stronger emphasis on human rights and so on?

---

[26] France stays firm on access to UK fisheries while Germany and Italy hold out for fair Brexit deal as Johnson's deadline arrives – RT UK News.

Books

Adam, Rudolf G. *Brexit, eine Bilanz*. Heidelberg: Springer Verlag, 2019.

Dittert, Annette. *London Calling: Als Deutsche auf der Brexit*. Hamburg : Hoffmann und Campe Verlag, 2017.

Grabuschnig, Ralf. *Endstation Brexit*. Baden Baden: Tectum Verlag, 2018.

Simms, Brendan. *Europe: The Struggle for Supremacy, from 1453 to the Present*. New York: Basic Books, 2014

Van Middelaar, Luuk. *Alarums and Excursions: Improvising Politics on the European Stage*. Newcastle upon Tyne: Agenda Publishing Ltd., 2019

Reports and articles

Aronsson, Lisa & Keller, Patrick. *British-German Defence Co-operation in NATO: Finding Common Ground on European Security*. Hertford: Stephen Austin & Sons Ltd., 2012.

Howard, Michael. Speech on Europe. *The Guardian*, 12 February 2004.

Meyer, Harmut & Stehling. Deutsch-*Britische Beziehungen und der Mythos Cadenabbia*. Konrad Adenauer Foundation, 2005.

10

The new relationship between the EU and the UK

Sophie Loussouarn

After forty-seven years of membership, the United Kingdom (UK) officially left the European Union (EU) on 31 January 2020 following the signing of the Brexit Withdrawal Agreement, but it remained in the EU single market and customs union until 31 December 2020, when the transition period ended. The UK and the EU reached a breakthrough after ten months of relentless negotiations which were made more difficult by Covid-19. Fisheries, the 'level playing field' and state subsidies – these were the three major hurdles on the path to reaching a deal. In the end, after ten months of endless negotiations, both sides compromised.

Finally, a week before the expiry of the transition period, a trade deal between the UK and the EU was reached on Christmas Eve 2020, four years and a half after the referendum of 23 June 2016 on the UK's membership of the EU. During her term in office, Theresa May failed to find a common approach on what kind of future relationship with the EU would best serve Britain's interests. When Boris Johnson became Prime Minister in July 2019, he managed to renegotiate the Withdrawal Agreement, thanks to his eighty-seat majority in the House of Commons in the general election of 12 December 2019. This enhanced Britain's reputation. The trade deal came as a relief given the anxiety over the prospect of leaving without a deal. It is an historic deal, but it reveals an inability to think strategically in the long run. There is no denying that it is the biggest bilateral trade agreement between the EU and any third country so far. There shall be no tariffs or quotas on the trading of goods between the UK and the EU, but there will be customs checks at the border. It will also pave the way for new free trade agreements. Prime Minister

Boris Johnson had promised that the UK would no longer have to abide by EU regulations on 1 January 2021 and henceforth this deal enabled the UK to take back control of its borders, its laws and its waters. As Prime Minister Johnson declared on Christmas Day 2020, 'We have taken back control of our laws and our destiny. We have taken back control of every jot and tittle of our regulation in a way that is complete and unfettered.' This represented a major success for Prime Minister Johnson, who had made a commitment to deliver Brexit and had won an eighty-seat Commons majority in the general election of 12 December 2019 on that platform.

Members of the House of Commons overwhelmingly backed the deal on 30 December 2020 by 521 to 73. The twenty-seven countries of the EU gave their support to the trade and security deal, although they delayed their votes in order to study the Trade and Cooperation Agreement in detail.

The deal came into effect on 1 January 2021, when the transition period ended. It was no doubt the beginning of a new era for the UK, though it is not the end of negotiations with the EU. The UK and the EU will spend years forging a new partnership together, and it will impact on farming, fisheries, pharmaceutical industries, car manufacturing, haulage and even the fashion industry.

Michael Gove has been relieved of his role of overseeing Britain's future relationship with Europe. On 1 March 2021, Lord Frost took over Gove as UK Chairman of the Withdrawal Agreement Joint Committee; he also joined the Cabinet. Lord Frost became the UK's Brexit and international policy representative to implement the UK–EU trade deal he had negotiated with Brussels in 2020. His far-reaching role includes maximizing the opportunities of Brexit in terms of international trade and economic issues, coordination with Brussels in areas of mutual interest and working on domestic reform to make the most of Britain's freedom from EU rules. Lord Frost is an outstanding civil servant who resigned from the Cabinet on 19 December 2021 over his disapproval of the government's restriction measures to control Covid-19 and taxation policy. He was replaced by Foreign Secretary Liz Truss who took over the Brexit portfolio.

The four pillars of the trade deal

The free trade deal is a 1,246 page agreement. It is an unprecedented international agreement, which focuses on economic issues at the expense of political cooperation. Its symbolic importance is immense, but its importance in economic terms is very low. It is a political symbol for the British government under Prime Minister Boris Johnson. The deal had to be translated into twenty-three EU languages before being ratified on 28 February 2021. Because of its complexity, a postponement of the deadline for the EU to ratify the deal was granted until 31 April 2021. This created uncertainty for businesses on both sides of the Channel.

A free trade agreement without tariffs or quotas

The agreement will enable the UK and the EU to trade goods without tariffs: 'customs duties on all goods originating in the other Party shall be prohibited.'[1] The trade agreement also covers digital trade, intellectual property and energy. The UK has secured some simplifications of customs checks procedures, but there will be scope for further new friction in this context between the UK and the EU, because there will be checks on food imports. Some products are to be certified by EU, rather than UK testing bodies.

There is, however, very little on services; these account for 80 per cent of the British economy. Furthermore, Section 5 focuses on financial services[2] and Title IV deals with capital movements and maintains the 'free movement of capital for the purpose of liberalisation of investment and other transactions as provided to in Title II (Services and investment) of this Heading'.[3]

This groundbreaking free trade deal is a considerable political achievement, which will bring stability and certainty to the UK and the EU. The landmark agreement belongs to international law, not to EU law. The free trade deal gives the UK access to the EU market without maintaining EU regulations. A free trade deal is much better than a 'no-deal Brexit', which – it has been estimated – could have adversely affected British economic growth and might have led to an 8 per cent fall of GDP in the forthcoming decade.

---

[1] *EU-UK Trade and Cooperation Agreement*, 24 December 2020, Article GOODS 5, p. 20.
[2] *EU-UK Trade and Cooperation Agreement*, 24 December 2020, pp. 107–11.
[3] *EU-UK Trade and Cooperation Agreement*, 24 December 2020, Article CAP 3, p. 123.

An economic and social partnership, the fight against climate change, non-discrimination

Title II of the trade deal is devoted to services and investment and asserts the commitment to protect the environment:

> The Parties reaffirm the right to regulate within their territories to achieve legitimate policy objectives, such as: the protection of public health; social services; public education; safety; the environment, including climate change; public morals; social or consumer protection; privacy and data protection or the promotion and protection of cultural diversity.[4]

The UK has agreed to maintain its existing standards on employment and the environment and will not distort trade unfairly.

The security of citizens : The fight against terrorism and organized crime

The UK and the EU will work together: there will be a respect of fundamental rights, and there will be a respect of personal data too. Since 2017, the Permanent Structured Cooperation was initiated including four-dozen projects which span a Eurodrone, a surveillance network and a school for 'spooks' run by Greece and Cyprus. Yet new defence schemes will take time. The UK and the EU will have much to discuss on security and defence matters. Will this be discussed in 2021, in five years' time or even in the forthcoming decade? A lot still needs to be done.

Customs checks

Customs checks were introduced at the border between the UK and the EU. Apart from this, goods moving from the rest of the UK to Northern Ireland, which remains part of the UK, are subject to checks and this is causing disruption to Northern Irish exporters, who are being blocked from sending

---

[4] *EU-UK Trade and Cooperation Agreement*, 24 December 2020, Article SERVIN.1.1, p. 74.

goods to the Continent. Shevaun Haviland, director general of the British Chambers of Commerce, declared in August 2021:

> Small and medium-sized exporters have found themselves consumed in an avalanche of red tape and blockaded by disruption, to the degree that many have simply been forced to cease selling to EU-based customers altogether. That is why we are calling on senior Ministers in the UK Government, as well as EU officials, to step in and urgently examine the issues that are currently plaguing SME [small and medium-sized enterprise] exporters.

'What we call the beginning is often the end and to make an end is to make a beginning' (T. S. Eliot)

The words of the president of the EU Commission Ursula von der Leyen on 24 December 2020 were borrowed from the last part of T. S. Eliot's poem *Little Gidding*, which deals with time, memory and meaning. As the British negotiator for Brexit, Lord Frost said: 'This is a moment of national renewal.' Yet the freedom of the UK comes at a price. Brexit will recreate barriers to trade in goods and services and to cross-border mobility and exchanges which have not existed since 1973.

The British Parliament debated the trade deal on 30 December 2020, and Boris Johnson delivered a conciliatory speech in the House of Commons:

> Having taken back control of our money, our borders, our laws and our waters by leaving the European Union on 31 January, we now seize the moment to forge a fantastic new relationship with our European neighbours, based on free trade and friendly cooperation. And at the heart of this Bill is one of the biggest free trade agreements in the world, a comprehensive Canada-style deal, worth over £660 billion, which, if anything, should allow our companies to do even more business with our European friends, safeguarding millions of jobs and livelihoods in our UK and across the continent.[5]

The leader of the Labour Party, Sir Keir Starmer, said in the House of Commons on 30 December 2020:

---

[5] *Parliamentary Debates, Hansard*, Commons, 30 December 2020, p. 513.

A thin deal is better than no deal, and not implementing this deal would mean immediate tariffs and quotas with the EU, which will push up prices and drive businesses to the wall. It will mean huge gaps in security, a free-for-all on workers' rights and environmental protections, and less stability for the Northern Ireland protocol. Leaving without a deal would also show that the UK is not capable of agreeing the legal basis for our future relationship with our EU friends and partners. That matters, because I want Britain to be an outwardlooking, optimistic and rules-based country – one that does deals, signs treaties and abides by them. . . . There is only one choice today, which is to vote for implementing this deal or to vote for no deal, and those who vote no are voting for no deal. So Labour will vote to implement this treaty to avoid a no deal and put in place a floor from which we can build a strong future relationship.[6]

There was a thumping 448-vote majority in the House of Commons. Not a single Conservative MP voted against the government. Two Conservative MPs, John Redwood and Owen Paterson, abstained from voting. Only seventy-three MPs voted against the deal. The Liberal Democrats joined the SNP, Plaid Cymru and the Democratic Unionist Party of Northern Ireland in voting against the bill. Thirty-six Labour rebel MPs defied Sir Keir Starmer and abstained, among whom was the former leader Jeremy Corbyn. Only one Labour MP, Bell Ribeiro-Addy, voted against the deal.

The veteran Eurosceptic Sir Bill Cash paid tribute to the Prime Minister Boris during the debate:

Against all the odds, (Boris Johnson) led us out of parliamentary paralysis that year to victory, delivering us from 48 years of subjugation to EU laws and European court jurisdiction and regaining our sovereignty . . . Churchill and Margaret Thatcher would have been deeply proud of his achievements, and so are we. This Bill for our future relationship with the EU provides a new exciting era for our trade with Europe and the rest of the world on sovereign terms, not those of the EU, as with the Chequers deal.

The House of Lords also debated the deal on 30 December 2020 and approved it. The legislation sped through all legislation stages in one day, which was unprecedented since 1912. The Queen gave the royal assent to the bill before

---

[6] *Parliamentary Debates, Hansard*, Commons, 30 December 2020, pp. 521–2.

the end of the transition period on 31 December 2020 and enshrined the legislation in UK law.

The legislation passed without the consent of the devolved Parliament in Edinburgh as SNP, Labour, Green and Lib Dem Members of the Scottish Parliament had voted to reject the post-Brexit trade deal agreed between the UK and the EU. Yet numerous negotiations will have to be carried out in the next decade. Doing a deal at the last minute is likely to maximize disruption in the short term. Besides, leaving the single market and the customs union requires the restoration of border customs, rules of origin and veterinary checks.

A debate in the Lords followed on 8 January 2021 in the afternoon with peers speaking remotely on Zoom due to the Covid-19 pandemic. Viscount Chandos approved of the 'implementation of this agreement'. Lord Loomba, a cross-bencher, praised 'a remarkable trade deal' and 'an opportunity to trade with other countries in the world'. In addition, Baroness Pidding paid tribute to the Brexit negotiator Lord Frost, who had 'delivered a deal which can meet the ambitions of both sides of the House'. Yet a cross-bencher peer, Lord Ricketts, a former head of the Foreign Office and ambassador in Paris, pointed out the treaty's lack of explicit cooperation on foreign policy. He is now a keen advocate of closer cooperation with the EU, not least because of the Afghanistan debacle.[7]

The impact of the trade agreement on the UK and the EU

The trade deal will preserve the benefits of free trade for the UK and the twenty-seven countries of the EU. The agreement to zero tariffs and zero quotas on the trade of goods will be mutually beneficial. Yet, as a senior Labour peer said: 'It is still a pretty damaging deal for the UK and when the public begin to face and feel the disadvantages they were not expecting, Labour cannot say they had nothing to do with it.' It will also have geopolitical consequences for the UK's relationships with China, the United States and Africa, let alone sustainable development or the protection of personal data.

---

[7] https://hansard.parliament.uk/lords/2021-01-08/debates/1EE2CDA0-A9E3-44F1-917A-4B9EA5EE8898/EU-UKTradeAndCooperationAgreement

The impact on the UK

It is too early to say what the impact of the new trade agreement will be on the UK. What will the cost of Britain's recovered sovereignty be?

About 60 per cent of British MPs believe that the trade deal will bring benefits to the UK. The UK was the second-largest net contributor to the EU budget and paid £13 billion into the EU budget in 2018. In 2019, the UK contributed £14.4 billion to the EU budget, while only receiving £5 billion of public sector receipts back from the EU.[8] That is why many politicians consider Brexit as a win for the UK. Taking back control of its finances was what mattered most to the UK government.

As cross-bencher Lord Bilimoria said in the Lords debate on 8 January 2021: 'No-deal would have been very costly.' He added: 'We have lots to look forward to. Let us make the most of it.' As for the Earl of Shrewsbury, he underlined that 'the future outside the EU looks exciting'. A Conservative peer, Lord Taylor of Holbeach, declared that it would entail 'chang(ing) our business model'. Furthermore, the Conservative peer Baroness Finn insisted that 'to succeed we need reform'. As the Cabinet Office Minister Lord True hinted: 'the agreement ensures preserving our right to regulate independently and cooperate in the fight against antimicrobial resistance', referring to the spread of Covid-19.

Zero tariffs and zero quotas to the EU

The Prime Minister described the trade agreement as being worth £660 billion and as 'the biggest trade deal yet'. This is significant, because it is the first zero-tariff, zero-quota deal which the EU has agreed with any other trading partner. It will provide stability for economic sectors such as agriculture, car manufacturing, aerospace and chemical industry. It will allow British goods to be sold without tariffs and quotas in the EU market. It will also enable British companies to do more business directly with the twenty-seven countries of the EU. As Cabinet Office Minister hinted in the Lords debate on 8 January 2021: 'The deal maintains zero tariffs in trading goods.'

---

[8] House of Commons Library.

The trade agreement should protect jobs in the UK. Yet there is very little on services which account for 80 per cent of Britain's GDP. The Chancellor of the Exchequer Rishi Sunak is therefore committed to negotiating a broader deal on financial services.

National independence

For the UK, Brexit has always been about taking back control and Britain is once again an independent trading nation recovering its sovereignty over British waters. Fishing was one of the major obstacles in securing a deal. The UK has made a compromise on fishing and will keep 25 per cent of EU boats' fishing quota in British waters during a transition period of five-and-a-half years. This will bring the share of the total catch taken in British waters by British vessels to around two-thirds. The UK has maintained tariff- and quota-free access to the EU market, where British fish is sold and this was what mattered most to British fishermen. Ten years after the historic referendum on British membership of the EU which took place on 23 June 2016, the UK will recover sovereignty over its entire territorial waters and will be a fully independent coastal state with full control over its waters for the first time since 1 January 1973. The EU could be cut off from British waters by 2026. After this period, there will be annual talks on the amount of fish EU boats can catch in British waters. According to the new rules, boxes of seafood and fish have to be offloaded from lorries and inspected by vets before they leave Scotland. In other words, regaining control of fishing waters will enable the UK to create jobs in the fishing community. 'The perishable nature of fish makes it vital to ensure the smoothest access to European markets', according to the Cabinet Office Minister, Michael Gove, who campaigned for Brexit in 2016. Scottish seafood traders are already complaining about the papers to be filled in order to export to the EU. Fishing is massively important politically, and Scottish fishermen are still unhappy about the deal as British fishermen are banned indefinitely from selling mussels, oysters, clams and cockles to EU member states unless they have been treated in purification plants. Prime Minister Boris Johnson had hoped to organize a meeting with EU officials to discuss the ban on UK shellfish exports, but the EU has refused to discuss this issue with the UK. Consequently, the UK is planning to hit back on EU goods under retaliatory measures, such as banning EU mineral waters.

Since May 2021, Jersey and France have been at loggerheads and Channel Island authorities tried to introduce post-Brexit licensing laws for fishing. A tense fishing row erupted after the European Commission complained about the closure of the English Channel for French vessels.

Control of British laws

While the UK was a member of the EU, European law prevailed over British law and became part and parcel of British law. As a consequence of Brexit, Britain will take back control of its legislation. British law will be made by the British Parliament, interpreted by British judges and the UK will no longer be under the jurisdiction of the European Court of Justice.

According to Title X, which focuses on the good regulatory practices and regulatory cooperation: 'Each party shall be free to determine its approach to good regulatory practices under this Agreement in a manner consistent with its own legal framework, practice, procedures and fundamental principles underlying its regulatory system.'[9] After Brexit, Britons will be limited to up to nine days travel at a time without a visa within a six-month period. There will no longer be automatic passport gates for the British, who will have to get their passports stamped. Furthermore, the EU has decided to make the British pay to go into the EU. In addition, accountants, concert performers and chefs will require a work visa and will need to be registered as local professionals. Before Brexit, European and British businesses were thoroughly intertwined. The hassle of the new VAT rules has already prompted some businesses to stop shipping to Britain.

The UK is no longer restricted to working within the EU and has secured bilateral trade deals with the rest of the world, especially Japan, Singapore, South Korea, Vietnam, Kenya, Turkey, Mexico and Ghana. The UK has now secured trade deals with a total of sixty-five countries outside the EU, especially Australia and New Zealand. The free trade agreement between the UK and New Zealand will encourage New Zealanders to buy British, as they will no longer have to pay 10 per cent tariffs on chocolate and gin, buses and clothes coming from the UK. In return, high-quality New Zealand

---

[9] *EU-UK Trade and Cooperation Agreement*, 24 December 2020, Art GPR.1, p. 174.

products including wine, other drinks and dairy products will be tariff-free in UK shops. This trade deal will enable British exports to be more competitive and British customers to enjoy lower prices. The trade agreements between the UK, Australia, Brunei, Canada, Japan, Malaysia, Mexico, New Zealand, Peru, Singapore and Vietnam will be a stepping stone to the UK's joining the Transpacific Trade Agreement, one of the most dynamic markets in the world in 2021.

On 26 January 2021 Prime Minister Boris Johnson visited India, where he was Prime Minister Modi's guest of honour for Republic Day. There could soon be a mammoth free trade deal in Africa which would amount to £2 trillion, as the African continent will account for 25 per cent of the world's population by 2050. A Tory peer, Lord Popat identified Africa as the next key area for the UK to kick-start post-Brexit plans, now that it is free from the shackles of EU bureaucracy. In 2020, Prime Minister Boris Johnson established the UK-Africa Investment Summit, which extended the Trade Envoy Programme to cover more African countries. In 2022, the Africa Continental Free Trade Agreement will be implemented and shall provide a huge market, offering a vital opportunity for the UK to build its trade portfolio and access Africa's abundant opportunities.

Yet the fashion and textile industry, which accounts for £35 billion of GDP and employs about one million people in the UK, could suffer from Brexit because of the burdensome regulations now affecting it. Businesses are suffering from the weight of red tape imposed by unbearable non-tariff barriers. The end of the transition period means the beginning of red tape for many businesses and citizens in the UK, while hauliers from the Continent will now need a Kent Access Permit to enter that county.

The UK asserted its commitment to enhance workers' rights. Number Ten will publish a keenly anticipated new Employment Bill later in 2021. On 19 January 2021, Prime Minister Boris Johnson convened the first online meeting of his Build Back Better Council. The Prime Minister detailed his plans for economic recovery post Brexit. Project Speed was launched by the Chancellor of the Exchequer, Rishi Sunak, in order to make business legislation more efficient and less bureaucratic.

For important economic sectors such as manufacturing industry and agriculture, the UK must choose to align with either EU regulations or American regulations.

The Northern Ireland question

Brexit meant that the border between Northern Ireland and Ireland became an external border between the EU and a non-member state. Such a border would normally require the full enforcement of customs and regulatory rules and with it checks and controls. But the Northern Ireland Executive urged the British prime minister against allowing such a hard border. The protocol now in place is the third version published. At the root of all of them is the question of how to avoid checks and controls at the Irish land border as it becomes an external UK–EU border and how to protect the Good Friday Agreement of 1998. These objectives are reflected in the details of the protocol. The version negotiated by Boris Johnson in October 2019 commits Northern Ireland to follow EU regulatory and customs rules, so as to avoid friction on movement of goods across the island of Ireland and meets the UK government's desire to be able to diverge from EU rules and conduct an independent trade policy.

As a consequence there is now a customs and regulatory border in effect on goods moving from Great Britain to Northern Ireland. The new version of the protocol is a permanent arrangement for the trade in goods, subject to the continued consent of the Northern Ireland Assembly in a vote, every four to eight years. The terms of this protocol came into full force on 1 January 2021 with the end of the transition period. The protocol means that there are no visible changes to the Irish land border and no changes in procedures for goods crossing. However, there are changes in the movement of services and people. The trade in services between Northern Ireland and the EU, including Ireland, is governed in the same way as between the whole UK and EU through the Trade and Cooperation Agreement. People can move freely across the border because the Common Travel Area (CTA, consisting of the UK, the Channel Islands, the Isle of Man and the Republic of Ireland), which predated EU membership and since 1948, has allowed Irish citizens to continue to be able to live and work in the UK and vice versa. Article 2 of the protocol states that the UK 'shall ensure that no diminution of rights, safeguards or equality of opportunity' – as written into the 1998 Belfast Agreement – occurs as a consequence of its decision to leave the EU. But non-Irish EU citizens in Northern Ireland lose their automatic right to live and work there, just as British citizens in Northern Ireland lose their EU rights to live and work in the EU.

As part of the protocol, Northern Ireland remains in the EU's single market for goods and enforces some of its customs arrangements. The application of these rules is implemented by UK authorities but overseen by the European Commission. They can be enforced by the European Court of Justice. Yet Article 4 of the protocol states that Northern Ireland remains part of UK customs territory. This means that the benefits of UK trade deals can apply to Northern Ireland too. Northern Ireland has benefited from its unique status by having access to both the UK and EU markets. There have been increased sales of Northern Irish goods into the Republic of Ireland in the first six months of 2021, according to Stephen Kelly, chief executive of Manufacturing NI.

Article 5 of the protocol applies the EU's Union Customs Code to goods entering Northern Ireland from third countries. Consequently, EU import formalities such as customs declarations must now be completed for all goods traded into Northern Ireland, including those from Great Britain.

According to the protocol, customs duties are payable on goods entering Northern Ireland from outside the EU if they are considered at risk of entering the EU or crossing the Irish border.

Even though the UK–EU Trade and Cooperation Agreement creates a zero-tariff deal for direct UK–EU trade, some goods which come into Northern Ireland from the EU via Great Britain are considered to be reimported and attract a tariff. The British government has said that it will refund any duties paid on goods that remain in Northern Ireland, but this reimbursement mechanism has yet to be established. The protocol therefore places new restrictions on trade between Great Britain and Northern Ireland, just as Brexit places new restrictions on trade between Great Britain and the EU.

Cabinet Office Minister Michael Gove and his counterpart, the Slovak diplomat and EU's Brexit negotiator Maros Sefcovic, met on 11 February 2021 to discuss the Northern Ireland border issues. Gove asked for change on the trade rules for goods going from Great Britain to Northern Ireland. Gove also asked for a lighter enforcement of EU rules over supermarket goods, pharmaceuticals, chilled meats and parcels coming from Great Britain and heading towards Northern Ireland until January 2023. Furthermore, Gove asked for a new deal between the UK and Northern Ireland on pet travel, for flexible movement of seed potatoes and plant products and mutual recognition of qualifications. Yet Brussels has so far refused to extend the current grace period, which provides derogations from EU safety rules for goods moving from the UK to Northern Ireland. The grace period on chilled meats expired on 30 September 2021, meaning that sausages and mince produced in England could be banned in Northern Ireland.

Tensions over the implementation of the Northern Ireland Protocol have damaged UK–EU relations since January 2021 and overshadowed the G7 Summit in Cornwall from 11 to 13 June 2021. Customs checks on goods travelling from Britain across the Irish Sea could undermine the Good Friday Agreement. The EU has threatened to launch a trade war against Britain if it does not abide by the treaty obligations and implement customs checks on goods entering Northern Ireland under the terms of the Brexit deal. The EU is threatening to introduce retaliatory measures. Electricity, fishing and the City of London could be the targets of the proposed trade war. France wants to block renegotiation of the Northern Ireland Protocol and President Macron even hinted that Northern Ireland was not part of the UK in his speech at the G7 meeting in Cornwall. Macron has consistently failed to understand the complex and subtle relationships between the three constituent kingdoms and one principality of the UK (let alone the Crown Dependencies of Man and the Channel Islands). Northern Ireland is a full part of the UK; as such it has a right to continue to enjoy the unfettered trade that it has enjoyed since the Act of the Union of Great Britain and Ireland of 1801. This act constituted the UK.

Prime Minister Boris Johnson threatened to invoke Article 16 to 'take appropriate safeguard measures' in situations where the application of the protocol 'leads to serious economic, societal or environmental difficulties that are liable to persist, or to diversion of trade'. A Joint Consultative Working Group has been established to facilitate dialogue between the EU and the UK on the implementation of the protocol and to smooth certain potentially contentious matters before they become issues. The EU and UK are still at odds over the Northern Ireland Protocol as imports to Britain are impeded by lorry driver shortages, red tape and Covid-19. The EU should have more trust in the UK. The animosity in the European approach is a threat to the peace process. The negotiators need to get to some pragmatic solution. The UK has so far been against triggering Article 16, which could lead to a retaliation from the EU and would damage already weak relations with Brussels. There has been additional costs of £7.5 billion a year handling customs declarations for British businesses as if there had been a no-deal Brexit. Besides, trading with the EU requires a great number of customs forms to be filled which is no different from a no-deal situation. A breakthrough was made on 6 September 2021 and the EU agreed to hold talks to improve the implementation of the Brexit deal. As it stands, the Northern Ireland Protocol agreed under the Brexit deal is a loss for the UK.

Nevertheless, Prime Minister Johnson is planning to make the UK the economic powerhouse of Europe, doing away with EU regulations. The British government is determined to make the most of the business opportunities offered by Brexit, looking forward to the future, adopting new ways of thinking. A meeting was held at Number 10 Downing Street on 18 January 2021 with the chairmen of British Petroleum, British Telecom, Unilever, Jaguar Land Rover and Tesco to discuss the deregulation of financial services and the restructuring of labour for the economic recovery.

Gibraltar

The 6.8 square kilometre enclave is a self-governing British overseas territory, like Bermuda or the Falklands Islands. Most of its 34,000 residents are British citizens, who voted almost unanimously in a 2002 referendum to remain under sole British sovereignty. In the 2016 Brexit referendum, 96 per cent of Gibraltarians voted in favour of remaining in the EU. Gibraltar's £2.35 billion services-based economy is dependent on the flow of frontier workers coming from Spain – the type of free movement which Brexit was meant to limit. Rules guiding border protocols are still in flux, even after the EU and the UK sealed their divorce. Gibraltar's border with Spain, like that between the Republic of Ireland and Northern Ireland, became a divide between the EU and non-EU. Gibraltar is not covered by the UK's Trade and Cooperation Agreement, and separate negotiations with the EU are set to take place to agree on a post-Brexit treaty. The UK and Spain made a last-ditch preliminary deal at the end of 2020 to avoid stricter controls on the movement of people and goods into Gibraltar when Brexit came into force. A last-minute agreement between the British government and Spain will enable Gibraltarians to move freely between the British overseas territory and the EU. Under the agreement, Gibraltar will be part of the EU's Schengen free-travel zone. During a four-year implementation period, the territory is to operate under passport-free Schengen terms, with officials from the European border agency, Frontex, helping with controls at Gibraltar's port and airports. As ever, the Spanish government has used Brexit to assert its authority and attempt to snatch back control of the British outpost. Madrid used the divorce talks to secure a veto over any future relationship pact applying to the region and to undermine British sovereignty. Spain would like to police the border between Spain and Gibraltar, even though Gibraltar has been a British territory since 1713 under the Treaty of Utrecht. Gibraltar is one of the last relics of the British Empire, and it has an emotional significance for many Britons. Its location on the narrow strait separating Europe and Africa makes it strategically important and the Royal Navy's Gibraltar Squadron patrols the territorial waters. The two Fast Patrol Boats of the Gibraltar Squadron, HMS *Dasher* and HMS *Pursuer*, keep watch over Gibraltar's shores and protect British and coalition vessels in the Strait of Gibraltar. A final treaty will address the question of border crossings and secure fluidity of movement for people. The aim is also to do away with paperwork required by Spaniards and residents of Gibraltar who cross the border daily.

The Lugano Convention

In accordance with Article 127 of the Withdrawal Agreement, the UK remained a party to this convention until 31 December 2020. On 2 April 2020, the UK applied for re-admittance to the Lugano Convention on jurisdiction and the recognition and enforcement of judgements in civil and commercial matters. Switzerland, Norway and Iceland, which are parties to the Lugano Convention, approved of the UK's re-admittance. Yet the European Court of Justice ruled that the EU should decide on the UK's request for accession. The EU refused the UK's request because of Brexit, which puts an end to Britain's close regulatory integration with the EU. According to UK lawyers, stopping Britain's accession to the convention could cause severe issues for UK and EU families with relations on both sides of the English Channel. This will weaken London's attraction as a centre for dispute resolution.

The impact on the EU

Without the UK, the EU has lost its financial clout, and its share in financial services has fallen from 20 per cent to 13 per cent. Yet for the EU, the UK remains a trusted partner and ally. As the president of the EU Commission Ursula Van der Leyen declared on 24 December 2020: 'The United Kingdom and the European Union will stand shoulder to shoulder to defend their values.'

Between 2006 and December 2020, the EU profited from having the UK as a members and sold exported goods worth £3.41 trillion to the UK, a trade surplus of £1.17 trillion. The goods sold to the UK amount to more than the exports to the United States, China, Russia or Japan. Brexit will put an end to this trade surplus.

A few days before the UK signed its Brexit Agreement with the EU on 24 December 2020, British troops left Bosnia and returned to the UK after contributing for sixteen years, leaving the EU alone to deal with Operation Althea. This is a major blow to the defence cooperation between the UK and the EU. Romania has offered to step in.

When the UK left the EU it was kicked out of the Global Navigation Satellite System (GNSS). But in June 2021, Timo Pesonen, head of the Directorate-General for Defence Industry and Space of the European Commission, indicated Britain could still have a role with Galileo. As he said, 'The European Union is open to negotiate with the UK on its participation in the EU space programmes.' The EU needs access to British territory for base stations.

Conclusion

There will be many changes in the relationship between the UK and the EU after forty-seven years of close cooperation since 1 January 1973 when the UK finally joined the European Economic Community (EEC). The UK has not been a superpower for 100 years, but it has the ability to be at the centre of alliances addressing future threats. The UK can forge its own policy based on full control of trade.

Yet British businesses trading with the EU have had to deal with new bureaucracy and rules, while EU companies trading with the UK have had to adjust. Customs checks were put in place and there is additional paperwork. The challenge for the UK and the EU is to find a new model of partnership. The UK will also have to strengthen bilateral relations with EU member states at a time when the EU is not yet reconciled to the UK departure and is an unreliable partner.

Prime Minister Boris Johnson has managed to unite the Conservative Party and the UK over Brexit, whereas Margaret Thatcher was deposed, John Major lost the 1997 election and David Cameron had to resign over Europe. The UK will free itself from the shackles of Brussels, but there will be great disruption of services, which account for 80 per cent of the British economy. There will be a process of continual negotiation with the EU which will remain Britain's staunch partner and ally as Boris Johnson asserted in the House of Commons:

> We are going to become a friendly neighbour – the best friend and ally the EU could have, working hand in glove whenever our values and interests coincide, while fulfilling the sovereign wish of the British people to live under their own laws, made by their own elected Parliament.[10]

The UK remains a European power, and the new relationship between the UK and the EU will be an aspect of Global Britain. In many respects the deal is an acrimonious divorce on unfavourable terms but the last-minute deal avoided the worst short-term chaos. The Brexit Trade Agreement creates new opportunities, removes barriers and also enables low tariffs with the Asia-Pacific area. There is nervousness among the business community that trades with the EU. Yet exports to the EU have grown by 31.5 per cent from 1 April until 30 June 2021, compared with the previous quarter. While a new relationship is being forged between the UK and the EU, Britain will look to new markets to help diversify its trade routes and supply chains in Latin America, the Middle East and the Indo-Pacific, which will account for 56 per cent of the global GDP growth by 2030.

On 1 February 2021, the UK applied to join the Comprehensive and Progressive Agreement for Transpacific Partnership in order to increase trade with eleven fast-growing countries of the Asia-Pacific area. Yet some politicians, among whom is Tony Blair, have been considering future options for the relationship between the EU and the UK.

Breaking the shackles of EU bureaucracy should enable the UK to thrive after the pandemic, in spite of the heavy death toll that the UK experienced. The roll-out of the vaccine has been very successful. The relationship with the EU is likely to remain close, as the UK shares many values with the EU27. Yet there will be a transition period of two to three years.

---

[10] *Parliamentary Debates, Hansard*, Commons, 30 December 2020, p. 521.

The UK failed to get a deal for financial services and a deal on mutual recognition of professional qualifications as the EU has raised undue difficulties, but foreign investors are investing in Brexit Britain, creating over 50,000 jobs since the UK left the EU on 31 January 2020. According to the Department for International Trade Foreign Investment report, foreign direct investment created around 55,319 jobs in the 2020–1 financial year. Yet Brexit has led to a scarcity of labour force in numerous economic sectors in the UK. British fishermen feel betrayed and small and medium sized businesses are facing extra costs to export their goods to the EU. British exports to the EU have risen by 6% or about £7 billion in 2021 compared with 2020, in a recovery from the worst economic slump due to the pandemic.

Over the summer of 2021, talks between the UK and the EU were at a standstill and started all over again in Brussels on 6 September.

Without the UK, the EU is a very different organization and the divisive issues between member states more striking. We can wonder how long the damage last and whether bitter divisions dwindle in the long run. The unity of the EU is being put to the test by Britain's withdrawal. Brussels diplomats are worried to see Britain leave, as Sweden and the Netherlands will miss the UK because they saw eye to eye on a number of key policy issues.[11] The power dynamics will change within the EU, now that a major player has left the table. Denmark and Spain are even thinking of holding referenda on EU membership; they are now viewing the EU with growing suspicion.

Bibliography

EU-UK Trade and Cooperation Agreement, 24 December 2020.
Parliamentary Debates, Hansard, 30 December 2020.
Ricketts, Peter. *Hard Choices: What Britain Does Next*. London: Atlantic Books, 2021.

---

[11] In a poll conducted by Redfield & Wilton Strategies for *Euronews* in August 2021, 76 percent of Dutch people surveyed believed national governments should be solely in charge of financial and economic regulations in the Netherlands. Besides, the poll was carried out in 12 other EU countries and most of them did not believe the EU should be in charge, especially Estonia, Germany, Greece, Italy and Portugal where 60 percent of people are in favour of more national sovereignty when it comes to financial issues.

Index

Acheson, Dean   144
Adenauer, Konrad   186
Afghanistan   130, 142, 150, 171, 191, 192, 200
Africa   175, 204, 209
Amsterdam   77, 95, 102, 103, 108, 147, 148, 174
Article 50   20, 30-2, 34, 35, 89, 118, 124, 183
artificial intelligence   109
AUKUS   vi, 175
Australia   vi, vii, 78, 122, 123, 127, 175, 203

Bailey, Andrew   103, 147
Bank of England   81, 89, 95, 97, 103, 105, 108, 147, 149
Barnier, Michel   94, 139, 173
Battle of Hastings   152
Bevin, Ernest   2, 180
Biden, Joe   109, 130, 141-6, 150, 191
Blair, Tony   130, 170, 171, 182, 211
Blum, Léon   160
Brexit party   21, 28, 35, 36
Brown, Gordon   133, 181
Brussels   83, 95, 97, 118, 132, 134-7, 139, 148, 173, 182, 195, 207, 211, 212
Bush, George W.   130, 131

Cabinet responsibility   17
Cambon, Paul   153
Cameron, David   3, 17, 20, 28, 30, 39, 85, 134, 135, 146, 175, 178, 181-3, 211
Canada   127, 198, 204
Carney, Mark   89
Change UK   21, 28, 34
China   9, 58, 110, 137, 143, 146, 149, 200, 210
Chirac, Jacques   170, 171
Churchill, Winston (Sir)   36, 129, 130, 154, 158-60, 170, 199
Clemenceau, Georges   157, 158

Clinton, Bill   143
Clinton, Hillary   132
Common Agricultural Policy   166, 168
Commonwealth   vi, 10, 122, 164, 165
Comprehensive and Progressive Agreement for Trans-Pacific Partnership (CPTPP)   127, 128, 204, 211
Conservative party   21-4, 28-31, 33, 35, 36, 38, 40, 46, 49, 52, 53, 86, 92, 117, 134, 135, 173, 182
Constitution   11, 13, 22
COP26   109, 122
Corbyn, Jeremy   23, 24, 29-31, 33, 34, 36-8, 130, 199
Council of Europe   161
Covid-19   39, 40, 62, 68, 105, 122, 123, 126, 139, 173, 176, 179, 188, 191, 194, 195, 200, 201, 207
customs union   vi, 31, 34, 155, 163, 164, 173, 194, 200

Davey, Ed   188
Davis, David   30, 33
devolution   5, 49, 51
Democratic Unionist Party   7, 32, 65, 199
Department for Exiting the EU (DExEU)   87, 118, 124
Department for International Trade (DIT)   118, 119, 124, 128
Disraeli, Benjamin   4
Douglas-Home, Sir Alex   3, 131
Draghi, Mario   133
Dublin   77, 95, 108, 148

Edinburgh   49, 77, 87, 158, 200
Entente Cordiale   152, 153, 155, 156, 170, 171, 175
Euro   54, 133, 145, 147, 148, 189
Eurobond market   80
Eurodollar market   79

European Central Bank   140
European Charter of
    Fundamental Rights   16
European Communities Act 1972   15
European Convention on Human
    Rights   14, 16, 138
European Court of Justice   16, 135, 138,
    203, 206, 209
European Free Trade Agreement
    163-5
European Monetary Union (EMU)   169
European Rate Mechanism
    (ERM)   133, 180
Europhiles   42-4
Euroscepticism   16, 170
Eurosceptics   24, 33, 44, 199
Exchange Rate Mechanism   3, 132

Falklands War   130, 167, 168
Farage, Nigel   32, 35, 63, 139
Fashoda   156, 160
financial services   vii, 76, 77, 83-6, 90,
    91, 93, 100, 106, 107, 109, 111, 112,
    139, 147, 148, 208, 209, 212
First World War   146, 153, 157, 160, 165
fishing   172, 176, 188, 202, 207
Five Eyes   vi
Fixed-term Parliaments Act   24, 49
Foch, Ferdinand   157
Fox, Liam   30, 118
France   141, 149, 157, 174, 176, 184, 186,
    189, 192, 203
Frankfurt   77, 83, 95, 108, 148, 174
Free Trade Agreements (FTA)   118, 121,
    122, 125-7, 143, 194
Frost, David (Lord)   150, 173,
    195, 198, 200

G7   122, 123, 176, 207
G20   122, 123
de Gaulle, Charles   154, 160,
    163, 165, 166
Germany   140, 146, 148, 154, 156,
    159, 161, 162, 178-81, 183-7,
    189, 191, 192
Gibraltar   66, 189, 208, 209
Global Britain   10, 126, 211
Good Friday Agreement   26, 58, 63, 65,
    70-2, 143, 173, 205, 207
Gorbatchev, Mikhail   168

Green finance   109, 189
Greens   6, 192, 200
Guizot, François   153

Haig, Douglas   157
Heath, Edward   3, 131, 166
Hedge funds   84
Hollande, François   175, 183
Holyrood   6
Hong Kong   77, 78, 82, 110
House of Commons   15, 17, 23, 28, 32-4,
    36, 39, 120, 133, 153, 158, 173, 194,
    195, 198, 199, 211
House of Lords   14, 23, 120, 199-201
Hunt, Jeremy   9, 35

Industrial Revolution   78
information technology (IT)   82
International Monetary
    Fund (IMF)   122
Iran   141
Iraq   142, 145, 154, 175, 186
Ireland   57, 59, 62, 63, 65, 67-72,
    89, 205, 208
Irish Republican Army (IRA)   8

Japan   122, 125, 127, 159, 203, 204, 210
Jenkins, Roy   3
Jersey   203
Johnson, Boris   2, 4, 20, 29, 33, 35, 36,
    40, 51, 63, 68, 77, 88, 111, 120, 135,
    137, 139, 141, 142, 171, 173, 176,
    188, 190, 194-6, 198, 202, 204, 205,
    207, 208, 211
Johnson, Lyndon   130
J.P. Morgan   107, 108, 148, 174
Juncker, Jean-Claude   183, 184

Kennedy, John   164
King, Mervyn (Lord)   149
King Edward VII   153, 156, 157
King George V   153, 159
King George VI   159
King Louis-Philippe   153, 155, 156
Kissinger, Henry   9, 131
Kohl, Helmut   133, 169, 181

Labour party   4, 16, 21-3, 28-30, 32-5,
    38, 39, 52, 53, 130, 180, 198, 200
Lancaster House Treaty   175

Leave   18–20, 24, 28, 30, 32, 33, 38, 39, 44, 46–53, 117, 179, 188
Le Maire, Bruno   100
Liberal Democrats   3, 35, 36, 38, 49, 52, 188, 199, 200
Lisbon Treaty   183
Lloyd George, David   158
Lloyd's of London   78, 88
London   19, 26, 27, 77–83, 86–8, 90, 102, 103, 107, 110, 111, 134, 147–9, 158, 174, 179, 184, 185, 190, 207
London Stock Exchange   78
Lugano Convention   209
Luxembourg   77, 108

Maastricht Treaty   3, 133, 170
Macmillan, Harold   2, 129, 154, 163–6
Macron, Emmanuel   136, 137, 139, 140, 146, 149, 154, 172–4, 176, 192, 207
Major, John   3, 143, 181, 211
Marshall Plan   161
May, Theresa   2, 3, 20, 29–35, 45, 85, 117, 135, 139, 154, 172, 173, 194
Merkel, Angela   133, 134, 140, 146, 172, 181, 183, 191
Michel, Charles   100
Mitterrand, François   131, 167–9
Monnet, Jean   155, 161, 162, 165, 167, 172

Napoleon Buonaparte   155
Napoleon III   156
National Health Service   144
NATO   vi, 130, 131, 142, 146, 147, 165, 186, 192
New York   76, 77, 80, 82, 103, 107, 110, 132, 147, 148
New Zealand   vii, 78, 122, 127, 203, 204
Nixon, Richard   131
no deal Brexit   36, 92, 176, 196, 207
North Atlantic Treaty   130
Northern Ireland   1, 5–9, 19, 26, 27, 57, 59, 60, 62–6, 68, 69, 71–3, 143, 173, 176, 180, 197, 205, 206, 208
Northern Ireland Protocol   vii, 8, 59, 64, 68, 176, 199, 206–8

Obama, Barack   131, 135, 145
Owen, David   3

Paris   77, 83, 95, 103, 108, 174
passporting   147
Plaid Cymru   199
Poincaré, Raymond   157, 158
Pompidou, Georges   166, 167
populist   191
protectionism   120, 122
Putin   147

Queen Elizabeth II   163, 170
Queen Victoria   153, 154, 156

Raab, Dominic   35
red wall   38
referendum   38, 42, 43, 45, 52, 117, 133–5, 178–81, 183, 194, 208
Remain   19, 21, 24, 26, 28, 30, 32–6, 38, 43, 44, 46–53, 117
Remainers   36, 134
Rocard, Michel   171
Roosevelt, Franklin Delanoe   129
Royal Air Force (RAF)   141, 142
Royal Navy   142
Russia   9, 143, 146, 191, 210

Sarkozy, Nicolas   131, 171
Schengen Agreement   62
Schuman, Robert   66, 161
Scotland   5, 19, 26, 27, 42, 43, 46, 48–51, 53–5, 144, 180, 202
Scottish National Party (SNP)   6, 36, 42, 43, 45–7, 49, 52, 53, 199, 200
Second World War   146, 154, 159–61
Sefcovic, Maros   206
Shanghai   77, 82, 110
Singapore   77, 78, 127, 136, 203
single market   vi, 26, 27, 30–2, 155, 172, 173, 181, 194, 200, 206
Slovakia   3
Slovenia   3
Smith, Adam   133
Soames, Nicholas   36
Soft Brexit   39
sovereignty   14, 16, 24, 42, 43, 63, 100, 120, 143, 146, 199, 201, 202, 208, 209
Spain   54, 184, 188, 208, 209, 212
special relationship   129, 131
Starmer, Keir (Sir)   138, 139, 198
Stewart, Rory   35

Sturgeon, Nicola   45, 51
Sunak, Rishi   98, 147, 202, 204
supranationalism   172
Sykes-Picot Agreement   153, 154
Syria   145, 154

Thatcher, Margaret   131, 167–9, 178, 180–2, 190, 199, 211
Tokyo   77, 82
Trade and Cooperation Agreement (TCA)   vi, vii, 1, 2, 98, 195, 205, 206
Treaty of Rome   163, 164
Treaty of Versailles   158
Trump, Donald   25, 109, 132, 133, 141, 142, 144–6
Truss, Liz   195
Turkey   186

UK Independence Party (UKIP)   32, 134, 139
UK Parliament   103, 107, 198, 211
Ukraine   145
UK Supreme Court   21

UK Trade & Investment (UKTI)   117
Union   185
Unionist   5, 8, 69, 71, 73
United States   9, 10, 122, 126, 127, 130, 132, 137, 142–8, 154, 158, 163, 175, 189, 191, 192, 200, 210

Von der Leyen, Ursula   139, 140, 146, 149, 186, 198, 210

Wales   5, 27, 32, 179
Washington   132, 190
Wellington   155
Westminster   14, 15, 17, 144, 163
Wilson, Harold   130, 154
Wilson, Woodrow   158
Withdrawal Agreement   1, 2, 4, 36, 70, 89, 194, 195, 209
World Trade Organisation (WTO)   118, 121–4, 145

Yalta   154

Zurich   82